P9-CMT-370

9-10-72

KIERKEGAARD
and
FAULKNER

KIERKEGAARD
and
FAULKNER

Modalities of Existence

GEORGE C. BEDELL

Louisiana State University Press

BATON ROUGE

ISBN 0–8071–0043–9
Library of Congress Catalog Card Number 71–181356
Copyright © 1972 by Louisiana State University Press
All rights reserved
Manufactured in the United States of America
Printed by Kingsport Press, Inc., Kingsport, Tennessee
Designed by Dwight Agner

1709159

For Bettie

". . . like gold to ayery thinnesse beate."

Contents

Contents

Acknowledgments

SØREN KIERKEGAARD and William Faulkner are, to my mind, the most seminal religious thinker and the most brilliant novelist of our time. For a good many years I admired their works from a distance. Then in 1966 or so, my good friend and teacher William H. Poteat of Duke University suggested that I get to know them better by doing an essay on them. This book is the result, though I by no means want to hold Professor Poteat responsible for anything but the merit of this venture, if, indeed, it has any. Fortunately for me, though, he loves Kierkegaard and Faulkner about as much as I do and could therefore enthusiastically lend support to my project as well as bring to bear his incisive critical powers.

I also want to acknowledge the encouragement and advice of Professor Harry Russell of the University of North Carolina at Chapel Hill, who carefully scrutinized the earliest versions of the manuscript and saved me from numerous grammatical and syntactical lapses. Professors Edwin Scott Gaustad of the University of California at Riverside, Weldon Thornton of the University of North Carolina at Chapel Hill, and Richard L. Rubenstein of the Florida State University

Acknowledgments

lent their moral support along the way and made valuable suggestions. Walker Percy of Covington, Louisiana, took time to read and comment upon the essay. I especially appreciate his sympathetic and provocative response. Two of my colleagues at the Florida State University, Robert A. Spivey and Walter L. Moore, were good enough to help me sharpen the focus of the introduction and consequently the book. My thanks also to Leslie E. Phillabaum of the Louisiana State University Press for having had the courage to accept my rather unconventional manuscript and stick with it, and my special thanks to Maureen Trobec for her sensitive and thoughtful editing and for guiding me through the mysteries of producing my first book.

My father, Chester Bedell of Jacksonville, was good enough to make available the competent services of his secretary, Agnes B. Rawls, who typed the penultimate version of the manuscript. I want to thank them and Lib Henderson, Janice Donahue, and my present secretary, Pat Hansard, who also helped in various stages of the typing.

I am particularly grateful to my students on whom many of the ideas of this book have been tested. They convinced me of its feasibility.

Finally, I am indebted to my wife, Bettie, and my sons, George, Frank, and Nathan, whose patience during the various phases of putting this book together has been exemplary.

George C. Bedell

Tallahassee
July, 1971

KIERKEGAARD
and
FAULKNER

1

Introduction

THIS BOOK about religion and literature has a special twist. More often than not, religion scholars make theological capital out of works of literature—by showing, for example, that writer X is dealing with theological problem Y, or that author A is basically a Calvinist, or that novelist B is exploring the meaning of *agape* (though he was unaware of it until some religion scholar told him so), or that writers of the twentieth century are our true theologians. Valuable as such enterprises may be, my project attempts a *tertium quid:* the result is not only an essay in theology, nor is it only an essay in literary criticism. Instead, I have sought to produce a kind of conceptual collage by juxtaposing the works of Søren Kierkegaard and William Faulkner and by interfering as little as possible with the new shapes that emerge.

The subject of this book may therefore be said to appear on three fairly distinct though interrelated levels.

On the most obvious level, the book is about these two giants of recent vintage. Though separated by geography, language, and custom, both Kierkegaard and Faulkner have

3

much to tell one another [1] about the various ways people live out their lives in relative degrees of hope or despair. I consequently do more than merely elucidate Faulknerian characters by means of the Kierkegaardian analysis. I also try to test the Kierkegaardian analysis by means of the concrete characterizations set forth by Faulkner.

On a second level, the book is about the crisis of modernity. Again, both writers address themselves to the peculiar problems that confront men in the midst of the severe cultural and axiological dislocations that have occurred in the Western world during the modern period. They both make shrewd analyses of contemporary society and provide useful tools with which one may conduct an investigation into the shape of modern civilization.

On a third and more fundamental level, the book is about human existence itself, or what I prefer to call "modalities of existence." That is, it attempts to depict the ways in which the individual human being may deploy himself as a mind-body totality in a world that is inescapably his but that also belongs to others—a world which makes him what he is and yet is, fundamentally, made by him. Though this may at first seem contradictory, it is merely an expression of the highly dialectical process of indwelling a *human* world. The phrase "modality of existence" signifies more than a purely intellectual process, which would be likely to produce something like a "mindset" or a "worldview." Rather, it denotes the ways in which the total human being (mind *plus* body) inhabits both history and nature as an incarnate being or embodied consciousness. The individual thus claims a *world*—not just an *idea* of a world—and makes it his own. And yet, as we all

---

1. I have frequently been asked if Faulkner knew Kierkegaard's work and have not yet discovered any evidence that he did. It is a fact that he did not own any volumes by Kierkegaard. See Joseph Blotner, *William Faulkner's Library: A Catalogue* (Charlottesville: The University of Virginia Press, 1964). However, the only conclusion we may safely draw from this evidence is that, if he was in fact acquainted with Kierkegaard's thought, it was at best a casual acquaintance.

know, all worlds are shared, for world-construction is by nature a collective enterprise. To be human is to dwell, however marginally, *in* community.

Faulkner, of course, as a novelist never attempted to write about existence abstractly but did write about characters who indwell the world in their own special ways. Kierkegaard found it *impossible* to write about existence directly. His great contribution to the discussion was to provide the categories by which we may talk about the various modalities (or, as he called them, stages) of existence.[2] But, like Faulkner, Kierkegaard also resorted to fictional and legendary characters to illustrate that vocabulary.

Although the book operates on these three levels, its basic methodology is quite simple. It first attempts to extract from Kierkegaard's pseudonymous works the vocabulary he employs and the illustrations he gives in setting forth the various modalities or stages. It then uses that same vocabulary in attempting to describe some of Faulkner's fictional characters. The result is a transaction that helps us understand the Kierkegaardian modalities of existence by drawing on the fictional characters in some of Faulkner's novels and sheds light on the fundamental nature of Faulkner's characters by enabling us to view them from the standpoint of the Kierkegaardian modalities. The transaction also yields a serendipitous bonus in that a larger comment is made on a larger issue—namely, being human in the modern world.

WHY KIERKEGAARD AND FAULKNER

It is clear that Faulkner never thought of himself as a novelist of ideas. He was essentially a storyteller who wanted to describe how various people react to the strains and pressures of life. That is why his work is so appropriate for this

2. "Modalities of existence" more adequately conveys the elastic quality of the categories of existence than does the more rigid term "stages" (*Stadier*). Lowrie points out that "existence-spheres" is the expression Kierkegaard himself was more fond of than "stages." See Søren Kierkegaard, *Stages on Life's Way*, trans. Walter Lowrie (Princeton: Princeton University Press, 1945), 8.

essay: he is describing people as he sees them act out their lives. It is, of course, important to make the distinction between fictional characterizations and real persons. Literature is not life. Faulkner's fictional world is exactly that—fictional. But the act of perceiving the fictional world requires the same kind of close attention that perceiving the ordinary world does, and the recorded results of what one has perceived are, in fact, the same. Malcolm Cowley put it this way: "Faulkner created the characters, with the stories—or properly speaking, the fables—in which they are involved, and the fact in itself reveals something about the bent of his mind. Simply because they *were* created—because he had given these characters a life that was independent of his own—their ideas belong in the dramatic or novelistic context. They may or may not be the ideas that Faulkner would express when speaking in his own person." [3] Faulkner was not trying to confer upon his characters some preconceived metaphysical construct about the meaning of existence. We have to assume, I think, that he sometimes "rigged" the situations within which the characters appear so that a maximum stress would be applied to their lives, but we can never accuse him of "rigging" the situation so that the final disposition of their careers could be predicated ahead of time. This is not to say that Faulkner did not have certain beliefs and convictions about man that affected his writing, for he readily admitted that a fairly well-defined anthropology informed his thinking and work. Moreover, he continually pointed out that religion is integral to life. But even so, he did not cajole the reader into accepting his notions about man or God; he merely tried to tell a story to the best of his ability.

Faulkner once told his friend Cowley that he had only one purpose in mind as an author and that was to repeat the human story as he saw it:

> I am telling the same story over and over, which is myself and the world. Tom Wolfe was trying to say everything, the

3. Malcolm Cowley, *The Faulkner-Cowley File* (New York: The Viking Press, 1966), 18.

world plus 'I' filtered through 'I' or the effort of 'I' to embrace the world in which he was born and walked a little while and then lay down again, in one volume. I am trying to go a step further. This I think accounts for what people call the obscurity, the involved formless 'style,' endless sentences. I'm trying to say it all in one sentence, between one Cap and one period. I'm still trying to put it all, if possible, on one pinhead. I don't know how to do it. All I know to do is to keep on trying in a new way.[4]

The "same story," of course, concerns "the problems of the human heart in conflict with itself,"[5] which is Faulkner's way of talking about what Kierkegaard considers the religious problem. This is not to say that Faulkner was or considered himself a religious writer. It simply means that he saw the agony and joy of life against the backdrop of eternity: "I think that no writing will be too successful without some conception of God, you can call Him by whatever name you want." He considered Sartre a second-rate artist because Sartre had no place for the religious dimension in his works. Hemingway's work suffered likewise: "Hemingway for years . . . didn't deny God but he assumed, he functioned, on the premise that . . . God might be all right but let God let me alone. His people functioned in a vacuum until his last book. In his last book . . . God made the great fish, God made the old man that had to catch the fish, God made the shark that had to eat the fish, and God loved all of them, and I think that Hemingway's work will get better."[6] Whether one agrees with Faulkner's interpretation and evaluation of Hemingway or not, it is important to note that he considers the religious point of view absolutely necessary for the artist to realize fully his creative powers.

Unlike Faulkner, Kierkegaard openly admitted to a definite apologetic purpose in his writing: to set forth the truth

4. *Ibid.*, 14.
5. William Faulkner, *Essays, Speeches, & Public Letters*, ed. James B. Meriwether (New York: Random House, Inc., 1965), 119.
6. William Faulkner, *Faulkner in the University*, ed. Frederick L. Gwynn and Joseph L. Blotner (New York: Random House, Inc., 1965), 161.

and power of the religious point of view. Midway in his literary career, he attempted "a report to history" which was an account of the meaning and plan of his authorship. Here he affirmed that he was, from the beginning, a religious author.[7] He states that when he began *Either/Or*, which was his first published work and a book ostensibly about aesthetics, he was "potentially as deeply under the influence of religion" as he had ever been. He was so wholeheartedly grasped by the religious point of view that he knew he could never compromise his position in order to secure for himself some comfortable *via media* as most people seemed to be able to do: "I had either to cast myself into perdition and sensuality, or to choose the religious absolutely as the only thing—either the world in a measure that would be dreadful, or the cloister." The second path was what he had already chosen, profoundly and irrevocably.[8]

Kierkegaard's commitment to the religious therefore determined his authorial strategy. As he looked out on his contemporary world, he saw that people lived under what he called "a prodigious illusion"—the illusion that they were somehow still living in an age when religion was a vital and moving force in people's lives. But for him, "Christendom" was a monstrous hoax which had to be exposed for what it was, and he conceived a deceptively simple strategy for exposing it. He proposed to meet the so-called Christians of his day on their own grounds, which meant that he had to begin with self-humiliation: "The helper must first humble himself under him he would help, and therewith must understand that to help does not mean to be a sovereign but to be a servant, that to help does not mean to be ambitious but to be patient, that to help means to endure for the time being the imputation that one is in the wrong and does not understand what the other understands." [9]

Kierkegaard adopted this strategy, because he assumed that

7. Søren Kierkegaard, *The Point of View for My Work as an Author: A Report to History* (New York: Harper & Row, Publishers, Inc., 1962), 5 and elsewhere.   8. *Ibid.*, 18.   9. *Ibid.*, 27–28.

"an illusion can never be destroyed directly." Since most of his contemporaries suffered the illusion that they were Christians, he felt it his duty to adopt a pose that would readily identify him with those living under such misconceptions. Obviously, the person who "vociferously proclaims" himself an authentic Christian but considers others inauthentic Christians would hardly be effective in his campaign to win them to his point of view. The careful strategist, therefore, obliquely approaches the person under illusion. That is, he temporarily lets "the prospective captive enjoy the advantage of being the Christian" in order to win a listener. But if these people are not authentic Christians, in what categories do they live? The answer is they live in "aesthetic" categories. Kierkegaard's term means that a person who lives "aesthetically" has abdicated all responsibility for his own life and allows his destiny to be determined by forces outside himself over which he has no control. Thus, Kierkegaard in saying that his contemporaries were dwelling in an "aesthetic" modality is suggesting that they had refused to make the kind of radical commitment which is the essence of Christianity. Furthermore, he meant that they were *unaware* that they had adopted a non-religious way of being in the world while calling themselves religious. This, he sensed, was the fundamental cause for the *taedium vitae* of his day, though no one seemed to know it.[10]

The first principle, then, is to get in touch with people by writing in the aesthetic mode. But, warned Kierkegaard, assuming the aesthetic pose can be a dangerous procedure, because the writer can so easily be seduced. Instead of freeing others from its enchantment, the aesthetic mode may acquire power over the writer as well as his audience. The secret is to know *when* to present the religious, so that the momentum gained by the reader's attraction to the aesthetic will thrust him "headlong into contact with the religious." If the religious is introduced too late in the process, one might receive the mistaken impression that becoming religious is simply a

10. *Ibid.,* 24–25.

9

natural process of maturation. But one does not mature into a religious state, for the aesthetical and religious modalities are completely separate and distinct spheres. Or, as Kierkegaard would say, there is a radical discontinuity between them. The only way from one modality to another is by way of a "leap," not a mediation—a leap across the chasm separating them.

If the religious is introduced too soon in the procedure, one sees no discontinuity between the modalities.[11] Therefore, the writer must choose exactly the proper moment in which to introduce the religious—neither too soon nor too late. He must present "the aesthetic with all its fascinating magic" so that the reader will be enthralled by it. He should not hesitate to use any device at his disposal to present his story with the feeling that exactly suits the reader: "merrily for the merry, in a minor key for the melancholy, wittily for the witty." But again, the writer must not lose his perspective; he must not forget his purpose, which is to bring forward the religious: "By all means do this, and fear not to do it; for truly it cannot be done without fear and trembling."[12] So the strategy is simple: find out where your audience is, go there, and begin there. Present the aesthetic in all its potency and attractiveness, and then at the moment when the reader is captivated introduce him to the category of the religious so that he cannot help stumbling across it, even if he will not accept it.

Although we have no record of Faulkner's having worked out such a careful strategy for his corpus, I think we can appropriately say that his work has some points of contact with Kierkegaard's formula. If, as he says, he wishes to depict "the human heart in conflict with itself," what he most wants to show about this conflict is the tragedy and disappointment that inevitably result from one's living in the aesthetic or aesthetic-ethical modalities. Those figures who manage to live meaningful and significant lives have, in some sense, managed to find themselves in the category of the religious, as I

11. *Ibid.*, 26.   12. *Ibid.*, 29.

think this essay will bear out. And if we take seriously Faulkner's comments on his own writing, as well as the works themselves, I think we will have to admit that there is a profoundly religious and moral quality to his work. It goes without saying that he captivates his reader by the allurement, both benign and malignant, of the aesthetic modality, but there is frequently (if not always) lurking in the background the potency of the religious. As John W. Hunt says, we must not conclude that essentially destructive elements are there because of some defect in Faulkner's character or "because he is exploiting sensationalism for money"; they are present in order to give the reader a "total vision in which these obvious qualities of his world take on the symbolic function of laying bare the moral nerve ends of the present human condition." [13]

KIERKEGAARD OUR CONTEMPORARY

Although he died in 1855, Kierkegaard more appropriately belongs to our century than to the nineteenth. Or, in terms of this essay, we could say that he bears a closer affinity to William Faulkner than to Hans Christian Anderson. The reasons for this anomaly are several.

In the first place, his use of pseudonyms and other indirect methods resulted in his readers not being able to grasp his intended meaning. Those who were not offended by his work merely scoffed at it. They could not believe that he meant to be taken seriously. More often than not, they were put off by his deliberately obscure technique. Even after his death those scholars who took the trouble to try to decipher his apparently confused work—most notably the Germans—also failed to penetrate the ironic mask with which he concealed his true purpose. Only recent scholarship has begun to unravel some of the more mystifying elements in the Kierkegaardian corpus. But why? Because the issues to which Kierkegaard addressed himself were only dimly perceived, if perceived at all, by his contemporaries. With almost clairvoyant power he

13. John W. Hunt, *William Faulkner: Art in Theological Tension* (Syracuse: Syracuse University Press, 1965), 7.

11

was able to grasp the contours of the cultural crisis that would one day grip the entire Western world—namely, the threat of depersonalization and loss of self in the face of a massive, urbanized, technological society. He was—like the prophets of old—speaking to a people of hardened hearts and deafened ears. They did not understand at all what he was trying to say. But when the insanity of the twentieth century reached its peak during the horrors of war, concentration camp, and extermination oven—and during an age when one's badge of identification has in fact turned out to be a Social Security number—Kierkegaard's prophetic discrimination has made sense to countless numbers throughout the world. Like many geniuses, he was a man far ahead of his time.

Translation has also contributed to his recent popularity. He wrote, of course, in a minor language and published his limited editions in the cultural backwaters of nineteenth-century Copenhagen—which simply meant that he had virtually no readers outside Denmark. But since his translation into the major languages of the world, he has exercised an enormous influence over some of the most important writers of the twentieth century: Karl Barth, Martin Heidegger, Gabriel Marcel, Miguel de Unamuno, Jean Paul Sartre, Karl Jaspers, Paul Tillich, Nikolai Berdyaev, Rudolph Bultmann, and others. When translated into English in the 1940's he found an immediate audience in the United States; a recent edition of his *Journals* even won the National Book Award.[14]

Kierkegaard is, therefore, very much our contemporary. His language and references do come out of the nineteenth-century environment in which he wrote, but his main concerns are peculiarly germane to the cultural crisis we face today.

14. *Søren Kierkegaard's Journals and Papers*, ed. and trans. Howard V. Hong and Edna H. Hong (Bloomington: Indiana University Press, 1967).

I

*The Structure
of Modernity*

2

A Critique of Modernity

KIERKEGAARD AND FAULKNER were keen analysts of the social scene. They both observed what they believed were specifiable forces at work in the modern world which account for the large dose of dissociation felt by most men today.

For Kierkegaard, "the present age" lacks passion and meaning because it is infected with the malaise of indifference or alienation. Although there may be brief moments when men burst into enthusiasm, they quickly lapse back into lassitude. "One is tempted to ask whether there is a single man left ready, for once, to commit an outrageous folly," he writes. The problem is that we spend much too much time in reasoning and reflecting rather than acting.[1] There was a day, he maintains, when men were known by their ability or inability to act; "nowadays, on the contrary, everyone idles about and comes off brilliantly with the help of a little reflection, knowing perfectly well what ought to be done."[2] Reflection itself is not the problem, but reflection may be used as a dodge for

1. Søren Kierkegaard, *The Present Age and Of the Difference Between a Genius and an Apostle*, trans. Alexander Dru (New York: Harper and Row, Publishers, Inc., 1962), 33.   2. *Ibid.*, 39.

15

personal responsibility. Thus a passionless age, like ours, ends up having no values at all, because the values or notions we might espouse with our lips never get translated into action. For us, everything is potential, nothing actual. Those ideas which seem broadly humane or true remain absolutely lifeless because they never become imbedded in history through human action.

The pseudonymous author of the first volume of *Either/Or* tells in a memorable way what has happened to the modern world because of its tendency toward reflection:

> Let others complain that the age is wicked; my complaint is that it is paltry; for it lacks passion. Men's thoughts are thin and flimsy like lace, they are themselves pitiable like the lacemakers. The thoughts of their hearts are too paltry to be sinful. . . . Their lusts are dull and sluggish, their passions sleepy. . . . Out upon them! This is the reason my soul always turns back to the Old Testament and to Shakespeare. I feel that those who speak there are at least human beings: they hate, they love, they murder their enemies, and curse their descendents throughout all generations, they sin.[3]

In almost an exact parallel, Faulkner says that he has little use for the New Testament because it is "full of ideas," whereas he likes the Old Testament and Shakespeare because they are "full of people, perfectly ordinary normal heros and blackguards . . . all trying to get something for nothing."[4] Both Kierkegaard and Faulkner, then, decry the tendency of modern men to run off into abstraction. Kierkegaard complains about the lack of passion and action, Faulkner about the tendency to reduce everyone to an impersonal and mechanical level. We have adopted, Faulkner says, an almost "mystical belief . . . that individual man cannot speak to individual man because individual man can no longer exist."

3. Kierkegaard, *Either/Or*, trans. David F. Swenson and Lillian Marvin Swenson with revisions by Howard A. Johnson (2 vols.; Princeton: Princeton University Press, 1959), I, 27.

4. William Faulkner, *Faulkner in the University*, ed. Frederick L. Gwynn and Joseph L. Blotner (New York: Random House, Inc., 1965), 167–68 and elsewhere.

That is because he has relinquished his individuality to "a regimented group of his arbitrary factional kind" which inevitably is arrayed against an "opposite opposed factional regimented group, both filling the same air at the same time with the same double-barreled abstractions." By so substituting the group for individual responsibility, we have successfully avoided personal encounter. We have unwittingly subscribed to "the mythology that one single individual is nothing, and can have weight and substance only when organized into the anonymity of a group where he will have surrendered his individual soul for a number."[5]

Thus, the great difficulty facing the young writer today is that he is condemned to work in what Faulkner calls "a kind of vacuum of the human race." He will have to write about characters who have not known "the moil and seethe of simple humanity." By contrast, men and women of earlier generations were "understandable and comprehensible even when antipathetical, even in the moment when they were murdering or robbing or betraying you, since theirs too were the simple lusts and hopes and fears uncomplicated by regimentation or group compulsion."[6] Our generation has not known that "simple" form of existence.

In a particularly illuminating exchange with scholars at the University of Virginia in 1957, Faulkner notes that there are no "blackguards" anymore, because respectability—the most abstracting of all powers in the modern world—will deprive men of themselves. The exchange concerns the Snopes clan. Faulkner has just said that no one is brave enough to be "an out-and-out blackguard or rascal" in our day:

Q. Why aren't they blackguards anymore?
A. They ain't brave and strong and tough like they used to be.
Q. Why not?
A. It's the curse of the times maybe, and maybe there's a— three-or-four-color printing of advertisements have been too seductive or a picture of a fine big car in two colors with a handsome young woman by it so that you almost

5. *Ibid.,* 242.   6. *Ibid.,* 243.

17

think the woman comes with the new car to make the installment payments and one is—there's so much pressure to conform, to be respectable.

Q. More than in the Victorians.

A. I think so, yes. In the Victorian they tried to force you to be respectable to save your soul. Now they compel you to be respectable to be rich.

Q. Are you saying that [one] has to be a scoundrel to be an individualist?

A. No sir, I say a scoundrel, to be a good one, must be an individualist, that only an individualist can be a first-rate scoundrel. . . .

Q. You could have some grudging admiration for Flem Snopes, who pretty well sticks to his character.

A. Well, until he was bitten by the bug to be respectable, and then he let me down. . . .[7]

In short, ultimately Flem Snopes lost his self by conforming to the abstracting principle of respectability, which is another way of saying that he let someone else make his decisions for him.

Kierkegaard's concept of "inwardness" is particularly helpful here. The real problem with trying to be respectable (something Flem Snopes was not, by nature) is that it lifts a man out of himself and out of history into the realm of the abstract. The man of real inwardness is a man of character, a man who acts on his inner convictions, no matter what they are. That is to say, whether one is "moral" or "immoral" is beside the question at this point. A man must be one or the other: "To be neither moral nor immoral is merely ambiguous, and ambiguity enters into life when the qualitative distinctions are weakened by gnawing reflection." The authentic person must therefore avoid a "theoretical knowledge of evil," for it is this which tends to blunt the distinction between good and evil.[8] When too much thought is given to the problem, all inwardness is lost, and to that extent no vital antagonism is maintained between good and evil. Instead, a

7. *Ibid.*, 33.   8. *The Present Age*, 43.

18

"stasis" is produced which signals the end of moral contradiction. The result is a bland existence in which all life is reduced to appeasement and the studied avoidance of conflict: "For a time committee after committee is formed, so long, that is to say, as there are still people who passionately want to be what they ought to be; but in the end the whole age becomes a committee." [9]

Finally, Kierkegaard says that there is a force in the modern world which wants to bring all superior achievements down to a common level: "At its maximum the levelling process is a deathly silence in which one can hear one's heart beat, a silence which nothing can pierce, in which everything is engulfed, powerless to resist." The levelling tendency is the victory of the abstract over the individual. The result is the creation of "the Public," an entity within which all individuality is obliterated. Just adding individuals together does not necessarily create an entity that is identifiable in its separateness.[10] Faulkner agrees:

> It is not men in the mass who can and will save Man. It is Man himself, created in the image of God so that he shall have the power and the will to choose right from wrong, and so be able to save himself because he is worth saving;—Man, the individual, men and women, who will refuse always to be tricked or frightened or bribed into surrendering, not just the right but the duty too, to choose between justice and injustice, courage and cowardice, sacrifice and greed, pity and self;—who will believe always not only in the right of man to be free of injustice and rapacity and deception, but the duty and responsibility of man to see that justice and truth and pity and compassion are done.[11]

Faulkner sometimes takes a rather romantic view of man's ability to combat the levelling forces within modern society, but Kierkegaard is less sanguine about the individual's ability to put a stop to the trend. The age of chivalry is dead, is gone,

---

9. *Ibid.*, 44.   10. *Ibid.*, 51, 53f.
11. Faulkner, *Essays, Speeches, & Public Letters*, ed. James B. Meriwether (New York: Random House, Inc., 1965), 119.

he says (Faulkner would readily agree), and the individual is no bedizened knight setting forth to conquer the dreadful dragon, the Public. Instead, each individual *may* use the experience of being overwhelmed by sameness and blandness as a means of discovering an "essentially religious attitude." To be more specific, Kierkegaard holds that we have the opportunity not only of seeing the levelling as evil but also as "the starting-point for the highest life." It may become an "education to live in the age of levelling," which is, for us, the highest calling. For this reason, he claims that there is no more concrete individual than he who springs directly from the infinite abstraction of "pure humanity." Thus, the levelling process may become the teacher, and "the man who learns most from the levelling and himself becomes greatest does not become an outstanding man or a hero—that would only impede the levelling process, which is rigidly consistent to the end." What then does he become? "A man and nothing else, in the complete equalitarian sense." [12] This complete equalitarianism Kierkegaard calls "the idea of religion." In *this* context, at least, the leap of faith is into the sea of the levelling process, which may sound contradictory, but is entirely consistent with his conception of the knight of faith depicted in *Fear and Trembling*.[13]

Therefore, the discipline of living within the abstractiveness of mass society *may* be and *can* be the means whereby the individual discovers himself, for he is given the opportunity to learn "to be content, in the highest religious sense, with himself and his relation to God, to be at one with himself instead of being in agreement with a public which destroys everything that is relative, concrete and particular in life." The secret to discovering real life is to learn to find peace within oneself and with God, "instead of counting hands." Counting hands is the way to create the Public, "a

12. *The Present Age*, 56, 57.
13. Kierkegaard, *Fear and Trembling and The Sickness unto Death*, trans. with introduction and notes by Walter Lowrie (Princeton: Princeton University Press, 1954), 49f.

deserted void which is everything and nothing." But we must also assert that the Public is the "gruesome abstraction through which the individual will receive his religious formation—or sink." [14]

It is significant that Kierkegaard, though he lashes out at the growing conformity and vacuity of the modern era, also sees it as a means by which one may discover one's true identity: "Just as reflection itself is not evil, so a very reflective age has its lighter [i.e., more positive] side, simply because a higher degree of reflection implies greater significance than immediate passion." The key, as always, is the religious, for it is this element which enters into the individual's life, grasps him, gathers the powers of reflection for decision, and catapults him into action. As Kierkegaard says, "Reflection is not the evil; but a reflective condition and the deadlock which it involves, by transforming the capacity for action into a means of escape from action, is both corrupt and dangerous, and leads in the end to a retrograde movement." [15]

From this *milieu* a very different kind of leader or hero will arise. He will be without authority, "because he will have divinely understood the diabolical principle of the levelling process; he will be *unrecognizable*." Moreover, the "support" he gets from the people will come in a negative form; that is, he will have to repel people. And the one thing he will have to guard against is being recognized or discovered. Moreover,

14. *The Present Age*, 62–64. In *Point of View* Kierkegaard makes another significant comment about the Public. "Perhaps it may be well to note here once for all a thing that goes without saying and which I never have denied, that in relation to all temporal, earthly, worldy matters the crowd may have competency, and even decisive competency as a court of last resort. But it is not of such matters I am speaking, nor have I ever concerned myself with such things. I am speaking about the ethical, about the ethico-religious, about 'the truth,' and I am affirming the untruth of the crowd, ethico-religiously regarded, when it is treated as a criterion for what 'truth' is" (p. 110*n*). All those ethicists who accuse Kierkegaard of unqualified privatism in ethics would do well to note what he says here: that in the realm of public policy, there is a place for 'counting hands' and democratic rule, but that when one wants to know what God has said, one does not call for a vote!   15. *Ibid.*, 67, 68.

the unrecognizable must use all precaution not to speak or to teach directly at the head of the masses. He must use the principle of inversion and indirection in order to guide their decisions and actions. He must not give support to the individual but free him to make his own decisions: "any other course would be the end of him, because he would be indulging in the short-sighted compassion of man, instead of obeying the order of divinity, of an angry, yet so merciful, divinity."[16]

Nor are the unrecognizables to attempt to thwart the principles of the levelling process, for to reverse the development would be a tacit admission that the unrecognizable one was in fact in charge, in a position of authority, a circumstance that must not be allowed to occur. In this respect Kierkegaard is most explicit: "Only by suffering can the "unrecognizable" dare to help on the levelling process, and, by the same suffering action, judge the instruments. He dare not overcome the levelling process directly, that would be his end, for it would be the same as acting with authority. But he will overcome it in suffering, and in that way express once more the law of his existence, which is not to dominate, to guide, to lead, but to serve in suffering and help indirectly.[17]

What is this describing, if it is not the principle at work in the life of one of Faulkner's grandest characters, Dilsey? In the emotion-packed pages of *The Sound and the Fury*, we receive an unforgettable portrait of that ancient Negro woman, the heroine of faith.[18] She gives of herself unstintingly and without complaint, and by so doing, she is the only figure of the tragic Compson household who has the serenity and grace to choose suffering instead of attempting to escape it. By choosing to suffer (rather than evading it or only passively accepting it) she has overcome the forces of the world that would de-humanize her—the levelling process. The law of her existence is that she will not dominate, guide, or lead but will

16. *Ibid.*, 80, 82.   17. *Ibid.*, 83.
18. Faulkner, *The Sound and the Fury and As I Lay Dying* (New York: Random House, Inc., 1946).

22

serve in suffering and thereby help those around her indirectly.

Kierkegaard says that those who have no inkling of what religiousness consists will not be able to perceive the nobility and worth in the actions and lives of people like Dilsey. Indeed, they will look upon "the unrecognizables" as failures or as completely impassive figures who have no other possibility but to live out their lives in meagerness and deprivation. But those who have been fortunate enough to become conversant with the religious or who have themselves moved into the realm of the religious will suspect that what looked like failure was actually victory in some mysterious and inexplicable way. But still they have no absolute certainty about this. For, as Kierkegaard says, if the unrecognizable should give "certainty to a single person it would be the end of him, because he would have been unfaithful to the divinity in desiring to play at being authority." [19]

The present age, then, though infected with the disease of indifference, though given to reflection instead of action, does possess some few individuals who, because they *are* just that —individuals—embody inwardness, religiousness, authentic existence. Or in Faulkner's terms, they endure. [20]

What we must consider now is the concatenation of events and experiences that have led us to "the present age." We did not arrive at this place by pure accident, for there is, according to Kierkegaard's analysis, a discernible structure of events that has brought us to the current situation. There is a conceptual framework to be uncovered.

19. *The Present Age*, 83.   20. *The Sound and the Fury*, 22.

3

The Informing Principle

INSTEAD OF attempting to write about the religious category directly, we have already seen how Kierkegaard first of all decided to make an oblique attack by ostensibly dealing with aesthetic categories. Or, as he put it, he engaged in Socratic "deception" in order to deceive his readers into accepting the "truth."[1] Therefore, in his first published work, *Either/Or*, he wrote about figures such as Don Juan, Faust, and the Wandering Jew; he delivered panegyrics on the ecstasies of the emotional life; he composed a seducer's diary—all in the interest of presenting sensuality in a variety of ways. But in the end, we discover that he had been addressing himself all along to the question of how pure Spirit can become incarnate in the world. For him the problem was not so much the academic question of the relationship between the sacred and the profane—how to set forth the relationship of religion to culture in some systematic way. Instead, it was the question of discovering the effects of the religiousness of Christianity

1. Søren Kierkegaard, *The Point of View for My Work as an Author: A Report to History* (New York: Harper & Row, Publishers, Inc., 1962), 39f.

24

on human life and how it might have informed the Western imagination throughout the centuries. The paradoxical doctrine of an embodied infinite Spirit has had a pervasive effect, he would say, which becomes particularly apparent to the person who has had some sort of first-hand knowledge of just what religiousness consists of, for in Kierkegaard's eyes the idea of the God-Man has been an intensely productive one in history, one that has had ramifications in every conceivable sector of human life, not the least of which has been the realm of the aesthetic. In one place he wrote very simply: "When a religious painter was aware of his talent, but this talent could not express itself in the productions which lie closest to the religious sphere, one has seen in this situation that such an artist could just as piously devote himself to painting a Venus, just as piously interpret his artistic calling as one which helped the Church by enthralling the eyes of the congregation with the sight of heavenly beauty."[2] The crux of the matter is that Kierkegaard was apparently convinced, as he read history and viewed man's artistic creations, that something of unique significance occurred in the arts when Christianity was posited. This, of course, is not the kind of assertion that can be proved. Nor is it necessary to embrace the details of Kierkegaard's intellectual-historical analysis to accept its heuristic value for this particular essay. Kierkegaard's point simply is that the religiousness construed by the Christian revelation accounts for both our origin and our destiny and that the individual person who lives in a spiritually determined universe without coming to grips with the Spirit will, of necessity, be alienated from the ground and source of his existence.

Here is one of the most fundamental distinctions underlying his work—the contrast between the ancient Greek world and the world inaugurated by the Christ-event. Kierkegaard speaks of Greek antiquity as a "psychically determined" or

2. Kierkegaard, *The Concept of Dread*, trans. with introduction and notes by Walter Lowrie (Princeton: Princeton University Press, 1946), 95.

"psychically qualified" cosmos. Although he is arbitrarily restricting the word "psychical" to suit his case, he nevertheless is drawing on historically valid connotations. He uses this word and its cognates to call attention to the rational, logical, humane world which is thought to have prevailed in ancient Greece. It is the world described by Socrates in the *Gorgias:* "Communion and friendship and orderliness and temperance and justice bind together heaven and earth and gods and men and . . . this universe is therefore called Cosmos or order, not disorder or misrule, my friend. But although you are a philosopher you seem to me never to have observed that geometrical equality is mighty, both among gods and men." [3] The soul (*psyche*) of this cosmos is harmony and order; in short, it is a human, finitely conceived world.

In contrast to this world stands the "spiritually determined" or "pneumatically qualified" universe of the Christian West.[4] Kierkegaard considers the Spirit (*pneuma*) to be the decisive influence in history subsequent to the Christ-event. For him, the Spirit is, above all else, an infinitely powerful spirit, absolutely transcendent to the world, who breaks open the contained and orderly Greek cosmos. This means that time is no longer cyclical and repetitious as in the ancient Greek world; instead, time rushes headlong into infinity (God). Therefore, Spirit, who in the final analysis is God, is not beauty and truth but energy and power. He is the source of holiness. He does not simply inspire poets or warriors as in the Greek world; he is the very foundation of freedom to be or to choose one's existence. This, of course, was a wholly unintelligible idea for the Greeks, as Paul discovered. For them freedom meant emancipation of the intellect or *nous* from the prison house of the body. For Paul and Kierkegaard, freedom meant the capability of the whole man (the body-

3. Plato, *The Dialogues of Plato*, trans. B. Jowett (2 vols.; New York: Random House, Inc., 1937), I, 569.
4. Kierkegaard alludes to the Pauline meanings surrounding *pneuma*, a word that gained new force and power in the Epistles. *Pneuma*, of course, is usually translated "Spirit."

mind totality) to escape the narrowness of an egocentric life.

For the Christian man, then, the *psyche* or intellect (which is finite) does not direct him; the Spirit (which is infinite) does. And the quality of existence enjoyed by this man is entirely different from the existence enjoyed by antique Greek man. This differentiation between the two ways of "being in the world" becomes one of the principal motifs in the Kierkegaardian canon. What difference has the irruption of the Spirit made for the Western consciousness? Kierkegaard says that one may grapple with the Spirit within any one of three broad categories. Within the aesthetical category, the Spirit is discovered under the cover of sensuousness. Within the ethical category, it is discovered as the infinite and unyielding demand of the universal law. Within the religious category, it is discovered as the absurd or the paradox precisely because it is illogical to hold that the infinite may become embodied in time.

FAULKNER AND THE INFORMING PRINCIPLE

One of the major problems in Faulkner criticism is religion. Just how much does Christianity inform his fiction? Are there myths from other great traditions at work? What was his own conception of this factor in his writing? One of the most revealing comments he makes in this respect concerns his understanding of the religious orientation of the society he writes about: "Remember, the writer must write out of his background. He must write out of what he knows and the Christian legend is part of any Christian's background, especially the background of a country boy, a Southern country boy. My life was passed, my childhood, in a very small Mississippi town, and that was a part of my background. I grew up with that. I assimilated that, took that in without even knowing it. It's just there. It has nothing to do with how much of it I might believe or disbelieve—it's just there."[5]

5. William Faulkner, *Faulkner in the University*, ed. Frederick L. Gwynn and Joseph L. Blotner (New York: Random House, Inc., 1965), 86.

Faulkner makes it clear that it is not properly our purpose to deal with his own private faith, whatever that might be. It is only important to understand the way in which the "Christian legend" informs his imagination. He wrote about people as he found them, and he discovered, as he says, that "the Christian legend" had had a profound effect on them, in both positive and negative ways. One has merely to observe the serene faith of Dilsey and the distorted Calvinism of Joanna Burden to see how integral Christianity becomes for the Yoknapatawpha saga. It is not only observable in distinguishable and discreet ways but it is also an underlying force in the entire Faulknerian canon. As he says, "it's just there" and must be taken account of.

One has only to thumb through the pages of his works to see how he uses religion. In one of Faulkner's most underrated novels, *The Wild Palms*, Harry Wilbourne cries out:

> There is no place for [love] in the world today, not even in Utah. We have eliminated it. It took us a long time, but man is resourceful and limitless in inventing too, and so we have got rid of love at last just as we have got rid of Christ. We have radio in the place of God's voice and instead of having to save emotional currency for months and years to deserve one chance to spend it all for love we can now spread it thin into coppers and titillate ourselves at any newsstand, two to the block like sticks of chewing gum or chocolate from the automatic machines. If Jesus returned today we would have to crucify him quick in our own defense, to justify and preserve the civilization we have worked and suffered and died shrieking and cursing in rage and impotence and terror for two thousand years to create and perfect in man's own image.[6]

In this passage one of Faulkner's protagonists sounds very much like the author himself in his critique of modernity, and the basis of this is thoroughly Christian. As Robert M. Slabey points out, it is not unlike Kierkegaard's attack upon Christendom which is not so much an attack upon the Church

6. Faulkner, *The Wild Palms* (New York: Random House, Inc., 1964), 136.

per se as upon "the *un*Christian situation in a presumably 'Christian' society; Kierkegaard indicted the complacent code of bourgeois ethics and formalized religious practice which had replaced the Christian ideals of love and self-denial."[7] Faulkner obviously indicted his generation for much the same reason.

But Wilbourne's (Faulkner's?) understanding of the current crisis is even more profound when he says, "If Venus returned she would be a soiled man in a subway lavatory with a palm full of French post-cards." The point here is that only in a society informed by Christianity can pagan love, which in itself is essentially innocent, be corrupted to the point where it becomes "dirty." As Kierkegaard says, there was a kind of "modesty" which rested over all pagan love; the idea of seduction was "entirely wanting" among them. He writes, "They fell in love with a girl, they set heaven and earth in motion to get her; when they succeeded, then they perhaps tired of her, and sought a new love." But this was essentially a faithful love, because it was carried on within the limits of what Kierkegaard calls "the psychically determined cosmos" of the ancient Greeks.[8] This cosmos was orderly and transparent; there was absolutely no place for disorder and obfuscation. A kind of graceful light played upon the Greek consciousness which gave the ancient world a pellucid quality. There were limits to all human endeavor, so that the finite was accepted as the rightful place within which one's life was to be acted out. But with the coming of Christianity, all of this changed. The infinite was introduced. Disorderliness (in the form of sin) was posited. The light that played upon the ancient world was eclipsed by the darkness of the human consciousness discovered by such astute psychologists as Paul of Tarsus and Augustine of Hippo. The paradigmatic figure

7. Robert M. Slabey, "Myth and Ritual in *Light in August*," *Texas Studies in Literature and Language*, II, 3 (Fall, 1960), 329.

8. Kierkegaard, *Either/Or*, trans. David F. Swenson and Lillian Marvin Swenson with revisions by Howard A. Johnson (2 vols.; Princeton: Princeton University Press, 1959), I, 92 and elsewhere.

for the Christian era, says Kierkegaard, becomes Don Juan
—one whose existence could not even have been imagined
prior to the positing of the Spirit through Christianity. The
word with which Kierkegaard described Don Juan was "sensuous." *His* love was "not psychical but sensuous, and sensuous love, in accordance with its concept, is not faithful, but
absolutely faithless; it loves not one but all, that is to say, it
seduces all." [9]

It therefore turns out that sensuousness is a crucial concept for this particular study, especially if we hope to use
Kierkegaard's insights to investigate the inner workings of
Faulkner's characters. Indeed, one must be able to grasp the
idea of the sensuous before the relationship between the
categories of the aesthetical and the religious in the modern
world may be understood. Sensuality and spirituality are
intimately connected.

9. *Ibid.*, 93.

4

Sensuousness and the Spirit

KIERKEGAARD'S FIRST ASSERTION regarding sensuousness is that it is more than an idea or an abstraction. It is a principle or force that has had immense historical consequences. But a corollary of this first assertion is the notion that the full effect of sensuousness was not felt until Christianity appeared and released it from its containment within the forms and structures of pagan societies: "In ancient times the sensuous found its expression in the silent stillness of plastic art; in the Christian world the sensuous must burst forth in all its impatient passion." [1] In one sense, then, Christianity "brought sensuousness into the world," but the converse is also true: Christianity has excluded sensuousness from the world. That is because "Christianity is spirit," and spirit and sensuality are essentially hostile to one another. They are hostile because sensuousness will ultimately "objectify" the human world, while spirit is the source for what Kierkegaard calls "sub-

1. Søren Kierkegaard, *Either/Or,* trans. David F. Swenson and Lillian Marvin Swenson with revisions by Howard A. Johnson (2 vols.; Princeton: Princeton University Press, 1959), I, 97.

31

jectivity"[2] or what we might call "personal authenticity." The great symbol for the objectifying sensuousness of the ancient Greek world is, of course, *Moira* or Fate, while in the Christian world the spirit can only be expressed in the abstract concept "absolute freedom." Thus, when the sensuousness of the pagan world meets spirit in Christianity, it is radically transformed. It is energized, potentiated, infinitized—or, as Kierkegaard says, it is "spiritually determined" or "spiritually qualified." That is to say, in the Christian world sensuousness is no longer controlled in some finite form but is broken out of all forms by the phenomenon of spirit. Sensuousness can no longer be expressed in the "silent stillness" of, say, Greek architecture or sculpture, but adopts a medium which can express the free and transcendent quality of a sensuousness which is energized and infinitized by confrontation with spirit—namely, the medium of music. Music is appropriate because it is in time in an unessential way: it is performed *in* time, but then, as soon as the performance is over, it is gone. Likewise, sensuousness in the spiritually determined universe is known only for brief and evanescent moments: it is here and then gone—immediately. It cannot be contained. It breaks out of all forms into storm and passion. Original sensuousness is thus rudely awakened from its tranquil state in the ancient Greek world and potentiated into absolute transcendence because it has become spiritualized. Of course, the Spirit that qualifies and determines sensuousness is the same Spirit that hovered over the face of the deep at Creation, it is the same Spirit that made the God-Man possible, it is the same Spirit that thrusts the church into time and up out of history into eternity. We can therefore begin to see the centrality of the Incarnation for Kierkegaard's thought.

2. The terms "objectify" and "subjectivity" and their cognates are unfortunate words to use, though thoroughly Kierkegaardian, because of their equivocal meaning in the post-Cartesian ethos. This is especially so since Kierkegaard himself is anti-Cartesian and gives his own special sense to "objectivity" and "subjectivity." These difficulties will be overcome as we proceed, however.

If the Spirit is to have its own way in the world, it must inevitably exclude the sensuous, but, paradoxically, it is precisely because of its being excluded that the sensuous gains power and validity as a principle. We might well ask what form it took prior to its liberation by Christianity. If sensuousness is "spiritually determined" beginning with the Christian era, what determined it prior to that? Kierkegaard holds that it was "psychically qualified," which means that it did not possess the qualities of "opposition" and "exclusion" that characterize its appearance under Christianity; instead, it possessed the qualities of "harmony" and "accord." The most exemplary expression of sensuousness in this "psychically determined" form is therefore found in ancient Greece, where it appeared not as a vital force or principle, but as part of the total Greek experience, assimilated into the Greek way of life.[3]

The clearest illustration of this occurred in the Hellenic conception of the erotic, where the sensuous was under the control of "the beautiful personality." Or, as Kierkegaard shows, it might be more accurate to say that it was not controlled at all, because "it was not an enemy to be subjugated, not a dangerous rebel who should be held in check." On the contrary, it was an effusion of life and joy that was harmonized and integrated into the being of "the beautiful personality." For this reason we cannot say that the sensuous was posited as a principle prior to Christianity, although it is impossible to think of the beautiful personality without also thinking of the sensuous. Kierkegaard says:

> Love was present everywhere as moment, and as such it was momentarily present in the beautiful personality. The gods recognized its power no less than men; the gods, no less than men, knew happy and unhappy love adventures. In none of them, however, was love present as principle; in so far as it was in them, in the individual, it was there as a moment of the universal power of love, which was, however, not present anywhere, and therefore did not exist for Greek thought nor for the greek consciousness.[4]

3. *Ibid.*, 59–60.   4. *Ibid.*, 61.

We can see that the "silent stillness" of the "psychically determined" love of the Greeks stands in radical contrast to the storm and urge of the "spiritually determined" love of the Christian era, represented in the figures of Don Juan and Faust.

If we turn to the structure of Greek mythology, we gain an even deeper insight into the psychically determined consciousness of the Hellenic people. Kierkegaard calls our attention to the fact that, in Greek mythology, although Eros was the deity of love, he was never *in* love himself: "In so far as the other gods or men felt the power of love in themselves, they ascribed it to Eros, referred it to him, but Eros was not himself in love." This apparent diffidence on the part of Eros is more than a quirk of mythology, for it represents the objective or what we might characterize as the externally oriented character of Greek consciousness. Kierkegaard suggests, for example: "If I imagined a god or goddess of longing, it would be a genuinely Greek conception, that while all who knew the sweet unrest of pain or of longing, referred it to this being, this being itself could know nothing of longing."

This is much more complex than appears on the surface, for Kierkegaard himself despairs of ever saying it well: "I cannot characterize this remarkable relation better than to say it is the converse of a representative relation." By "representative relation" he meant chiefly the Incarnation, which occurs when "the entire energy" or "the absolute idea" is concentrated into a single individual and other individuals are thereafter free to participate in whatever it is that constitutes this representative. But Eros, instead of having some kind of personal power, was universalized; he was, in a sense, everywhere at once but never within himself. He was free to give the energy or the idea of love to others, but he himself did not know love. He was, in short, the image of the discarnate Platonic idea (*eidos*) of erotic power which becomes incarnate only in individuals or particulars, who, because they are able to incarnate erotic power, become endowed with it. Eros, on the other hand, was never centered, never incarnate in

34

himself, never in the world. He was therefore deprived of power precisely because he was unembodied. That is, he was form without matter, being without power (*dunamis*). Kierkegaard sums it up this way: "That which constitutes the power of the god is not in the god, but in all the other individuals, who refer it to him; he is himself, as it were, powerless and impotent, because he communicates his power to the whole world. The incarnated individual, as it were, absorbs the power from all the rest, and the fullness is therefore in him and only so far in the others as they behold it in him." [5]

It is impossible, therefore, to find the sensuous as a principle or as a force operative within Hellenic culture. When we are able to point to sensuousness in any of its various manifestations in the Greek consciousness, we are not able to see it as a concentration of energy but as a radiation of power from a point which, in effect, seems not to exist, or at best is "identifiable by the fact that it is the only point which does not have that which it gives to all the others." Or, as Kierkegaard is continually saying, the psychical and the sensuous within the Greek mind are in concord. To talk about the sensuous within pagan culture, then, is to talk about a completely benign phenomenon, a factor that is in almost every respect pre-ethical—anterior to the invocation of the ethical dichotomy: either/or. 1709159

The difference between sensuousness in such a society and that found within Christianity is also pointed to by Kierkegaard in his discussion of the problem of sin in *The Sickness unto Death*. Here he maintains that the selfishness found in paganism "in spite of all that can be said about it, is not nearly so 'qualified' as that of Christendom," the point being that until Christianity posits the spirit there is no way for natural man or pagan man to know the radical nature of sin. "Psychically determined" human error does not result in the radical disjuncture in the God-relationship known to the "spiritually determined" person who has been confronted by the Infinite. Sin for Socrates was ignorance, but for the

5. *Ibid.,* 62.

Christian, sin is willful disobedience. Socrates could think the way he did about human error because his measure of right and wrong had to be found within the limits of human experience, but for one to appreciate the absolute quality of human degradation there must be a revelation from God which will show "that sin does not consist in the fact that man has not understood what is right, but in the fact that he *will* not understand it, and in the fact that he *will* not do it" (Italics added). We are at liberty to say, therefore, "that the pagan did not sin in the strictest sense, for he did not sin before God." [6]

In sum, Kierkegaard is arguing that modern Western civilization is inescapably informed by the Christian myth. Whether we are a-Christian or even anti-Christian, the fact is that we always find ourselves in *some* kind of relation to the Incarnation. It is at the center of our consciousness. Whatever our *de jure* professions may be, we are all to some extent *de facto* Christian.

Faulkner's world certainly bears out this contention, for it is a world "qualified" by the Spirit. The sin he writes about is not the wrong done within the limits of human experience as in Greek drama; it is the sin of infinite proportions depicted in Biblical stories. Moreover, the sensuous plays an important role in the novels. Faulkner sees that sensuousness is not allowed free expression in our society but is suppressed by our puritanical distortions of human life, all of which results in the violence and terror of novels like *Sanctuary* and *Light in August*. What Eliot calls the "dissociation of sensibility" has indeed taken place, and the demonic has rushed into the vacuum left when the sensuous has been removed or suppressed.

6. Kierkegaard, *The Sickness unto Death*, in *Fear and Trembling and The Sickness unto Death*, trans. with introduction and notes by Walter Lowrie (Princeton: Princeton University Press, 1954), 121, 211–12, 226.

5

The Nature of Tragedy

KIERKEGAARD MAKES another attempt to ferret out the essence of Christian culture by discussing the nature of tragedy. To do this contrasts the drama which developed in the psychically determined cosmos of Greek civilization with the drama composed in a culture informed by the principle of the Incarnation. Once more, we are being confronted with what is apparently an essay on aesthetics while it is at the same time an incisive discourse on religion.

Kierkegaard says that the peculiarity of ancient tragedy is that "the action does not issue exclusively from character," but in a sense is already decided by the historic past out of which Greek drama springs. But more than this, characters are prevented from determining the action because "subjective reflection and decision" are not really possibilities for Hellenic man. He is so reliant upon the processes outside himself that he is never able to act on his own or to accept the fact of his own individuation in any significant way. In the language of phenomenology, he is never able to see himself primordially as a body which inhabits the world. For the Greek man, the soul (the most real thing about him) inhabits a body, in an uneasy coalition that has great difficulty in ever getting firmly situated in the world.

Because there is so little "subjective reflection and decision" in ancient tragedy, the action is characterized by a "suffering" (*passio*) of circumstances. The hero is more acted upon than actor. His dialogue is not developed to the point where "everything is absorbed in it," which further indicates that his individuality is secondary to the plot. Moreover, the action and dialogue of a play require supplementation and elaboration by the devices of the chorus and the monologue. All of this, Kierkegaard says, shows the "objective" nature of Greek drama. In contrast to the ancients, however, modern drama reveals how much of the "subjective" can be crammed into dialogue; here a character sets out quite deliberately and self-consciously to attempt to alter the course of his own destiny and is acutely aware that his choices will have consequences, not only for himself but for others as well. Accountability looms as a big factor because choice is mandatory. One cannot avoid responsibility, because no decision in itself constitutes a choice of a kind—a negative one. On the other hand, the dialogue and action of ancient tragedy are not personally accredited or backed up in so positive a way. Decisions, though performed, are made in the presence of Fate. Indeed, "the Greek hero rests in his fate" and is thereby prevented from discovering his own radical individuality.[1] That is discoverable only after the representative individual (Christ) has made its appearance.

It is well known, of course, that Greek audiences attending the theater were already familiar with the stories of the heroes and heroines before seeing them acted out on the stage. The legends and myths which formed the plots for ancient tragedy rested in the known past or what is called the "epic background." Kierkegaard once again attributes this to the lack of inwardness in Greek culture: "The ancient world did not have subjectivity fully self-conscious and re-

1. Søren Kierkegaard, *Either/Or*, trans. David F. Swenson and Lillian Marvin Swenson with revisions by Howard A. Johnson (2 vols.; Princeton: Princeton University Press, 1959), I, 141, 149.

flective."[2] What this means is that it was impossible for an ancient author to take a group of characters, place them in a given situation, and let them assume a kind of independent existence and work out their own problems within the limits of the situation. This, of course, is precisely the technique employed by Faulkner, who throughout his literary career kept following in his imagination the loves and hates, the lives and deaths of the people who made up his famed Yoknapatawpha County. The Snopeses and Compsons and Sartorises all have their independent existence within his mind. Nowhere is this more forcefully shown than in his creation of the appendix to *The Sound and the Fury*, originally done for the Viking *Portable Faulkner*. Malcolm Cowley records the way in which Faulkner, without even owning a copy of his favorite novel, was able to write the appendix, because "the true Compson story was the one that lived and grew in his imagination."[3] He once told a group of students that "when the characters come alive, all the writer has to do is jog along with his notebook and record what they say."[4]

In this connection, it is instructive to note Kierkegaard's attitude toward his pseudonyms. In the "First and Last Declaration," which is appended to *The Concluding Unscientific Postscript*, we read:

> In the pseudonymous works there is not a single word which is mine, I have no opinion about these works except as third person, no knowledge of their meaning except as a reader, not the remotest private relation to them, since such a thing is impossible in the case of a doubly reflected communication. One single word of mine uttered personally in my own name would be an instance of presumptuous self-forgetfulness, and dialectically viewed it would incur with one word the guilt of annihilating the pseudonyms. Just so far am I from being the Seducer or the Judge in *Either/Or*, just so far am I from being the editor Victor Eremita.[5]

2. *Ibid.*, 141.   3. Malcolm Cowley, *The Faulkner-Cowley File* (New York: The Viking Press, 1966), 47.

4. Joseph Satin, "Resist the Mass," *Time*, LXIX, 22 (June 3, 1957), 40.

5. Kierkegaard, *The Concluding Unscientific Postscript*, trans. David F. Swenson and Walter Lowrie (Princeton: Princeton University Press, 1941), 551.

This passage reveals Kierkegaard's attitude toward the pseudonyms and "their" works as essentially ironic but fundamentally literal: they were characters who gained independent status in his imagination. They were "real" to him and required the same kind of attending to that an ordinary person would—a technique unknown to writers of classical antiquity. In ancient Greece neither historical personages nor imaginative figures possessed that kind of autonomous existence. Instead, says Kierkegaard, they rested "in the substantial categories of state, family, and destiny." [6]

With the advent of the representative individual, however, these substantial categories subside, and the individual is left on his own to become primarily responsible for his own destiny. Kierkegaard goes so far as to say that one becomes one's own creator. But when a man is thus put on his own, sin takes on a much more abrasive quality as a consequence. Sin no longer is ignorance or the failure of reason to control the will; instead, it is disobedience or a fundamental distortion of the will. This automatically means that the idea of the tragic is nullified. The essence of tragedy is that no matter what one may choose to do, his destiny is still decided by Fate. But when he is freed and held responsible for his actions, choices have ultimate or infinite significance. Kierkegaard puts it this way: "The concept of guilt and sin does not in the deepest sense emerge in paganism. If it had emerged, paganism would have foundered upon the contradiction that one might become guilty by fate. This indeed is the supreme contradiction, and in this contradiction Christianity breaks forth. Paganism does not comprehend it; for that it is too frivolous in its definition in the concept of guilt." [7] It is for this reason, of course, that many theologians have wanted to maintain that tragedy is no longer possible within a Christian setting, and in a strict sense, this is so. The rationale runs this way:

6. *Either/Or*, I, 141.
7. Kierkegaard, *The Concept of Dread*, trans. with introduction and notes by Walter Lowrie (Princeton: Princeton University Press, 1946), 87.

In the modern world, "the tragedy of suffering has really lost interest" for the spectators. That is because the hero in modern tragedy has become responsible for himself. But the spectator can commiserate only with a hero who *cannot* help himself, one who *suffers* the blows of Fate. Therefore, when the fatalistic element is removed from tragedy and the hero becomes accountable for his actions, an entirely new relationship exists between the spectator and the action on the stage. Choice now becomes of paramount significance and responsibility is agonizingly present. Kierkegaard correctly observes, "The tragic hero, conscious of himself as a subject, is fully reflective, and this reflection has not only reflected him out of every immediate relation to state, race, and destiny, but has often even reflected him out of his own preceding life." This means that we now become concerned not so much with what brought the hero to his present dilemma but with the present dilemma itself. A specific moment of his life is considered in its singularity "as his own deed" and no one else's. This is why, for the modern theater, the action can be "exhaustively represented in situation and dialogue, since absolutely nothing of the immediate remains anymore." The dramatist cannot really point to other factors and call them responsible for the dilemma; the hero is fundamentally his own master in will and deed.[8]

However, Kierkegaard is quick to point out that it would be a misunderstanding of the tragic "to let the whole tragic destiny" of the hero "become transubstantiated in individuality and subjectivity." That is because we would thereby know nothing of the hero's past life, his origins, the forces and powers that have influenced and helped shape his character. We would be tempted to "throw his whole life upon his shoulders, as being the result of his own acts" and would consequently "make him accountable for everything." This cannot be true for drama, for by doing so, we would transform "his aesthetic guilt into an ethical one," a move which

---

8. *Either/Or*, 147, 141.

41

would be inimical to the dramatic enterprise. If we hold the tragic hero totally responsible for his actions, he becomes "bad" and "evil becomes precisely the tragic subject; but evil has no aesthetic interest, and sin is not an aesthetic element." What Kierkegaard wants us to see here is "the infinite gentleness" of the tragic: "It is really in the aesthetic sense with regard to human life, what the divine love and mercy are; it is even milder, and hence I may say that it is like a mother's love, soothing the troubled." By contrast, the ethical is seen to be "strict and harsh." [9] It would therefore be contrary to all aesthetic principles to hold the hero to be absolutely and unambiguously guilty.

Another way Kierkegaard approaches the same theme is to contrast sorrow with pain. "In ancient tragedy the sorrow is deeper, the pain less; in modern, the pain is greater, the sorrow less. Sorrow always contains something more substantial than pain. Pain always implies a reflection over suffering which sorrow does not know." Kierkegaard holds that the sorrow of ancient tragedy is deeper because the guilt of the hero is in fact aesthetically ambiguous. Sorrow shrouds the action because he is only dimly aware of what has happened to him; were he to apprehend transparently just how much his life has been shaped and determined by the substantial categories of the past, he would be outraged. No, he "rests" in his fate—a fate which has been "gentle"—and for this reason he is not compelled to engage in self-reflection. This is why Kierkegaard says the profound sorrow cannot grasp the modern spectator of an ancient tragedy, for we cannot really understand how sorrow can lie "within" the drama itself. In order to grasp what is meant here, one must be able to indwell the Greek consciousness, which, of course, is patently impossible for those of us who live within a pneumatically qualified universe. Kierkegaard therefore derides his contemporaries who "profess to admire Greek tragedies; for it is obvious that our age, at least, has no great sympathy

9. *Ibid.,* 142, 143.

with the specific character of Greek sorrow." In contrast to heroes of ancient times, the hero of modern drama knows greater pain. That is because he "suffers entirely according to his own desert" and is acutely aware of his own folly. The Infinite has opened up for him infinite possibilities. Thus, the results of decisions are not only felt sometimes to be painful, but the very process of making decisions becomes a painful burden. "It is a fearful thing to fall into the hands of the living God," Kierkegaard reminds us, for when one is faced with the Absolute, a radically new dimension is added to human consciousness.[10]

Kierkegaard also distinguishes the ancient from the modern idea of the tragic by contrasting anxiety with sorrow. Anxiety comes as a result of reflection whereas sorrow requires little or no reflection. If we are anxious about something, it is because we have considered it reflectively, but the word "sorrow" can be used in both objective as well as subjective ways. We can sorrow over some untoward event, but "one's personal sorrow" can also be discussed as an objective reality. Anxiety, on the other hand, can only involve subjective response to something that has already occurred or is about to occur. This would suggest, then, that we can never be anxious in the present tense. But sorrow, says Kierkegaard, "like the whole of Greek life, is in the present tense, and therefore the sorrow is deeper but the pain less." The heightened ability for self-reflection is what differentiates the spiritually determined hero from the psychically qualified hero of ancient Greece.[11] It might be well summed up this way: "Christianity has never subscribed to the notion that every particular individual is in an outward sense privileged to begin from scratch. Every individual begins in a historical nexus, and the consequences of natural law are still as valid as ever. The difference now consists only in this, that Christianity teaches us to lift ourselves above that 'more,' and condemns him who does not do so as not willing to do so." [12]

10. *Ibid.*, 145–46.   11. *Ibid.*, 152–53.
12. *The Concept of Dread*, 65.

43

It will now be our purpose to see what emerges when the categories developed by Kierkegaard are placed next to one of the great characters of Faulkner's most productive period —Joe Christmas. In particular, we shall scrutinize the world in which Christmas lives to determine what influence, if any, the Incarnation might have had on that world.

6

Joe
Christmas
and the
Incarnation

AT THE University of Virginia, Faulkner was asked about the possible parallels between Joe Christmas and the Christ of the gospels. His answer could have been predicted: that there was no intended parallel, that the Christ story is simply part of our heritage, and that, if a writer finds it convenient to use this story or any part of it in order to do his job, he should feel free to do so.[1] A more penetrating question would have inquired about the ways in which the life-styles of a Joe Christmas or a Joanna Burden might have been affected by the Incarnation. For no matter how interesting and important it might be for the scholar to trace the use Faulkner makes of religious themes and motifs, a much more basic inquiry concerns the existential modalities of the characters who populate a given novel. This, after all, is what compelled Faulkner's attention for the most part: characters in their concrete settings in life. When he did self-consciously attempt to retell the Christ story in fictional form, as in *A*

1. William Faulkner, *Faulkner in the University*, ed. Frederick L. Gwynn and Joseph L. Blotner (New York: Random House, Inc., 1965), 75. See above, p. 27.

Fable, he overextended himself. Indeed, there is widespread agreement today that this novel, as good and as powerful as it might be, is not able to carry the freight of the sacred story so directly told. As almost everyone agrees, *A Fable* is one of his lesser achievements.

This chapter, then, will explore the extent to which the world of Joe Christmas is a world informed by the irruption of the Infinite Spirit in history; it concludes that a life such as his could *only* have occurred after the Incarnation. He could never have dwelled within the limits of that contained, orderly world Kierkegaard calls "the psychically determined cosmos" of ancient Greece. That is because the Infinite Spirit is the qualifying factor in Joe's consciousness, whereas beauty is the qualifying factor for Hellenic consciousness.[2] When the Spirit irrupts in history, the infinite yawnings of the chasm of nothingness are opened up and dread becomes the vital force in men's lives. They are made uneasy by their precarious position in the face of the Infinite Spirit.[3] This is the world in which Joe Christmas finds himself—a world of extremes and absolutes.

The first appearance of Christmas in the novel presages his dread-filled condition. A group of men working at the sawmill where he was employed looked up one day to see a "stranger" who seemed to have appeared from out of nowhere. The stranger "did not look like a hobo in his professional rags, but there was something definitely rootless about him, as though no town nor city was his, no street, no walls, no square of earth his home."[4] And as the novel progresses,

2. Where beauty is the synthesizing principle of a culture as in ancient Greece, Spirit is excluded (or Spirit is only there potentially). Beauty, instead, accounts for the serenity and quiet solemnity of ancient Greece because beauty is finite, orderly, transparent, graceful.

3. Søren Kierkegaard, *The Concept of Dread,* trans. with introduction and notes by Walter Lowrie (Princeton: Princeton University Press, 1946), 58.

4. Faulkner, *Light in August* (New York: Random House, Inc., 1950), 27. Subsequent references to this edition in this chapter will appear in the text.

46

we find that this transient and evanescent figure was, as Faulkner might have said, "doomed" to spend his life running and running and running. Or, as Kierkegaard might have said, his manner of existence would ultimately break forth in "force, life, movement, constant unrest, perpetual succession; but this unrest, this succession, does not enrich it, it remains always the same, it does not unfold itself, but it storms uninterruptedly forward as if in a single breath."[5] Not that Christmas had "chosen" to indwell the world in a dreadful (full-of-dread) way. In a sense, he was not even aware of the anxiety at the base of his existence. But his dread was derived from the very fact that he could find no place in which he could gain perspective on himself. He was profoundly and hopelessly without roots—anywhere. Which means that we have great difficulty in assigning any content to his existence; it was poverty-stricken. In short, he was a model aesthete.

It is, of course, impossible to assign any content to the aesthete's modality of existence, because, as Kierkegaard says, we are confined to talking about the "how" of human existence, not the "what." A *way* of being in the world defies definition; it may only be described. But beyond this rather routine methodological observation, Kierkegaard also ascribes poverty to the aesthetical modality for very specific reasons. An aesthete's existence is poverty-stricken not only because his *telos* is "the moment," an entirely specious and illusory goal for anyone, but it is poverty-stricken because his *modality* of existence, his *way* of being in the world, does not allow him to be discovered or met. That is why a Joe Christmas or a Don Juan are not situated in history in any significant way and why music is their perfect medium, for music passes away in time and is *in* time only in an unessential way. Joe Christmas rarely speaks or acts in such a way as to enter history. Rather, he is acted upon, and the words

5. Kierkegaard, *Either/Or*, trans. David F. Swenson and Lillian Marvin Swenson with revisions by Howard A. Johnson (2 vols.; Princeton: Princeton University Press, 1959), I, 70.

47

he does manage to utter do not allow him to declare himself publicly. He is still hidden from everyone's view as he dwells on in his sensuousness.

Joe's sensuousness may be traced to circumstances that drove him into an uncertain future. Orphaned from birth, he was never able to gain a perspective on himself. Because he remained totally unaware of his antecedents, he was cursed with the lack of a history that he could know about, much less claim. Rootlessness was not something he at first "chose" but was something laid upon him by circumstance and Fate. His problem was not so much one of refusing to accept his past as it was not knowing what his past was so that he could choose it. The people who could divulge his parents' identity to him willingly refused to do so and deliberately set about to create uncertainty in his mind about his heritage—especially with respect to whether or not he possessed Negro blood. Old Doc Hines, Christmas's natural grandfather, believed his daughter Milly to have been "the walking shape of bitchery and abomination" because she gave birth to a bastard child. Since Joe was the living evidence of Milly's betrayal of the Hines family name, Doc understood his appointed task to be that of making Joe suffer for Milly's sin (327).

But even if he could have eventually discovered who his parents were with certainty, it is clear that Christmas's personality was so maimed and scarred by the Doc Hineses in his life that it would have been extremely difficult, if not impossible, for him to sink down roots anywhere. The chances for self-identity were slim. For example, his foster father, Simon McEachern, attempted to force upon him the harsh and unbending demands of a rigid Calvinism, which, instead of providing the intended boundaries for a wayward youth, further exacerbated Joe's feeling of outrage and hopelessness. Even his first love, the waitress-slut Bobbie Allen, was unable to provide any lasting relationship. In short, Joe's situation in life was always such that there was little or no opportunity for stability and order. Dread issued in disorder and despair.

Joe Christmas and the Incarnation

What we witness in this character, of course, is sensuousness, for Joe Christmas is the embodiment of "exclusion" and "opposition." He was certainly excluded by Hines—excluded because he was the constant reminder to the old man of "bitchery and abomination." After delivering the newborn child to the doorsteps of the Memphis orphanage, Hines took a job as janitor there in order to keep an eye on the child and to act, so he thought, as the instrument of God's will in seeking the destruction of the child:

> It was the Lord. *He* was there. Old Doc Hines give God His chance too. The Lord told old Doc Hines what to do and old Doc Hines done it. Then the Lord said to old Doc Hines, 'You watch, now. Watch My will a-working.' And old Doc Hines watched and heard the mouths of little children, of God's own fatherless and motherless, putting His words and knowledge into their mouths even when they couldn't know it since they were without sin yet, even the girl ones without sin and bitchery yet: Nigger! Nigger! in the innocent mouths of little children. 'What did I tell you?' God said to old Doc Hines. 'And now I've set My will to working and now I'm gone . . . , because I have set My will a-working and I can leave you here to watch it.' So old Doc Hines he watched and he waited. From God's own boiler room he watched them children, and the devil's walking seed unbeknownst among them, polluting the earth with the working of that word on him. Because he didn't play with the other children no more now. He stayed by himself, standing still, and then old Doc Hines knew that he was listening to the hidden warning of God's doom, and old Doc Hines said to him, 'Why dont you play with them other children like you used to?' and he didn't say nothing and old Doc Hines said, 'Is it because they call you nigger?' and he didn't say nothing and old Doc Hines said, 'Do you think you are a nigger because God has marked your face?' and he said, 'Is God a nigger too?' and old Doc Hines said, 'He is the Lord God of wrathful hosts, His will be done. Not yours and not mine, because you and me are both a part of His purpose and His vengeance.' (334–36)

The point simply is this: Eupheus Hines, by the invocation of the name of the transcendent God of the Christian tradition, was putting himself within the sphere of the Infinite.

49

His image of God was, to be sure, not of a just yet merciful God of the classical Christian tradition but of a grotesque and hideous tyrant. His wife remarked, "And so sometimes I would think how the devil had conquered God" in old Doc Hines (330). His religious fanaticism carried him to the extreme of interrupting services in remote Negro churches: "In his harsh, dead voice and at times with violent obscenity, [he would] preach to them humility before all skins lighter than theirs, preaching the superiority of the white race, himself his own exhibit A in fanatic and unconscious paradox. The Negroes believed that he was crazy, touched by God, or having once touched Him" (301). His possession by such demonic powers could only have transpired in a post-Incarnational world, where the principles of "opposition" and "exclusion" were possible. Indeed, Kierkegaard would say that Doc Hines lived in dread of the good, a dread which is manifest either in ravings of the maniac or in "shut-upness," [6] a sporadic muteness. This was precisely Hines's way. He either remained silent, uncommunicative, almost in a trance; or he would break forth with passion and howling. (One is reminded of Christ's confrontation with the demoniacs in the New Testament.) That is because Hines indwelt evil and dreaded the good. When anyone appeared who represented the possibility of the good—whether it was his wife, the people at the orphanage, the sheriff who wanted to maintain orderly procedures after the capture of Christmas—the muteness so characteristic of the demoniac Doc Hines was sprung open and the "demon" became actively destructive in an attempt to obliterate the good.

Just as "shut-upness" was Doc Hines's problem, so it became Joe's. He was never able to break out of his confined and shut-up existence. Our first glimpse of him shows a man who was either unable or who refused to speak. "He did not talk to any of them at all," but kept to himself, living in dread

6. This term, awkward as it is, probably conveys as well as any expression what Kierkegaard intended by *det Indesluttede* or *Indesluttedhed*. See *The Concept of Dread*, 110 and elsewhere.

of the nothingness which seemed to undergird his life (28–29 and elsewhere). Not that he understood he was living out his life within the realm of the demoniacal (it was all too immediate for him; he lacked the self-transcendence to be able to see what was happening), but that he had lost freedom, the opposite of the demoniacal. The possibility of freedom—of being able to choose one's own life—was too awesome for Joe to face. He therefore gave himself over to the external forces that would thereafter shape his life. He submitted to forces that would automatically proscribe meaningful relationships with all others. When Joanna Burden, after months of a clandestine sexual involvement with Joe, began to talk to him about marriage, he resisted the idea instantaneously: *"She wants a child no more than I do* 'It's just a trick,' he thought. 'I should have known it, expected it. I should have cleared out of here a year ago.'" But then he wavered: *"Why not? It would mean ease, security, for the rest of your life. You would never have to move again. And you might as well be married to her as this* thinking, 'No. If I give in now, I will deny all the thirty years that I have lived to make me what I chose to be'" (231–32). But he only deceived himself about having chosen anything, and his relationship to Joanna Burden was no exception. At the mention of marriage his being was volatilized still further. He was afraid of marriage, but then he was also afraid of rejecting marriage. He would therefore let things work themselves out naturally; he would simply put himself at the disposal of Fate.[7] All of this, of course, contributes to a discussion of Joe Christmas's modality of existence. It is clear that he did not dwell in a universe where the concept of beauty rules but in a universe of Spirit and anti-Spirit. Though Fate played a large part in his life, it was not the Fate of the antique pagan world, but a Fate qualified by the appearance in history of the absolutely unqualified Spirit of the Christian revelation. It was a world

7. As we shall see in chapters nine and ten, refusal to enter into marriage is one of the characteristics of the aesthetical stage of existence.

in which sin was defined as "radical discontinuity" with the transcendent and holy God. Joe Christmas's error—and the error of most of those around him—was not the error of ignorance, but the error of men within whom wrong has been infinitized before God. Thus, in addition to Doc Hines's rantings about sin and abomination, we see that Simon McEachern had a view of man and God that was equally twisted and savage. It was under his tutelage that Joe was first introduced to the category of sin—distorted, to be sure, yet still within the spiritually determined universe Kierkegaard speaks of.

In the poignant scenes in which McEachern attempted to force the boy to learn the Presbyterian catechism, we are confronted with a version of frontier religion in its most violent and obscene form. The harder McEachern pushed, the stiffer became Joe's resistance so that the omniscient author could report, "There was a very kinship of stubbornness like a transmitted resemblance in their backs" as they walked out to the barn for the beating—"the two backs in their rigid abnegation of all compromise more alike than actual blood could have made them" (130). It is clear that Joe was able to possess what identity he did because of the exclusion and opposition afforded by such rigidity. McEachern's fault lay in his totally unbending attitude. It was not that he was deliberate in his meanness, only impersonal, "cold, implacable, like written or printed words" (130). The punishment meted out by the wrathful executor of the will of a wrathful God is painfully memorable:

> Then the boy stood, his trousers collapsed about his feet, his legs revealed beneath his brief shirt. He stood, slight and erect. When the strap fell he did not flinch, no quiver passed over his face. He was looking straight ahead, with a rapt, calm expression like a monk in a picture. McEachern began to strike methodically, with slow and deliberate force, still without heat or anger. It would have been hard to say which face was the more rapt, more calm, more convinced.
>
> He struck ten times, then he stopped. "Take the book," he said. "Leave your pants be." He handed the boy the cate-

chism. The boy took it. He stood so, erect, his face and the pamphlet lifted, his attitude one of exaltation. Save for surplice he might have been a Catholic choir boy, with for nave the looming and shadowy crib, the rough planked wall beyond which in the ammoniac and dryscented obscurity beasts stirred now and then with snorts and indolent thuds . . . on the exact second of the hour McEachern returned the watch to his pocket. "Do you know it now?" he said. The boy didn't answer, rigid, erect, holding the open pamphlet before his face. McEachern took the book from between his hands. Otherwise, the boy did not move at all. "Repeat your catechism," McEachern said. The boy stared straight at the wall before him. His face was now quite white despite the smooth rich pallor of his skin. Carefully and deliberately McEachern laid the book upon the ledge and took up the strap. He struck ten times. (131–32)

But this was not the end. The self-righteousness of this bitter and uncompromising judge was displayed after Joe regained consciousness when McEachern asked the boy to kneel down with him:

The boy knelt; the two of them knelt in the close, twilit room: the small figure in cutdown underwear, the ruthless man who had never known either pity or doubt. McEachern began to pray. He prayed for a long time, his voice droning, soporific, monotonous. He asked that he be forgiven for trespass against the Sabbath and for lifting his hand against a child, an orphan, who was dear to God. He asked that the child's stubborn heart be softened and that the sin of disobedience be forgiven him also, through the advocacy of the man whom he had flouted and disobeyed, requesting that Almighty be as magnanimous as himself, and by and through and because of conscious grace. (133)

Joe, in turn, was to think of himself as the prime example of sinfulness and wretchedness in comparison with the pious Simon McEachern. For Joe, sin was not simply missing the mark; it was not just disproportion or ugliness; sin was the radical departure from the ways of God—ways he would never hope to accomplish because he felt himself to be so fundamentally depraved and without hope and because the

God he was taught to believe in was so grindingly despotic. McEachern's religiousness, which he attempted to impose on Joe, was no less distorted than Doc Hines's. Both men came out of a background that was only residually Christian, though it was not a return to the pre-Christian pagan world. It was a universe in which one despaired by the despair of defiance, which could only occur in the pneumatically qualified universe. A defiance of not willing to be the man one is— a sinner—and for this reason willing to dispense with the forgiveness of sins.[8] Neither Doc Hines nor Simon McEachern could see the depths of their own depravity nor the possibility for the grace and forgiveness of a merciful God. But even so, their misconception of religion is not the point just now. What we must see are the infinite dimensions of the world they inhabited and that Joe Christmas came to inhabit because of their influences on his life.

This is why it would be incorrect to hold that this modern tragic hero is subject to Fate in the way, say, that Oedipus was. The crime for the ancient classical hero consisted in the "choice" of existence. As William H. Poteat points out, "Existence, as such, is the *hybris* of the hero. His suffering is brought upon him at the hands of the gods through the necessity of having to choose." Rather than submit himself to the eternal decrees of an inexorable Fate, Oedipus attempts to be "outstanding"—that is, to stand out from the substantial categories of family, race, and nation. "Or, to put the matter in terms of the dramatic form itself, the hero breaks out of the Chorus" and thereby commits his primordial sin of simply being a man.[9] So his sin is laid upon him by Fate, by the gods, by the eternal order of things. He is, in a word, *made* guilty. It is not willful disobedience to a free and transcendent God who demands of his creature, man, that he also

8. Kierkegaard, *The Sickness unto Death*, in *Fear and Trembling and The Sickness unto Death*, trans. with introduction and notes by Walter Lowrie (Princeton: Princeton University Press, 1954), 244.

9. William H. Poteat, "Tragedy and Freedom," *The Carolina Quarterly*, VIII, 2 (Winter–Spring, 1956), 20–21.

be free and self-transcending. It is, instead, simply the "choice: to be what one is required to be—an existant. That is the first sin, the basic sin." (Of course, in this context the word "choice" has, at best, an equivocal and ambiguous status.) To be human is to be heroic and to become guilty at one and the same time. Thus, one is made human, suffers his humanity, and accepts the conditions of his humanity as something from which he cannot, ultimately, escape. Poteat continues:

> The hero's original crime is existence itself and everything that happens from the beginning works itself out in inexorable grandeur. Everything bears home to him this necessity: the more intensely he tries to escape, the more inevitably he seems to become entangled. In trying to exercise foresight, wisdom and responsibility for himself—e.g., Oedipus' flight when told he will kill his father and marry his mother—; in seeking to extricate himself from his situation, to outwit the gods, to overcome by increase of knowledge and responsibility; he only hastens his downfall. For it is the exercise of foresight, wisdom and responsibility for himself which produces the situation in the first place. To extend these is to exacerbate the problem still further, to compound the crime.
>
> All of this implies, of course, that if man had never "chosen himself," he would never have had to choose at all; and that if he had never had to choose, he would never have become guilty of particular crimes. Yet, this is the greatness of the man. At the same time this greatness seems somehow an anomaly in the universe. Therefore man shows his ultimate greatness in this ultimate reach of self-knowledge which enables him to see that he is an anomaly, to acknowledge it, and to acquiesce to it.[10]

But this is not Joe Christmas's world. He is an inhabitant of the post-Incarnational universe in which man is made in the image of God. That is, he is potentially active, free, and capable of self-determination. There is, in fact, a profound sense in which he is not made human but makes his own humanity such as it is. The very fact that Christmas *refuses* to make this choice forms the very shape of his existence.

10. *Ibid.*, 22.

He does, beyond question, "passively acquiesce" to his fate. What *appears* to be action on his part is not action but capitulation to despair and confusion. Or, as Kierkegaard would describe it, Christmas lives in a state of dread—a state defined as "sympathetic antipathy or an antipathetic sympathy." In other words, we are both drawn to and repelled by the nothingness which undergirds our existence. Dread can be the cause of existential paralysis when one seeks to withdraw from activity in the hopes of avoiding dread rather than engaging life and thus conquering dread, if only temporarily. We find Joe Christmas characteristically enthralled to dread. The dread that is in him becomes the energy of his life. Kierkegaard would not call it "a subjectively reflected dread" but "a substantial dread."[11] Christmas is unaware of its presence in his life and yet it is the very force or principle which gives substance to and informs his life. He has not chosen dread nor has he really chosen anything. The despair that *we* see inherent in his existence is not really grasped or understood by him. His existence is *given over* to the whole power of sensuousness—exclusion and opposition—which is born of dread.

The first indication of his subservience to the external world occurs relatively early in the novel. He is so overwhelmed by his hatred/attraction for Joanna Burden that he feels some outside force will compel him to destroy her: " 'Maybe I have already done it,' he thought. 'Maybe it is no longer now waiting to be done' " (97). Or again, after a wild dash through Freedman Town in Jefferson, he is not even thinking, and yet deep down in his subconscious the same theme drums on: *"Something is going to happen. Something is going to happen"* (103). Here is a man who is acted upon more than he acts, it would seem, and yet this passivity is not the result of the gods having irrevocably decided what his destiny would be; instead he is suffering the torpor and malaise which result from acquiescence to despair. Even in

11. *Either/Or*, I, 128.

those moments when he attempts to assert his selfhood in the face of the domineering Simon McEachern, we get the feeling that the very intensity of his rebellion against his foster father manifests his surrender to the external. After he murders the old man, he feels an exhilaration that seems only to come with violence. Like Faust,[12] he feels he has put behind himself "once and for all the Shalt Not" and is "free at last of honor and law" (180). Perhaps so. Perhaps he is free of the demands of the law drilled into him by McEachern, but he soon finds himself (again like Faust) in slavery to an even more stringent master: sensuousness as insatiable desire. Not simply the desire of sexuality—though that yearning was there in all its strength—but also the desire to discover his true identity. It is not merely coincidental that these themes—sex and identity—are frequently found in juxtaposition in the novel, as in the case when Joanna Burden urged "Negro! Negro! Negro!" in the midst of sexual intercourse. Or, there is the incident when he tries to avoid paying a white whore by telling her he was a Negro: "What about it? You look all right. You ought to seen the shine I turned out before your turn came . . . Say, what do you think this dump is, anyhow? The Ritz hotel?" (196). According to the omniscient author that episode made him sick and for a long time. "He stayed sick for two years."

The point is clear. In the Christian West sexuality is discovered within the context of radical individuality, because it is the Spirit which posits individuality. Indeed, sexuality becomes the extremest expression of individuality, because individuality is the result of what Kierkegaard calls "the leap"—a leap out of the Chorus, out of the substantial categories of family, race, and nation into discreet personhood. Prior to that, individuality is there only in a dreaming state and is not gained in its fullest until the Spirit is posited. It is the Spirit—as the representative relation, as the Individual— who makes individuality a possibility. But more *impor-*

12. One cannot dismiss the fact that both Kierkegaard and Faulkner think of Faust as a symbol for the demoniacal.

tantly, because this all takes place before God, in the presence of God, man discovers his own discrepancy and incommensurability with God, which is to say he discovers sin. Sexuality is not sinfulness, in itself, but without sin (which is actualized by the leap but derived from itself) there is no sexuality.[13] This is what the relationship with Joanna Burden is all about. Appropriately enough, she swings wildly between the extremes of hysterical sexuality and asexual indifference. But, like Christmas, her sometimes apparent lack of sensuousness and sexuality is not like that of the ancient Greeks. It is not the harmless phenomenon of sensuousness and sexuality that is distributed in an orderly and beautiful manner throughout the psychically determined cosmos where everyone has his being within the epic background, where sexuality is only an incidental characteristic of the Greek personality. Joanna's sexuality is "shut-up" as in the demoniacal personality, waiting to break forth in the storm of passion that marks her sexual encounters with Christmas. Early in the relationship he found her participation in the sex act to be "hard, untearful and unselfpitying and almost manlike yielding of that surrender. . . . There was no feminine vacillation, no coyness of obvious desire and intention to succumb at last. It was as if he struggled physically with another man for an object of no actual value to either, and for which they struggled on principle alone" (205).

In brief, Joe Christmas and Joanna Burden, though enthralled by external stimuli, do not dwell in a soulishly determined cosmos. Sensuousness for them is not some benign force. It is not dissipated throughout the lambent August landscape as with Lena Grove. Instead, it is concentrated into sexual aggression, verbal violence, and physical attack. And most significantly for Christmas, sensuousness is concentrated in an unquenchable desire to search out and find through frightening and yet alluring relationships with others his true identity, his individuality. Because he has such diffi-

13. *The Concept of Dread*, 44, 47, 71, and elsewhere.

culty in making and maintaining relationships, he frequently is seen, in Kierkegaardian terms, to be hovering in dread *above* history rather than becoming incarnate, as was true also for Don Juan in the first volume of *Either/Or:* "Don Juan constantly hovers between being an idea, that is to say, energy, life—and being an individual. . . . So Don Juan is an image which constantly appears, but does not gain form and substance, an individual who is constantly being formed, but is never finished, of whose life history one can form no more definite impression than one can by listening to the tumult of the waves." [14] This is why the trembling evanescent quality of music is perfect for presenting the figure of Don Juan.

In the same way Christmas—whose life history one can form no constant impression about (least of all himself)— hovers just above history. He appears and then almost as quickly disappears. He lives in a world in which the order and beauty of the ancient Hellenic cosmos has been destroyed but in which the infinite power of dread keeps teasing him away from making a decision to choose himself finally and irrevocably. Or, as Kierkegaard says in *The Sickness unto Death*, his despair is one which is unreflective. He does not stop long enough to reflect upon the cause for his perpetual running and vanishing. After the Bobbie Allen affair, he seeks the avenue of escape:

> From that night the thousand streets ran as one street, with imperceptible corners and changes of scene, broken by intervals of begged and stolen rides, on trains and trucks, and on country wagons with he at twenty and twentyfive and thirty sitting on the seat with his still, hard face and the clothes (even when soiled and worn) of a city man and the driver of the wagon not knowing who or what the passenger was and not daring to ask. The street ran into Oklahoma and Missouri and as far south as Mexico and then back north to Chicago and Detroit and then back south again and at last to Mississippi. It was fifteen years long: it ran between the savage and spurious board fronts of oil towns. . . . It ran through

14. *Either/Or*, I, 91.

yellow wheat fields waving beneath the fierce yellow days of labor and hard sleep . . . : he was in turn laborer, miner, prospector, gambling tout; he enlisted in the army, served four months and deserted and was never caught. And always, sooner or later, the street ran through cities, through an identical and wellnigh interchangeable section of cities without remembered names, where beneath the dark and equivocal and symbolical archways of midnight he bedded with the women . . . (195–96)

Two days later the last word to come directly from his consciousness shows that the ambiguity is still there for him. He is riding toward Mottstown on a wagon driven by a Negro youth with his shoes resting on the dashboard of the wagon, "the black shoes smelling of Negro: that mark on his ankles the gauge definite and ineradicable of the black tide creeping up his legs, moving from his feet upward as death moves" (297). But the significant note in this passage is that the "blackness" is still down around his ankles; it has *not* moved irrevocably up his legs into his whole body.

In this connection it is instructive to note the community's attitude toward Christmas's origins. The rabble was as confused as the protagonist: "He dont look no more like a nigger than I do, either. But it must have been the nigger blood in him" that drove him to murder Miss Burden (306, 303). Gavin Stevens, who had a much more sophisticated way of putting things, said pretty much the same thing. He talked about a war, within Christmas, between "white blood" and "black blood," but in the end the white blood won out:

It was the black blood which swept him by his own desire beyond the aid of any man, swept him up into that ecstasy out of a black jungle where life has already ceased before the heart stops and death is desire and fulfillment. And then the black blood failed him again, as it must have in crises all his life. He did not kill the minister. He merely struck him with the pistol and ran on and crouched behind that table and defied the black blood for the last time, as he had been defying it for thirty years. He crouched behind that overturned table and let them shoot him to death, with that loaded and unfired pistol in his hand. (393–94)

But no matter how the community assesses the man's heritage, *he* never knows who he is and is therefore never able to choose himself. Or conversely because he does *not* choose, he never has a self with which to be identified. He therefore finds that his running, which he has been doing for thirty years, is down the same old street he had run down before:

> He is entering it again, the street which ran for thirty years. It had been a paved street, where going should be fast. It had made a circle and he is still inside of it. Though during the last seven days he has had no paved street, yet he has travelled farther than in all the thirty years before. And yet he is still inside the circle. 'And yet I have been farther in these seven days than in all the thirty years,' he thinks 'But I have never got outside that circle. I have never broken out of the ring of what I have already done and cannot ever undo.' (296)

That is to say he is trapped within a world that is both posited for him and in which he refuses (we *must* use this or a similar verb) to exercise "subjective reflection and decision." He is responsible yet caught. He is not some Greek tragic hero whose destiny is predetermined by necessity or *Moira*—he lives in a universe where the possibility of freedom exists—but he never chooses. Though he has a past—however uncertain and dim the knowledge of this past might have been—we still have the feeling that anywhere along the line he could appropriate the past he does know, make it his own, establish himself and thereby call a halt to the volatilization of his being which is so aptly illustrated by the metaphor of wind. One of the most significant, but little noticed, passages in the novel occurs when Joe goes to the whorehouse to take Bobbie away to marry her. It is the one time that he has felt anything like closeness to another human being. He has, in the first place, just killed old man McEachern in a brawl at a roadside tavern and thinks himself liberated from the tyrannical rule of this seemingly omnipotent force in his life. Next, he has stolen Mrs. McEachern's life's hoardings in order to finance the marriage to Bobbie.

In brief, he has overturned the old order and is free to establish a new one. It is a time in which he feels he is making a move to consolidate his life against the arbitrary outside forces which have threatened to mould and shape his destiny in a way that would be repugnant to him. *But*, as soon as he discovers that Bobbie has rejected him, his own person, self, or consciousness is described by the volatile, insubstantial qualities of wind—he becomes pure spirit:

> "What did—" Joe said. "What did I . . ." he said, in a tone of fainting amazement, glaring from face to face with a sort of outraged yet still patient exasperation. "What did I come for? I came to get Bobbie. Do you think that I—when I went all the way home to get the money to get married—" Again he completely forgot, dismissed them. . . . *Very likely at that moment the two men were blown as completely out of his life as two scraps of paper.* Very likely he was not even aware when Max went to the door and called and a moment later the blonde woman entered. He was bending above the bed upon which sat the immobile and downlooking waitress, stooping above her, dragging the wadded mass of coins and bills from his pocket, onto her lap and onto the bed beside her. "Here! Look at it. Look. I've got. See?"
> *Then the wind blew upon him again.* . . . He stood in a quiet, dreamlike state, erect now where the upward spring of the sitting waitress had knocked him, and saw her, on her feet, gather up the wadded and scattered money and fling it; he saw quietly her face strained, the mouth screaming, the eyes screaming too. . . . "Bastard! Son of a bitch! Getting me into a jam, that always treated you like you were a white man. A white man!"
> But very likely to him even yet it was just noise, not registering at all: *just part of the long wind.* He just stared at her, at the face he had never seen before, . . . *Then she too seemed to blow out of his life on the long wind like a third scrap of paper.* (188–89; emphasis added.)

Utterly passive and dependent upon outside forces, he had not really chosen himself. If he had, the event would not have been so devastating to him as a person.

The tragedy of Joe Christmas was, therefore, a modern tragedy. He was not the tragic Greek hero whose sin was having been born. He was, instead, one who had the possibility of stepping out of the epic background into "subjective reflection and decision." He was free, in a way that the classical Greek hero was not, to speak and to act, and yet he never exercised that freedom. He fits Kierkegaard's description of the *immediate* man in every way:

> This is pure immediacy, or else an immediacy which contains a quantitative reflection.—Here there is no infinite consciousness of the self, of what despair is, or of the fact that the condition is one of despair; the despair is passive, succumbing to the pressure of the outward circumstance, it by no means comes from within as action. . . .
>
> The *immediate* man (in so far as immediacy is to be found without any reflection) is merely soulishly determined, his self or he himself is a something included along with "the other" in the compass of the temporal and the worldly, and it has only an illusory appearance of possessing in it something eternal. Thus the self coheres immediately with "the other," wishing, desiring, enjoying, etc., but passively; even in desiring, the self is in the dative case, like the child when it says "me" for I. Its dialectic is: the agreeable and the disagreeable; its concepts are: good fortune, misfortune, fate.
>
> Now then there *happens*, befalls (falls upon) this immediate self something which brings it to despair; in no other way can this come about, since the self has no reflection in itself, that which brings it to despair must come from without, and the despair is merely passive. That wherein immediacy has its being, or (supposing that after all it has a little bit of reflection in itself) that part thereof to which it especially clings, a man is deprived of by "a stroke of fate," in short, he becomes, as he calls it, unfortunate, that is, the immediacy in him receives such a shock that it cannot recover itself—he despairs.[15]

15. *The Sickness unto Death*, 184–85.

II

The Structure
of Existence

7

The Modalities of Existence

THE MOST ORIGINAL and lasting contribution Kierkegaard made to the development of modern intellectual history is his analysis of human existence.[1] His "stages" or "modalities" of existence form the foundation for all his work and have influenced subsequent writers in the existentialist tradition.

Delineation of the basic ways in which the human mind-body totality may deploy itself in its ambience was a natural extension of his fundamental concern with subjectivity. He was not merely speculating about the ways men live their lives but was undertaking to show how their life-styles express something more fundamental. He was not merely depicting psychological types but was describing the kinds of structures which inform reality. In short, he was developing a conceptual presentation of the kinds of worlds there are.

Kierkegaard was therefore suspicious of any attempts to fit the processes of living into an *a priori* scheme and was particularly wary of efforts by Hegel and other nineteenth-century idealists to construct a system into which all the

1. See James Collins, *The Mind of Kierkegaard* (Chicago: Henry Regnery Company, 1953), 42.

fragments of life might fit. In fact, he held that an existential "system" was beyond formulation; [2] the best one could do is observe and describe available data as accurately as possible. For this reason John Wild suggested some time ago that Kierkegaard may be considered a "radical empiricist." [3] Today, he might be called an "existential phenomenologist." In any case, he eschewed generalizations altogether and took as his subject the individual person in all his discreteness and concretion. This does not mean, however, that Kierkegaard had an easier task than the system builder. Quite the contrary:

> It is more difficult to describe one actor than to write a whole philosophy of art, and more difficult to describe one of his performances than to describe the actor. The more limited the material the more difficult the task . . . because it is a direct test of the powers of description.
>
> The more one can depend upon generalisation the easier it is, for the material is so vast that all the completely abstract observations, which anyone can learn by heart, seem to mean something. But the more concrete the observation the more difficult it is. God knows how long philosophers will continue puffing themselves up with the fantastic notion with which they deceive both themselves and others, that generalisation is what is difficult. [4]

But Kierkegaard felt philosophy was not entirely useless. Indeed, he saluted philosophy for contributing to our civilization and fervently encouraged his reader to use its methods. Moreover, he said, to deny the value of speculation would

2."Does this mean that no such system exists? By no means; nor is this implied in our assertion. Reality itself is a system—for God; but it cannot be a system for any existing spirit. System and finality correspond to one another, but existence is precisely the opposite of finality." Søren Kierkegaard, *The Concluding Unscientific Postscript*, trans. David F. Swenson and Walter Lowrie (Princeton: Princeton University Press, 1941), 107.

3. John Wild, *The Challenge of Existentialism* (Bloomington: Indiana University Press, 1955), 29.

4. Kierkegaard, *The Journals of Søren Kierkegaard*, ed. and trans. Alexander Dru (London: Oxford University Press, 1951), 147.

have been particularly unwise in his own case, because he had to rely so heavily on its services in his work as author and critic. But he did not sense that the Hegelians were under the same compulsion to attend to life as he was. Moreover, he repudiated the Hegelian confidence in language—that words can ever completely encompass "the truth" or that any ideational construction can ever be more than an exercise in thought. Therefore, Kierkegaard's alternative method was to describe from a direct and primitive standpoint, free of all generalizations, the sheer facticity of the subject under investigation.

Kierkegaard wished to accept the world and history as "already there" and possessing its own meaning prior to his reflection about it. That is why he conceived his task to be not so much one of explaining as describing. It is instructive to note in this respect that he saluted a forerunner of the modern phenomenological movement, Friedrich Schleiermacher (1768–1834), as a "thinker who could talk of what he has known, whereas Hegel, in spite of his remarkable and colossal learning, reminds us nevertheless again and again by his performance that he was in the German sense a professor of philosophy on a big scale, who *a tout prix* must explain all things."[5] But Kierkegaard wished to speak only of what he, personally, had known and of what was known to other men before him. This does not mean that the tangible, concrete entities in time or space are the only knowable things and that art or myth possess no validity. On the contrary, they are as much a part of what can be known as any other phenomenon, and Kierkegaard drew heavily on the works of the imagination to speak of "the truth" as he grasped it. He felt he could speak of anything that could be known experientially, anything that could become a part of his phenomenal field, or literally any-*thing*. The idea was not to strain phenomena through some sort of ideational sieve

5. Kierkegaard, *The Concept of Dread*, trans. with introduction and notes by Walter Lowrie (Princeton: Princeton University Press, 1946), 18.

69

or force them into the limits of a system, but to know them in their primordial and prereflective simplicity and vitality.

Kierkegaard's most powerful guns were trained on the Hegelian treatment of human existence, for their speculations were predictably disastrous: to speculate about existence only results in altogether abstracting the personal out of existence. To speculate about living only causes a perpetual vanishing from oneself.[6] The fact is that existence simply cannot be grasped as an object of thought. As John Wild says, "When I look at myself in this way, something eludes me. When I look at another as a cognitive object, something eludes me."[7] And this "something" we are attempting to pin down is existence itself, which may only be grasped by the individual by a completely different mode of awareness—certainly not in an objective mode. One is aware of oneself not as an object but as an agent who is caught up in the business of living and is forced to act. In the same way, the supreme question of one's own personal happiness is beyond objective grasp. Kierkegaard himself puts it this way:

> The difficulty of speculative thought increases according to the degree in which one makes existential use of what one has speculated upon. A man who with contrite heart needs the relief of believing in the forgiveness of sins at every moment: if he were to speculate, then everything would go amiss. But usually the philosophers (Hegel as well as all the rest), like the majority of men, exist in quite different categories for everyday purposes from those in which they speculate, and console themselves with categories very different from those which they solemnly discuss. . . .
>
> In relation to their systems most systematisers are like a man who builds an enormous castle and lives in a shack close by; they do not live in their own enormous systematic buildings. But spiritually that is a decisive objection. Spiritually speaking a man's thought must be the building in which he lives—otherwise everything is topsy-turvy.[8]

6. *Postscript*, 54.
7. Wild, *The Challenge of Existentialism*, 54.   8. *Journals*, 156.

Speculation can therefore be used as a dodge by the person who wishes to remain uninvolved with the hard decisions of life. It is simply another guise for the aesthetical modality, as Kierkegaard often points out in the *Postscript*. It is a way for one to avoid having to deal with the rigors of making "the absolute distinction between good and evil."[9]

Furthermore, the aesthetic-metaphysical modality can be the downfall of all serious learning. Kierkegaard, as an acutely sensitive student of his era, was especially insistent that the newly-won confidence in historical investigation was misplaced. The trouble with historical knowledge, he said, is that it is neither factual nor capable of being appropriated by the individual: "In historical knowledge, the subject learns a great deal about the world, but nothing about himself. He moves constantly in a sphere of approximation-knowledge, in his supposed positivity deluding himself with the semblance of certainty; but certainty can be had only in the infinite, where he cannot as an existing subject remain, but only repeatedly arrive. Nothing historical can become infinitely certain for me except the fact of my own existence . . . , and this is not something historical."[10] But the most insidious quality of historical knowledge is what it does to the private relationship between the individual and God. It forces the historian or philosopher to view "the world-historical process" *ex post facto*, whereas the relationship to God is an immediate experience. Because the historian must of necessity ignore God as sovereign of "the world-historical process," the whole God-hypothesis is brought into serious question, and "if he is not seen as sovereign, he is not seen at all."[11] Kierkegaard, therefore, warns against fatuous trust in the power and validity of the historical-critical method.

To the argument that subjectivity will ultimately lead to madness, Kierkegaard responds that the same could be said

9. *Postscript*, 120.   10. *Ibid.*, 75.   11. *Ibid.*, 139–40.

of objectivity. He admits that an exclusive dependence on subjectivity can easily lead one to believe that truth and madness are indistinguishable, but that is because both have inwardness. Nevertheless, he says, the *absence* of inwardness can also be a form of insanity: "The objective truth as such, is by no means adequate to determine that whoever utters it is sane; on the contrary, it may even betray the fact that he is mad, although what he says may be entirely true, and especially objectively true."[12]

In a sense, Faulkner agrees with Kierkegaard: "I don't have much confidence in the mind," he once told a group of university students. He trusted instead the intuition and the emotions. He thought men had become abstracted from their origins in nature and history. He therefore had no desire to read about ideas or to peddle them in his fiction. He conceived his job to be one of describing things as he perceived them, and on the occasions when he did resort to promoting one idea or another, he frequently lapsed into triviality or dubious polemic. The clearest example of this is seen by comparing his essays concerning the racial problem in the South with his fiction depicting the tragedy of racial conflict. His position in the essays would have to be acknowledged as "moderate" or "conservative," but his novels and stories are eloquent testimony to the imperative of securing justice in the arena of human relations today. The point is that he had no "System" to which his fictional output could

12. *Ibid.*, 172. Kierkegaard elucidates his occasionally bewildering notions of subjectivity and inwardness when he asks, *"What is certitude and inwardness? . . . I would say that it is seriousness. . . .* When Macbeth had murdered the King he cried:
> From this instant
> There's nothing serious in mortality.
> All is but toys: renown and grace is dead;
> The wine of life is drawn, and the mere lees
> Is left this vault to brag of.
. . . 'There's nothing serious in mortality, all is but toys'; for inwardness is precisely the fountain which springeth up unto eternal life, and what issues from this fountain is precisely seriousness." *The Concept of Dread*, 130.

be subjected. His own personal convictions and prejudices in the matter were subverted by his accuracy in the perception and recording of the social scene in which his characters were placed.

In short, Kierkegaard and Faulkner are kindred spirits, though they express themselves in different modes. Kierkegaard was a manic dialectician who suspected reason (the System) because he dialectically surpassed it. Faulkner was no dialectician at all, except insofar as his involuted style ("putting it all on the head of a pin") is dialectical in itself. But the kinship is pronounced in subject matter: both men brilliantly depict human beings in the concrete settings of their various worlds. Faulkner did it to "tell it all"; Kierkegaard did it to "wound from behind."

TRUTH AS SUBJECTIVITY

The task before every individual, then, is to seek to become the person he is and to do so with all the subjective intensity he can muster. It is "the highest task" each one of us has to face and one that can occupy us all our lives long, so that it is only the "restless" individual who "manages to be through with life before life gets through with him." Moreover, the pursuit of authenticity requires great effort. No one simply falls into inwardness; indeed, most of us have "a strong and natural bent and passion to become something more and different" than who and what we are. While it is true that there is a kind of givenness about our subjectivity, a great deal of effort is required when choosing inwardness.[13]

The very essence and meaning of life is at stake here, according to Kierkegaard. If it is true that we all hunger for truth, we will eventually discover that truth is known *only* in a subjective way:

> In an attempt to make clear the difference of way that exists between an objective and a subjective reflection, I shall now proceed to show how a subjective reflection

13. *Postscript*, 116, 146.

makes its way inwardly in inwardness. Inwardness in an existing subject culminates in passion; corresponding to passion in the subject the truth becomes a paradox; and the fact that the truth becomes a paradox is rooted precisely in its having a relationship to an existing subject. . . .

When the question of truth is raised in an objective manner, reflection is directed objectively to the truth, as an object to which the knower is related. Reflection is not focussed upon the relationship, however, but upon the question of whether it is the truth to which the knower is related. If only the object to which he is related is the truth, the subject is accounted to be the truth. When the question of the truth is raised subjectively, reflection is directed subjectively to the nature of the individual's relationship; if only the mode of this relationship is in the truth, the individual is in the truth even if he should happen to be thus related to what is not true.[14]

Kierkegaard chooses the question of God in order to press forward his argument. If we proceed objectively to consider the truth about God, we are immediately faced with the question of who or what the true God is. This becomes a highly dubious inquiry, because there are no standards against which the truth or falsity of a given deity may be measured. Subjectively, however, the question is not directed toward God as object, but it is directed toward the question of whether or not "the individual is related to something *in such a manner* that his relationship is in truth a God-relationship." The tendency of some thinkers, of course, is to seek a kind of mediating position between the poles of objectivity and subjectivity, but Kierkegaard flatly rejects this. It is impossible for the existing individual to be in a state of mediation, because mediation represents a finished and completed state, while existence is a state of becoming. Moreover, the individual cannot simultaneously encompass the opposing poles of the dialectic; one cannot be both subjective and objective at the same time. However—and this is one of Kierkegaard's crucial points—when a person is "nearest to being

14. *Ibid.*, 177–78.

in two places at the same time he is in passion; but passion is momentary, and passion is also the highest expression of subjectivity." [15]

The peril attending the objective search for God is the exposure to the dangers of the approximation-process. One cannot know God objectively or approximately "because God is a subject," says Kierkegaard, "and therefore exists only for subjectivity in inwardness." Accordingly, the person who follows the subjective path becomes impatient with all attempts to get at God through some objective method. He is impatient because he considers every moment in which one does not have God a wasted moment. He is perturbed with the objectivist who constantly deliberates about the nature of God but who never gets around to having a relationship with God. In the subjectivist's mind, one has a relationship with God *not* because of deliberation but "by virtue of the infinite passion of inwardness," and those who try to speak of God in objective terms do so at their own spiritual risk. We therefore have a choice. We can either accept the "urge of passion" to think existentially about that which we know we have experienced, or we can ramble comfortably on "by way of the long road of approximation" and never discover the urgency of becoming what we already are. [16]

The resolution comes, of course, when the two paths have been tried and evaluated. Is the most truth on the side of those who seek God objectively? Or is it on the side of the individual "who, driven by the infinite passion of his need of God, feels an infinite concern for his own need for God in truth?" For Kierkegaard the answer is never in doubt. He phrases it with the familiar ring of the parable: "If one who lives in the midst of Christendom goes up to the house of God, the house of the true God, with the true conception of God in his knowledge, and prays, but prays in a false spirit; and one who lives in idolatrous community prays with the entire passion of the infinite, although his eyes rest upon the

15. *Ibid.*, 178.   16. *Ibid.*, 178–79.

image of an idol: where is there most truth? The one prays in truth to God though he worships an idol; the other prays falsely to the true God, and hence worships in fact an idol." In this spirit Kierkegaard formulates one of his best-known aphorisms: "The objective accent falls on WHAT is said, the subjective accent on HOW it is said." [17] Reverberations from his strongly stated position are felt throughout all his work and especially in his discussion of "the stages on life's way."

From the very first, we must understand that he does not use the notion of stages or modalities as a rigid formula to be applied to the persons he describes; rather, he uses it as what Collins calls "a supple tool" for the interpretation and analysis of existence as he perceives it.[18] He is not approaching existence as a possible object of speculative thought; instead he is attempting to apprehend, on a radical level, what it means to say that one exists. His intensely personal involvement in his work, as has been conclusively demonstrated by his biographers, shows through convincingly when he begins to talk about the various categories of existence. His concerns are both practical and particular. He is the prototypical phenomenologist in his attempts to apprehend in a preobjective and prereflexive way the concrete matters of human existence. Indeed, the distrust of speculation and the urge to describe the concrete led Kierkegaard to use characters out of literature and history as well as creatures of his own imagination to express his insights into the modalities of existence. Such characters serve a dual purpose for him. They not only are the subjects of his investigation, but they also are illustrations for his conclusions. They are used as case histories. It obviously made sense to him to speak in terms of a Faust or an Abraham or a Judge William while attempting to describe the various stages. And this is why a discussion of Faulkner's characters can be so appropriately carried on in terms of the Kierkegaardian categories. In both cases, we are dealing with the concrete.

17. *Ibid.*, 179–80, 181.
18. Collins, *The Mind of Kierkegaard*, 44.

The Modalities of Existence

Because Kierkegaard writes in a discursive and rambling style, there are no extensive passages in which he discusses the stages in any systematic or definitive way. What we have instead are comments and occasional paragraphs which briefly mention the modalities within the larger discussion of another matter. It therefore is necessary to mine the writings for these allusions in order to outline the modalities. One result of the mining process is that we soon discover Kierkegaard's notions shifting as he moves from work to work. He is difficult to pin down. This could have been anticipated from everything we have learned about his writing up to this point, especially the fact that he quite self-consciously set out to avoid the pitfalls of the *a priori* by writing instead about actual and concrete personages. This technique naturally militates against too quickly forming generalizations into which individuals might automatically be dropped. He could not, however, and probably did not want to, do away with categorization altogether. He established categories so imaginative and creative in scope that they could cover a wide range of personages while illumining the salient features of each individual under discussion rather than force him into some *ideé fixe*. Kierkegaard's categories do, in fact, turn out to be extremely broad—much broader than scholars are prone to admit—and we have to resist the temptation to believe that we have exhausted their possibilities when we have said all we can about them.

In addition to the occasional comments Kierkegaard makes about the modalities, we also discover that nearly all his books are discussions, in one way or another, about them. For example, *Either/Or* deals primarily with the aesthetic and the ethical, *Fear and Trembling* with the ethical and the religious, *Repetition* with the aesthetic and the religious. Two works, *Stages on Life's Way* and the *Postscript*, deal explicitly with all three categories, and it could even be held that *The Concept of Dread* deals with the phenomenology of dread

77

as it is manifested differently in each of the stages and that *The Sickness unto Death* is a description of the varying forms of despair appearing in the several modalities of existence. All of this suggests that it is necessary to use not only the mining process or the inductive method in treating the categories; we also have to resort to the more intuitive methods of judgment and interpretation in trying to discern the patterns as they come to the surface.

8

The Three Stages

KIERKEGAARD CONCEIVES his task to be primarily descriptive. He continually turns to the historical or the concrete, because it is there the contours and textures of existence may be revealed and not in some abstract construct. He is not much concerned with essences, which are elusive, but with the discreteness of things which exist and are in process. Essences, if there are such, are fundamentally static and hence abstractive. Frater Taciturnus, one of the pseudonyms, makes this point well in *Stages on Life's Way* when he says that we must think of the "existence spheres" only in terms of the concrete. They are not metaphysical entities: "The metaphysical is abstraction, there is no man who exists metaphysically. The metaphysical, ontology, *is* but does not exist; for when it exists it is in the aesthetic, in the ethical, in the religious, and when it *is* it is the abstraction or the *prius* for the aesthetic, the ethical, the religious." [1] This is an extremely simple but shrewd observation. Metaphysics has reality, says the Frater, but if it exists, it exists *in* one of the modalities

1. Søren Kierkegaard, *Stages on Life's Way,* trans. Walter Lowrie (Princeton: Princeton University Press, 1945), 430.

or is an expression of one of them. Metaphysics is neither the truth of a modality nor does it comprehend the whole of a modality. It is, finally, hypothetical.

If the first fact about modalities is that they give an account of the concrete, the next is that they elucidate the particular. This returns us to Kierkegaard's refusal to deal with great groups or classes of people, for this is essentially an abstractive process. He believed that the malaise of modernity could be traced in part to the failure of his contemporaries to appreciate the radical truth and irreducibility of the individual. Although it is possible to talk about great groups of people suffering, it is only the individual in all his solitariness who knows the real meaning of suffering. Indeed, one of the ways to take the sting and bite out of suffering is to think about it in terms of groups. Six million Jews exterminated by the Nazis! It rolls off our tongues with only a momentary second thought. But to stand in the presence of the lone individual who suffers—or, better still, Kierkegaard says, to talk about *my* suffering is quite another matter. He expresses his ultimate stand with great power in prayer:

> Thou hearest also the most miserable, the most abandoned, and most solitary man—in the desert, in the multitude. And if the forgotten one has separated himself from all others; and if in the crowd he has become unknown—having ceased to be a man except as a number on a list—Thou knowest him. Thou hast not forgotten him. Thou rememberest his name; Thou knowest him where he is, retired, hidden in the desert, unperceived in the crowd, in the multitude. And if in the thick shadows of dread, in the prey of terrible thoughts, he was abandoned by men, abandoned almost by the language men speak, still thou wouldst not have forgotten him.[2]

There are, of course, scholars who criticize Kierkegaard for not taking more interest in the social dimension of human life. H. Richard Niebuhr, for example, who is one of the

2. Papier, VII, A, 132 in *The Prayers of Kierkegaard*, ed. Perry D. LeFevre (Chicago: University of Chicago Press, 1956), 15–16.

more responsible critics, objects because Kierkegaard "abstracted the self from society as violently as any speculative philosopher" and "ignores the responsibility of the self to and for other selves."[3] There are two replies to be made to this criticism: first, Kierkegaard did not set for himself the task of discussing *social* ethics but of determining what the individual must do in order to come to terms with himself in the presence of the Infinite. Or to put it in more traditional terms, he wanted to know what one must do to be saved. To blame him for not doing what he did not set out to do is a little beside the point. Second, if one examines closely enough the Kierkegaardian corpus, one may discover there some very useful foundation blocks on which a social ethic could be formulated. It is certainly not unthinkable that had Kierkegaard decided to write about that particular subject, he could have done it superlatively. His enterprise may be looked upon as a prolegomenon to all possible questions about society.

Moreover, according to Kierkegaard, the individual cannot possibly exist in isolation from his environment. That is to say, every man as Kierkegaard views him has a special kind of relationship to history. The person in the aesthetic modality, for example, finds meaning for his existence outside himself. He is without sufficient internal resources and is consequently dependent on external stimuli for making any sense out of the apparent nonsense of his environment. This passivity means that he will take on a peculiar relationship to his body and the physical world. He will either absolutely transcend his body, as Don Juan does, or will take up a highly equivocal relation to his body. That is, he will think of his body as an object among other objects and often thinks of other people in similar terms. Although the aesthete is generally conceived to be one who lives almost exclusively in terms of the sensuous and the flesh, the truth of the matter is that the aesthete is one who does not *choose* his body in

3. H. Richard Niebuhr, *Christ and Culture* (New York: Harper & Brothers, 1951), 244.

any serious or permanent way. Just the fact that he relies on the sensuous and on the moment indicates that the body is important only in a fleeting and uncertain way because the *moment* is perpetually vanishing. The aesthete therefore has an accidental relationship to the body.

Next, the aesthete puts himself at the mercy of Fate and thinks of events as fortunate or unfortunate, depending on how they affect him. He never assumes responsibility for his actions and more often than not thinks of himself as the one acted upon rather than as the actor. Because he is passive, passion may become his mode of existence in the sense that he depends upon external stimulation for the substance and meaning of his life. He is not in control of his destiny; something else is.

The person who dwells in the ethical modality, on the other hand, is of the opinion that he *can* choose and choose unalterably what his relationship to the external world will be. He believes that he can make choices with relative ease. He thinks that when he uses the first person singular pronoun in the nominative case, he is asserting himself in his "eternal validity"—which is to say that he can choose his best self, his ideal self. The ethical person has great confidence in his abilities. He is convinced that his utterances and decisions, because they are his, are accredited with power and authenticity. He does the good thing because he knows the good thing. He shapes his life so that it will be in keeping with the principles and norms common to civilized societies.

The ethicist's relationship to his body is one of control. His body is used as a tool or as a means by which he is able to assert himself in his "eternal validity." The paradigm of this modality is marriage and especially the marriage vows. Here, the ethical person believes he can choose his partner with complete and absolute ingenuousness. He also believes that marital sex is a basic symbol of the conjugal alliance; his relationship to his body is therefore entirely instrumental.

The person in the religious modality may exist in one of two broadly-conceived ways. In the category Kierkegaard calls "religiousness *A*," one is self-consciously a part of history but allows himself to be destroyed as an existing individual in order that God might have his way in the world. The person in this stage believes there is no other way. Because he finds his own selfhood an obstruction to a relationship with God, the self must be annihilated. He sees a complete identification of time with eternity and worships an immanental God. This means that the spheres of nature and history become especially important. Sacraments and ritual take on extra significance. In "religiousness *B*," on the other hand, the person is not destroyed, but his relationship to the world becomes highly dialectical. He is in it but not of it. He is transcendent to the world in the sense that it no longer controls him, and yet he does not feel compelled to remove himself from the world in order that God may appear. That is not the way God appears to him. Instead, he is given the grace and the wisdom to grasp fully the absurdity that the Eternal *is* in time, that the Infinite *is* in the realm of the finite. This understanding gives a completely new definition of time and eternity and of their relation. Existence is no longer a process of gradually working one's way *back* into favor with God but of working *forward* toward God while at the same time discovering that God has come, now, in the present moment. This person's view of life is essentially eschatological in that he sees history caught up in the future as the "place" where the Eternal will appear. In the *Postscript* Kierkegaard summarizes it this way:

> If the individual is in himself undialectical and has his dialectic outside himself, then we have the *aesthetic interpretation*. If the individual is dialectical in himself inwardly in self-assertion, hence in such a way that the ultimate basis is not dialectic in itself, inasmuch as the self which is at the basis is used to overcome and assert itself, then we have the *ethical interpretation*. If the individual is inwardly defined by self-annihilation before God, then we have *religiousness A*. If the individual is paradoxically dialectic, every vestige of original immanence being annihilated and all connection cut off, the individual being brought to the utmost verge of

existence, then we have the *paradoxical religiousness.* This paradoxical inwardness is the greatest possible, for even the most paradoxical determinant, if after all it is within immanence, leaves as it were a possibility of escape, of leaping away, of retreat into the eternal behind it; it is as though everything had not been staked after all. But the breach makes the inwardness the greatest possible.

Again, the various existence-communications rank in accordance with the interpretation of what it is to exist. . . . *Immediacy, the aesthetic,* finds no contradiction in the fact of existing: to exist is one thing, and the contradiction is something else which comes from without. *The ethical* finds the contradiction, but within self-assertion. *The religiousness A* comprehends the contradiction as suffering in self-annihilation, although within immanence, but by ethically accentuating the fact of existing it prevents the exister from being abstract in immanence, or from becoming abstract by wishing to remain in immanence. *The paradoxical religiousness* breaks with immanence and makes the fact of existing the absolute contradiction, not within immanence, but against immanence. There is no longer any immanent fundamental kinship between the temporal and the eternal, because the eternal itself has entered time and would constitute there the kinship.[4]

THE RELATIONSHIPS AMONG THE STAGES

Although there is not a great deal of evidence to support any absolutely clear view of the relationships among the three stages, certain conclusions may be drawn.

The first is that the stages are discreet and isolable. That is to say, one cannot live in two of them simultaneously. They are, as Swenson says, "rival views of life," which vie for our allegiance.[5] As we face the day-to-day facts of our lives, we must choose between alternatives that are constantly being pressed upon us. Either that, or choose *not* to choose, which is an aesthetic choice in itself.

4. Kierkegaard, *The Concluding Unscientific Postscript,* trans. David F. Swenson and Walter Lowrie (Princeton: Princeton University Press, 1941), 507–508.

5. Why not say "rival *modes* of life," since existence is more than a looking or a seeing? David F. Swenson, *Something about Kierkegaard* (Minneapolis: Augsburg Publishing House, 1948), 162.

Opting to live within one of three basic categories does not mean, however, that one is thereby lumped together with all others who fall into the same broad category. There are innumerable ways of being in the world within each category. For example, in the "In Vino Veritas" section of the *Stages*, Kierkegaard shows a half dozen aesthetes of varying shades and intensity, while in *Fear and Trembling* there are a good many illustrations of various ways of being in the world ethically. And, it is significant that the Judge William of *Either/Or* is a different character from the man having the same name in the *Stages*. The point is that there are many and sundry ways of being in the world within the larger, fundamental categories. The dialectical mania and subtlety with which Kierkegaard explores these modalities more than sustains his resolve to deal always with the concrete and the particular. We are *never* in a position of being able to deal with man in the mass; we must always confront the individual.

It is also noteworthy that Kierkegaard talks about "boundary zones" between the three major spheres: "irony, constituting the boundary between the aesthetic and the ethical; humor, as the boundary that separates the ethical from the religious."[6] There are two conclusions we may draw from this. First, if there are *boundary* zones, Kierkegaard himself must have thought the stages were discreet categories. Next, if there are boundary *zones*, he is talking about still more existence spheres than those already mentioned. Kierkegaard says as much by enumerating the following list of modalities one might conceivably dwell in: "immediacy; finite common sense; irony; ethics with irony as incognito; humor; religiousness with humor as incognito; and then finally the Christian religiousness, recognizable by the paradoxical accentuation of existence, by the paradox, by the breach with immanence, and by the absurd."[7] The proliferation of zones and spheres simply means that, although Kierkegaard values attempting

6. *Postscript,* 448.   7. *Ibid.,* 473 n.

to see individuals categorically, he is nevertheless more devoted to the individual than the category. Indeed, he only uses the language, thought forms, and categories he does in order to be able to look more closely and more accurately at the concrete exister. He merely wants to affirm the notion that each person inhabits his own special or particular modality, which may conveniently be subsumed under one of the major ones.

In the same spirit, Kierkegaard admits that categories may overlap. That is to say, although one cannot indwell two modalities simultaneously, one may indwell a modality that combines characteristics of two or more categories. Thus, we often hear Kierkegaard speak of "the ethico-religious" individual, "the aesthetic-ethical" person, "aesthetical religiousness," and so forth. Lowrie observes in this connection:

> Kierkegaard defines the three spheres only in the briefest and most general terms, but he is copious in depicting the characters who exemplify them. They do not exemplify any stage purely, as a logical system would require, for they represent the existential possibilities which lie between immediacy and spirit. The logical delimitation of the spheres is confronted by the movement in which each individual is involved, the *direction* of this movement is the prime consideration, and this is aptly indicated by the word "stages." "There are many ways which lead to the same truth, and each man takes his own." So said S. K.[8]

In sum, a person dwells in his own discreet and peculiar sphere, although it must fall within one of the three major stages. One is consequently not made to conform to an apriority but is in the world in his own special way. He *exists*, instead of being an abstraction. Because existence is not static and because each person's whole existence is an intentionality, each person does have a "direction," as Lowrie puts it, for his life.

If this is all correct, then what is the relation between one

8. Lowrie, Introduction to Kierkegaard, *Stages*, 9.

stage (or sub-stage) and another? Is there a logical sequence from one to the next? Can we expect continuous progress from the aesthetic through the ethical to the religious? Kierkegaard says not: "In the world of the spirit the various stages are not like towns on a route of travel." Nor does one move from one stage to another in the manner of Hegelian dialectics: from thesis to antithesis and then synthesis.[9] The transition is abrupt and sometimes even traumatic. That is because each one of the modalities possesses a kind of infinity.[10] Accordingly, it is impossible to reach another stage by mere development. Something much more drastic is required: a leap. One of the more important terms in the Kierkegaardian lexicon, the leap distinguishes his method from Hegel's. It is the opposite of mediation, for it recognizes the conflicting poles of life without trying to synthesize them. It affirms and protects the integrity of the contradictions and refuses to subject existence to some process by which the rough edges may be smoothed over. It accepts life in the concrete and does not attempt to rationalize it or make it conform to some informing Principle or overarching Idea. This, of course, is what is meant by the "dialectical" in Kierkegaard's works. He becomes suspicious when any definitive answer is given to the problems of life and is much happier when the relationship between them is one that admits and cherishes distinctions and conflicts.

But what happens to a previous stage in the radical transition? Has it been destroyed by the leap? By no means. The earlier stage has simply been "dethroned" by or subordinated

9. *Postscript*, 250, 261.
10. This, of course, is true only of modalities within the Christian West. In Kierkegaard's mind, there is a difference between the modalities of existence in pagan Greece and those of modernity. In the ancient setting the stages are under the control of the finite. The aesthetic is in harmony with its environment, as is illustrated by the stillness of Greek sculpture; the ethical is capable of being achieved, as is demonstrated by the "golden mean" of Nichomachean ethics; and the religious is diffused in the polytheism of Mt. Olympus. It is a psychically determined cosmos that is eventually broken open by the Incarnation when the stages of existence become infinitized.

to the new stage. "*A*," the author of "Shadowgraphs," says, "To reproduce another stage does not mean merely to become this stage, but to become it with all the elements of the preceding stage within oneself." And Judge William, the prototypical ethicist, could not have agreed more heartily, for the whole thrust of his essay on "the aesthetic validity of marriage" attempts to prove to his younger companion that one can be ethical but not lose the sweet taste of the aesthetic in the process.[11] Presumably this would mean that the dethroning occurs no matter in what direction one moves— whether, say, from the aesthetic to the ethical or in the opposite direction. Under any circumstance, it is apparent that we do not have to remain continually within a single stage but are free to move from one to another, if we are willing to make the leap.

In the last analysis, Kierkegaard's only purpose was to elucidate the meaning of the Infinite in time, and, as any careful reader of the works will attest, the Infinite may be discovered *incognito* within all the categories—the aesthetic and ethical as well as the religious. The aesthetic is necessarily preliminary and ends in despair because it wishes finally to exclude and deny the Infinite. The ethical is necessarily preliminary and ends in despair because it wishes to do what it cannot do: choose the Infinite by way of obedience. It is only in the category of the religious that the Infinite is present in all of its paradoxical glory. That is to say, one discovers one's authenticity not by following the absolute demands of the Infinite or even by removing oneself in order that the Infinite might be present. One discovers authenticity in the very midst of the historical where God is present.[12]

11. Kierkegaard, *Either/Or*, trans. David F. Swenson and Lillian Marvin Swenson with revisions by Howard A. Johnson (2 vols.; Princeton: Princeton University Press, 1959), I, 230, 204; II, 5–157. Judge William is one of the most brilliant creations in the array of pseudonyms and mythical characters that appear in Kierkegaard's works.
12. *Postscript*, 512.

The Three Stages

It is enlightening to see how people indwelling the three basic modalities respond to the special circumstances of suffering, pathos, and the comical.

The aesthete responds to suffering in many different ways, depending on the type of aestheticism he pursues. He could cherish suffering, for example, as a way to avoid choosing himself. He could turn his back on suffering as though it were non-existent. He could allow himself to be overcome by it and determined by it. But in all cases, he would consider it something directed at him from the outside, external to himself, accidental to his true nature. So far as the aesthete is concerned, suffering or not suffering is a matter of fortune or misfortune; it is something over which he has no control.

The ethical individual, on the other hand, while also considering the source of suffering to be Fate, will nevertheless struggle to overcome suffering in some way. In fact, he will deliberately choose it as an act of heroism that will allow him to confirm himself in his "eternal validity." He hopes to wipe out the accidental by deliberately choosing; he therefore incorporates suffering as an integral part of his perfect self.

The religious person, by contrast, deliberately chooses suffering as a way of life and something worthwhile in itself, because, like everything else in his existence, he considers it a gift—part of what is bestowed upon him as his portion in life. So far as he is concerned, suffering is essential. He has passed through the strenuous stage of resignation and ideality and has once more been able to choose the finite (suffering) by virtue of the fact that the Eternal has made Itself known to him in the midst of the finite (and, incidentally, in the form of suffering). Suffering, then, is not foreign. It is part and parcel of finite existence where God is known. For the religious person existence is not so much a case of having to cope with suffering as it is a way of putting oneself into a

89

new posture before suffering. The important thing for him is not an immanental or direct relationship to God through suffering (religiousness *A*); it is, rather, becoming edified through a new kind of externality—putting oneself at the disposal of the Infinite who appears as the finite. Which means, very simply yet deceptively, to serve one's fellows. One suffers because that is the way it is; one suffers because God was made flesh.[13]

Since the individual who exists aesthetically is oriented primarily toward enjoyment, he avoids suffering if at all possible unless he derives some kind of pleasure from pain. In that case, masochism may be considered a form of aestheticism. One who exists ethically also avoids suffering, if at all possible, but will attempt to deal with it heroically when it is unavoidable. The person in the religious modality, however, holds suffering to be something more than a "transitional movement" toward a satisfactory way of life; it is instead the persistent and characteristic element of an authentic existence. And the most painful and yet most earnestly sought for suffering is the Frater's seventy thousand fathoms over which the religious man continually treads water, which is to say that he dwells fundamentally in a modality of risk. The individual allows himself to be thrust into the absurd position of believing the Infinite is to be apprehended precisely in the concrete particularities of history. Yet, paradoxically, he is set free from any enthralling connections with the historical, because the historical is put in its proper perspective. The suffering of this modality, then, is the suffering attendant upon becoming absolutely and completely absorbed in the existential, which in the end drives one into a transcendent relationship to nature and history. The religious man sits loosely to the world.

Kierkegaard also discusses the stages' relation to pathos, for pathos may be discerned in three fairly distinct ways. The aesthete dwells in pathos as passivity; the ethical person

13. *Ibid.*, 389, 256, 498, and elsewhere.

dwells in pathos as the passion which is imposed on him from the outside but which he accepts and hopes to ennoble; the religious person dwells in pathos as something he has actively sought and now cherishes.

Aesthetic pathos perpetuates passivity, because the real self wants to escape involvement. The aesthete "abandons himself to lay hold of something great outside himself," such as Hegel's Idea or a similar abstraction. Or, alternatively, he may lose himself in the towering passion of a great love affair, always managing in the end to keep it from developing into an alliance where real commitment is required. In brief, "aesthetic pathos keeps itself at a distance from existence, or is in existence as a state of illusion." [14]

One of the highest degrees of pathos for the aesthete is the "pathos of words," because language may be the means of maintaining everything at the level of possibility. As an existing individual he has little interest in securing himself or claiming himself as an actual and concrete person in history, and one of the most effective devices for keeping oneself at a distance is talk. Even if the aesthetic person does become involved in some kind of action, this does not necessarily mean that he is existentially caught up in what he is doing: "All such action is therefore only aesthetic pathos, and its law is the law for aesthetic relationships in general; the non-dialectical individual transforms the world, but remains himself untransformed, for the aesthetic individual is outwardly changed, but remains inwardly unchanged." [15]

The pathos of the ethical modality moves the individual decisively toward an existential relation to the ideal. If a person fails to allow the ideal to transform his life and if he entertains it only as a possibility, then he remains in an aesthetic modality. But if he chooses the ideal in order to transform his *inner* life, then he has attained an ethical stage. Ethically speaking, the "question of the individual's mode of existence is of infinite importance." He cannot delay; he must act:

14. *Ibid.*, 350, 387.   15. *Ibid.*, 387–88.

He begins by exercising himself in the absolute relationship through renunciation. The task is ideal, and has perhaps never been completely realized by anyone, for it is only on paper that one begins without further ado, and has at once completed the task. In order that the individual may sustain an absolute relationship to the absolute *telos* he must first have exercised himself in the renunciation of relative ends, and only then can there be a question of the ideal task: the simultaneous maintenance of an absolute relationship to the absolute, and a relative relationship to the relative.[16]

But, as we shall see, this noble act is finally too strenuous, too demanding for even the noblest character. The quality of resignation required is beyond our capacities to achieve, because it is ultimately unrealizable existentially. That is to say, the basic ingredients of existence—the concrete, the particular, the finite—are renounced when the ideal, abstract, infinite self is chosen. In effect, this choice thrusts oneself out of life and induces despair because of one's inability to reach the ideal.

The pathos of the religious stage consists neither of words nor of action. It is pathos of the absurd—a situation in which one is not convinced intellectually or morally that Christianity is "right" or "workable" but a situation in which the understanding is "crucified." Christianity, in this stage, is seen to be "existence communication" and is not arrived at by reading books or speculating or even acting heroically; it is, in short, a way of being in the world. The "what" is not important; the "how" is everything: "The possibility of knowing what Christianity is without being a Christian must therefore be affirmed. It is a different question whether a man can know what it is to be a Christian without being one, which must be denied." Instead, one breaks with the understanding and becomes more and more deeply immersed in existence. In this process one discovers *existentially* what is meant when it is said that God is enfleshed in time just as he, the exister, is. This is a break with the religion of immanence because the

16. *Ibid.*, 349, 386.

individual does not find God within himself or by annihilating himself. He only finds God as a Subject outside himself, and in this new paradoxical relationship to the God-in-history the believer himself is made transcendent to the very history in which God is discovered—a transaction that flies in the face of all rationality and common sense. It is ultimately a case of existing "constantly on the extremest verge of existence by virtue of the absurd" and seeing the absolute contradiction between time and eternity: "Precisely the thought that the eternal *is* at a definite moment of time, is an expression for the fact that existence is abandoned by the concealed immanence of the eternal. In the religiousness *A* the eternal is *ubique et nusquam*, but concealed by the actuality of existence; in the paradoxical religiousness the eternal is at a definite place, and precisely this is the breach with immanence." [17] Thus, the pathos created by paradoxical religiousness is a pathos characterized by the Frater's seventy thousand fathoms over which one constantly treads water. It is the essence of absurdity. This does not mean, however, that the leap of faith is an act taken without thought. Stephen Crites states the case well:

> It is common enough, to be sure, to hear [Kierkegaard] accused of advocating sheer irrationality. He did oppose speculative rationalism as the alternative. He did oppose prudential calculation and 'cleverness' as a sufficient guide to life, but he did not suggest that life ought to be lived, ethically or religiously, without the guidance of rigorous thought. He did attack a 'reflective age' because it lacked passion, and insisted the reflection could neither provide a sufficient substitute for the passionate decision to act nor in itself, without passion, provide a sufficient springboard for the decision to act. Yet he never suggested that decisions ought to be made without reflection; on the contrary, the more a man reflects the more he is of significant decision. Kierkegaard's own authorship is devoted to stimulating the kind of reflection that will make authentic decision possible (though, of course, not inevitable), and one of his central

17. *Ibid.*, 332, 506.

points is that no man can really make the decision of faith without understanding its implications.[18]

Kierkegaard also uses the category of the comical in measuring the intensity of the existential commitment within the stages: "The comical is present in every stage of life (only that the relative positions are different), for wherever there is life, there is contradiction, and wherever there is contradiction, the comical is present. The tragic and comic are the same, in so far as both are based on contradiction; but *the tragic is the suffering contradiction, the comical, the painless contradiction.*" The stages take rank, therefore, by the ways in which they are related to the comical and by "whether they have the comical within themselves or outside themselves." For example, the aesthetic stage has the comical outside itself, because the aesthete seeks at all costs to avoid contradiction. Thus, the truly comical aspect of the aesthete's plight is that, no matter how hard he attempts to avoid the contradiction, he is the first to be caught in it. Contradiction and the comical overtake him in the same manner that suffering does. It is a matter of Fate and not of his own choosing.[19] His situation is not unlike a man caught in quicksand; the more vigorously he protests and attempts to escape, the deeper he sinks into his problem. For example, a person dwelling in what Kierkegaard calls "finite worldly wisdom" is victimized by the intrusion of contradiction from the outside. This modality, one that Kierkegaard does not mention until the *Postscript*, is comical because the person who dwells in finite worldly wisdom sees the comical in others but fails to see it in himself. It has no existential validity for him. And so he is the "expert" who is generous with his advice to others but fails to see the flaws and contradictions of his own state. His is therefore "an illegitimate comic apprehension" in that he cannot appropriate the comic for himself. Kierkegaard goes on to say that

18. See Kierkegaard, *Crisis in the Life of an Actress*, trans. with introduction and notes by Stephen Crites (London: Collins, 1967), 38n.
19. *Postscript*, 459, 463.

where a contradiction exists the only way of dealing with it is to correct it by integrating it into something higher. But when one has no "higher" resource to call on or when one has a specious resource with which one tries to resolve the contradiction, the comical is compounded. That is the situation with finite worldly wisdom, an aesthetical modality.

The comic is also seen by Kierkegaard to have special force in the "boundary" category of irony, which may be possessed by both the ethicist and the aesthete. But the ethicist has the advantage in that irony is "justified" over against immediacy, because it is a movement toward the ethical and toward choice. It is therefore "higher" than the aesthetic and may become the *incognito* of the ethicist. Kierkegaard asks why the ethicist uses irony as his *incognito* and answers: "Because he grasps the contradiction there is between the manner in which he exists inwardly, and the fact that he does not outwardly express it. For the ethicist does indeed reveal himself, in so far as he pours himself forth in the tasks of the factual reality in which he lives; . . . and what makes him an ethicist is the movement of the spirit by which he sets his outward life inwardly in juxtaposition with the infinite requirement of the ethical, and this is something that is not directly apparent." Irony, therefore, comes into play when one sees that the particularities of the finite are placed next to the infinite ethical requirements, "thus permitting the contradiction to come into being." But, as always, it is a mistake to speak of irony in the abstract instead of the ironist: "Irony is indeed an abstraction, and an abstract putting together of things, but the justification of the existential ironist is that he expresses this himself existentially, that he preserves his life in it, and does not toy with the grandeurs of irony while himself having his life in Philistinism; for then his comic apprehension is illegitimate." [20] From the beginning, irony was an important ingredient in Kierkegaard's own personal life and thought. His master's thesis at the University of Copenhagen

20. *Ibid.*, 450, 464.

was on the concept of irony, and his affair with Regine Olsen reflected an exquisite use of irony. He discovered, however, that irony has an erosive effect. This category, like all the others, except paradoxical religiousness, can be used as a means to escape existential responsibility.

Humor is the "boundary" modality between the ethical and religiousness. Humor can stand up and hold its own against every other modality except paradoxical religiousness. That is because the comical reaches its limit in humor and is not able to penetrate the inwardness of paradoxical religiousness and expose within it any contradiction. Indeed, there is no contradiction at all in religiousness *B;* "thus it is absolutely secured against the comical." That is because the religious man is absolutely related to the absolute *telos* and may only relatively be related to the relative. Humor, therefore, is seen to be "the concluding stage within the immanent" (religiousness *A*) and the last sphere before the leap into the absurd. It is the modality within which the contradictions of existence are seen in all their pathetic power, and yet the contradictions inherent in the paradox remain a mystery: "The humorist constantly . . . sets the God-idea into conjunction with other things and evokes the contradiction—but he does not maintain a relationship to God in terms of religious passion." The humorist simply does not know how "to absorb the suffering side of the paradox." Humor's justification, then, lies "precisely in its tragic side, in the fact that it reconciles itself to the pain," which everyone else seeks to escape but which humor does not know how to elude.[21] It remains for religiousness *B* to point the way to an ultimate solution.

THE STRUCTURE OF EXISTENCE

As one becomes immersed in Kierkegaard's work, it is possible to discern a definite form or structure for the stages. The aesthete is usually controlled by outside stimuli. He lives in a category of immediacy. He is subject to Fate and thinks of

21. *Ibid.,* 465, 451, 464.

events as fortunate or unfortunate. He relies heavily on the tangible and visible world and yet has no ultimately serious commitment to that world. In fact, the aesthete will often deny it. The ethical modality, on the other hand, is inwardly determined to a large degree, though it also receives the stimulus of outside forces. Perhaps it would be more accurate to talk about the ethical in terms of reciprocity. The ethical man passively accepts the dictates of Fate, but then he attempts to overcome that which is destructive or wrong through heroic action. The primary question for him is, "Guilty/not guilty?" But the ethical man also wishes to take this essentially inward question and expose it to the world. He believes he must, above all else, be transparent to his fellow men and therefore talk about rewards and punishment, which eventually have to become apparent to others.

In the religious modality one takes up a stance almost parallel to the aesthetic, for one is directed to that which is outside oneself—the Infinite in history. There is also an immediacy about this category and consequently no way to measure religiousness in objective terms. The greatest man and the most destitute are on equal terms in faith. Religiousness is finally the great equalizer between men in all walks of life.

There is a difference, however, between the aesthetical and religious stages, and the difference is decisive. In the aesthetic stage one is absolutely related to relative ends and only relatively related to the absolute *telos*, whereas in the religious stage the situation is reversed. One discovers, through the passion of a heightened inwardness, one's absolute *telos* in the God-relationship. One is not required to have a rational and understandable relationship with the Infinite; instead, one is given the answer to the question of his existence in the dynamics of the relationship itself.

This discussion of the stages is, at best, preliminary and programmatic. The next step will be to attend more specifically to each of the three major existence spheres to see the depth and variety of each one.

9

The
Aesthetical
According
to
Kierkegaard

ON SEPTEMBER 11, 1834, the young Søren Kierkegaard made a very revealing entry in his Journal. He wrote that he had the ability to "enjoy" a work of art because he knew how to find the "archimedean point" or "idea" that a given work of art seeks to express. "I can then follow the one great thought," he continued, "and see how all the details serve to throw light upon it." This seems to infer that he accepted the place and validity of the aesthetical. But, he said, people get in trouble when they try to view the works of God in the same way: "The works of God are too great for me; I inevitably lose myself in the details. That is also why people's expressions when they look at nature: it is lovely, magnificent, etc. are so insipid, for they are all too anthropomorphic, they stay at the outside; they cannot express the depths within."[1]

There is in this entry the germ of a larger thesis in his later work. On the one hand, the artistic would always fascinate him and would play an important part in his life. No matter how consumed he would become in his battle with the decay-

1. Søren Kierkegaard, *The Journals of Søren Kierkegaard*, ed. and trans. Alexander Dru (London: Oxford University Press, 1951), 1–2.

ing Danish church and society, he nevertheless would maintain an interest in art until the very last. This is amply illustrated by one of the later works of his career, *The Crisis in the Life of an Actress,* and other minor pieces published in *The Fatherland.* On the other hand, it is impossible to be related to God aesthetically.

There is, however, a popular tendency to think that a kind of incipient Puritanism drove Kierkegaard away from the arts toward the end of his life. Not so at all. What he deplored was treating religious or existential matters in an aesthetical way, for anyone who tried to talk about eternal happiness in this way was doomed to severe disappointment and frustration. He nevertheless always maintained a place—indeed, a cherished place—for the artistic in his life. Anyone who could write about Mozart or Fru Heiberg in the manner he did could not be accused of being anti-aesthetical.

It is important, then, to distinguish these two ways in which he uses the word "aesthetical." The basic meaning of the word never changes, but the value he places on it varies according to the uses he makes of it. What he is trying to describe, of course, are modalities of existence: if one takes up an aesthetical attitude toward art, that is entirely consistent and valid; but if one takes up an aesthetical attitude toward existence, despair can be the only result.

The essential characteristic of the aesthetical modality is objectivity. The person who inhabits this stage—whether *vis-à-vis* the arts or religion—attempts to maintain distance between himself and the object which stands over against him. It is a viewpoint which everyone adopts at one time or another and is appropriate under certain circumstances. Thus the art appreciator, the philosopher, the scientist, all of whom have valuable and necessary roles to play in modern society, assume the objective viewpoint in their work in attempting to discern patterns and forms within the reality they are investigating. But what Kierkegaard strenuously protested was the notion that the "objective" way was the only way of experiencing reality. In fact, it can and often does lead to distortion.

Men do not just stand over against the world and view it objectively; men are *in* the world. They are embodied consciousnesses. They exist. And Kierkegaard took as his principal task in life the exploration of and the description of existence. He continually asked the question, "What does it mean to exist?" Or better still, "What does it mean to say, 'I exist?'" If one takes up the objective or aesthetic standpoint toward existence, one immediately removes oneself from being able to *know* existence from the inside. Indeed, one exister cannot explain himself to another. He may only exist. This is why so much of Kierkegaard's work is taken up with describing actual personages.

THE AESTHETE: A COLLECTOR OF INTERESTING EXPERIENCES

Stephen Crites in his introduction to *The Crisis in the Life of an Actress* describes the person who lives exclusively in the aesthetical modality as "a collector of interesting experiences." He is the one who wishes to transform all existence into an art so as not to become directly and deeply involved himself. Another description of the aesthete is given by Judge William, a somewhat pompous exemplar of an ethical way of existing. He is writing his young friend:

> In case enjoyment were the chief thing in life, I would sit at your feet as a pupil, for in this you are a master. At one moment you are able to make yourself an old man in order to imbibe in slow draughts through recollection what you have experienced; at another moment you are in the first blush of youth, inflamed with hope; now you enjoy in a manly way, now in a womanly; now you enjoy immediately, now you enjoy reflection upon your enjoyment, now reflection upon the enjoyment of others; now you enjoy abstinence from enjoyment; now you devote yourself to enjoyment, your soul is open like a city which has capitulated, reflection is mute, and every step of the foreigner echoes in the empty streets, and yet there always remains a little observant outpost; now your mind is closed, you entrench yourself brusquely and unapproachably. Such is the situation, and at the same time you will see how egoistic your enjoyment

is, and that you never give yourself out, never let others enjoy you. You may be right enough in scorning men who by every pleasure are consumed and wasted; for example, the lovelorn men with tattered hearts, since you on the contrary understand capitally the art of being in love in such a way that it throws your own personality in relief. Now you know very well that the most intensive pleasure consists in holding fast to the enjoyment with the consciousness that the next instant it perhaps will vanish.[2]

The aesthete, then, wants to avoid having to make decisions, for he believes that "the true eternity does not lie behind either/or, but before it." Indeed, it is not really possible for the aesthete to choose. The Judge also writes his young friend about this theme: "Your choice is an aesthetic choice, but an aesthetic choice is no choice. The act of choosing is essentially a proper and stringent expression of the ethical. Whenever in a stricter sense there is a question of an either/ or, one can always be sure that the ethical is involved. . . . The aesthetic choice is entirely immediate and to that extent no choice, or it loses itself in the multifarious."[3] In any case, the aesthete abandons the existential in favor of the purely detached mode of the dilettante. He wishes to keep life "at bay."

Because he has great reservations about the value to him of decision-making and of becoming involved in the actual happenings of the concrete world, the aesthete always lives in the state of possibility. The young man writes: "If I were to wish for anything, I should not wish for wealth and power, but for the passionate sense of the potential, for the eye which, ever young and ardent, sees the possible. Pleasure disappoints, possibility never. And what wine is so sparkling, what so fragrant, what so intoxicating, as possibility!" This is preeminently so of the most binding of human relationships, the love between a man and a woman. At all costs, he wishes

2. Kierkegaard, *Either/Or*, trans. David F. Swenson and Lillian Marvin Swenson with revisions by Howard A. Johnson (2 vols.; Princeton: Princeton University Press, 1959), II, 25.
3. *Ibid.*, I, 31; II, 170–71.

to steer clear of marriage and all its encumbrances. For him the highest form of pleasure is a flirtation, a love relationship which can be thought of as a work of art: "I simply do not care to possess a girl in the mere external sense, but to enjoy her in an artistic sense." The point is that he wishes to remain detached. He will gladly accept love—"the highest conceivable enjoyment lies in being loved"—but he will carefully avoid giving love in return. Not especially because he is a cad or wishes to be mean; it is simply a matter of aesthetics: "To poetize oneself into a young girl is an art, to poetize oneself out of her is a masterpiece." [4]

With this heavy case of dissociation, is it any wonder that the aesthete looks on life as empty and meaningless? The young man writes: "We bury a man; we follow him to the grave, we throw three spadefuls of earth over him; we ride out to the cemetery in a carriage, we ride home in a carriage; we take comfort in thinking that a long life lies before us. How long is seven times ten years? Why do we not finish it at once, why do we not stay and step down into the grave with him, and draw lots to see who shall happen to be the last unhappy living being to throw the last three spadefuls of earth over the last of the dead?" [5]

So long as one is expecting others to meet one's needs, it is predictable, Judge William would say, that life will be empty. The problem arises because the aesthete wishes to remain enigmatic. Although it is true that no man is able to make himself completely transparent to others, the aesthete seems deliberately to obscure himself. "But," says the Judge, "he who cannot reveal himself cannot love, and he who cannot love is the most unhappy man of all." It is simply a matter of refusing to become involved with anyone else on any significant level. The only real pleasure the aesthete can claim to have is to "march seven times around existence and blow the trumpet and thereupon let the whole thing collapse," but the resounding crash is one of emptiness. No victory has been won. [6]

4. *Ibid.*, I, 40, 368, 363–64.   5. *Ibid.*, 28–9.   6. *Ibid.*, II, 164–65.

Because of his lack of commitment to the concrete, the aesthete also finds the category of time to be an anomalous and uncomfortable dimension of existence. He seeks to evade the consuming demands of time and throws himself instead into the pleasure and emotion of the moment. "Everything is cut out except the present."[7] The only difficulty with this strategy is that the "moment" is completely illusory.[8] The moment may indeed be everything for the aesthete, but alternatively, it is essentially nothing, for immediacy is fortune. Because the individual in the aesthetic modality refuses to choose and exercise discretion, he puts himself at the mercy of Fate. Contradiction strikes from the outside and is immediately labeled misfortune by the aesthete, because he "never becomes dialectical in himself." Because he fails to dispose of the contradiction, he will eventually give way to despair, a state characteristic of those who remain within the aesthetic stage.[9]

This syndrome also accounts for the highly ambiguous character of the aesthete's relation to memory. On the one hand, in a passage in the "Diapsalmata," the young man holds that a life "lived wholly in memory is the most perfect conceivable," because one is no longer involved with the concrete existence immediately before one. On the other hand, he says in the "Rotation Method" that we should *forget* all that has happened. To this end, "forgetting" should be developed as an art: "It is easy to see that most people have a very meager understanding of this art, for they ordinarily wish to forget only what is unpleasant, not what is pleasant. This betrays a complete one-sidedness . . . forgetting is really a tranquil and quiet occupation, and one which should be exercised quite as much in connection with the pleasant as the unpleasant." But again, the purpose of forgetting is to detach oneself from any commitment to existence, and the ability to forget

7. *Ibid.,* 21.   8. See chapter thirteen below.
9. Kierkegaard, *The Concluding Unscientific Postscript,* trans. David F. Swenson and Walter Lowrie (Princeton: Princeton University Press, 1941), 265.

depends precisely on the way one experiences reality. If one should plunge into life's experiences with "the momentum of hope," then one will never be able to forget. But if one looks neither to the past nor the future and lives only for the moment, then it will be impossible to remember or forget—the moment will be all. However, if one does live only for the moment, one must be careful not to become too deeply engrossed in the pleasure of immediate experience. It will then acquire "too strong a hold upon the mind," and the victim will be tempted to stop a moment for the purpose of remembering. The point is this: "From the beginning one should keep the enjoyment under control, never spreading every sail to the wind in any resolve; one ought to devote oneself to pleasure with a certain suspicion, a certain wariness." [10]

Clearly the pleasure enjoyed by the Kierkegaardian aesthete is not simply the purely physical pleasure we might be tempted to think it is. So far as the aesthete is concerned, pleasure may be derived from any number of sources, noble or base. They may include the highly sophisticated objectivity of a philosopher as well as the sensualism of a Don Juan. As Regius Jolivet observes, "To enjoy ideas, to be charmed by intellectual landscapes without one's own life being involved, is at bottom nothing more than the pursuit of carnal pleasure, for enjoyment is still taken as the final aim." [11] The key to understanding this phenomenon is to see that the *object* of enjoyment is secondary to the *way* of enjoyment; the "what" is less important than the "how."

Kierkegaard nowhere more brilliantly illustrates the range of possibilities for the aesthetical modality than in "The Banquet" section of *Stages on Life's Way*. Here he records the speeches given by a group of men who were gathered without notice to enjoy the pleasures of a sumptuous dinner. The setting, as the author describes it, was the epitome of fastidiousness. Besides the delicacy of the menu and the elegant fra-

10. *Either/Or*, I, 31–32, 290, 289.
11. Regius Jolivet, *Introduction to Kierkegaard*, trans. W. H. Barber (London: Frederick Miller, 1950), 125.

grance of the flowers, exquisite music by Mozart came from an orchestra on an adjoining terrace. All the furnishings and appointments of the banquet room were meticulously fashioned anew for the special occasion and were subsequently to be destroyed. "In vino veritas" was the password for the gathering, because, "though speeches were to be allowed as well as conversation, no speeches might be made except *in vino*, and no truths were to be heard except such as one *in vino*, when wine vindicates the truth and truth vindicates the wine." [12] The subject of the speeches, according to the host, Constantine Constantius, was to be love or the relationship between man and woman. He warned, however, that no actual love experiences could be alluded to, for this would introduce into the conversation a note of positiveness or reality that would have to be by-passed.

The first speaker was "the young man," a high intellectualized aesthete, who had successfully avoided any entanglements with women. He argued that love brought nothing but bitterness and grief to those who became involved in it and for no apparent reason. That is because love is "inexplicable":

In case the purport of love were to fall in love with the first comer, it would be easy to understand why no one could explain it more exactly; but since the purport of love is to fall in love with one only, the one only person in the whole world, it seems as if such a prodigious act of segregation and choice must contain in itself a dialectic of reasons which one might decline to hear, not because it explained nothing, but because it would be too prolix to listen to. But, no, the lover is not able to explain anything. He has seen hundreds and hundreds of women, he perhaps has reached a certain age, he has felt nothing, suddenly he sees *her*, the only one, Catherine! Is it not comic that this thing, love, which is to transform and beautify the whole of life is not like a grain of mustard seed from which there grows a great tree, but is even smaller than that, is at bottom nothing at all; for there is not a single antecedent criterion that can be alleged (as if, for example, there was a certain age at which the phe-

12. Kierkegaard, *Stages on Life's Way*, trans. Walter Lowrie (Princeton: Princeton University Press, 1945), 41.

nomenon occurred), and there is not a single reason that can be alleged why he chose her, her alone in the whole world—and this not at all in the same sense in which "Adam chose Eve, because there was no other." Or is not the explanation which the lovers give equally comic, or rather does it not serve precisely to throw into sharp relief the comic character of love?

For the young man, the most serious member of the group, love thus becomes the essence of the comic, for it contains within itself nothing but contradiction:

> Behold, for this reason I have renounced love, for to me my thought is all in all. If love be the most blissful pleasure, then I renounce the pleasure, without wishing to offend anyone or to envy him; if love constitutes the condition for performing the greatest benefaction, then I disavow all claim to such an opportunity, but my thought is safely preserved. I am not without an eye for the beautiful, my heart is not unmoved when I read the songs of the poets, my soul is not untouched by sadness when I dreamily reflect upon those conceptions of love, but to my thought I will not be unfaithful, and what would it avail anyway, when for me there is no blessedness where my thought is not safely preserved to me . . . , which I dare not desert to cling to a wife, since to me it is my eternal essence, and so is of still greater value than father and mother and of still greater value than a wife.[13]

By means of reflection this speaker managed to escape the commitments of love.

Although Johannes the Seducer immediately wished to reply to the young man, Constantine reminded the group that no *logical* discussions were to take place—only the effusions of speech *in vino*. Constantine himself then decided to address the group. He thought the young man had been entirely too earnest about woman:

> She can only be rightly construed under the category of jest. It is man's part to be absolute, to act absolutely, to give

13. *Ibid.*, 50–51, 59.

expression to the absolute; woman has her being in relationship. Between two such different beings no genuine recipro-
cal action can take place. This incongruity is precisely what
constitutes jest, and it is with woman jest first came into
the world. . . .

Jest is not an aesthetic but an imperfect ethical category.
Its effect upon thought is like the effect upon one's frame
of mind at hearing a man who begins a speech, and after
reciting a phrase or two with the same eloquence, says,
"Hm"—and then dead silence. So it is with woman. One
aims at her with the ethical category, one shuts one's eyes,
one thinks of the absolute in the way of requirements, one
thinks the thought of man, one opens one's eyes, one fixes
one's glance upon the demure little miss upon whom one is
experimenting to see if she meets the specifications; one becomes uneasy and says to oneself, "Ah, this surely is jest."
For the jest consists in applying the category, in subsuming
her under it, because with her the serious never can become
serious; but precisely this is jest, for if one might require
seriousness of her, it would not be jest. . . .

If one does not regard woman in this way, she may do
irreparable harm; with my interpretation she becomes
harmless and amusing.

That was precisely the young man's failing; he could not see
woman in a light enough vein. Constantine concludes his
speech:

Forgive me now, dear boon companions if I have spoken too
long, and now drain a glass to love and woman. Fair is she
and lovely when regarded aesthetically—that no one can
deny. But since it so often is said, I too will say: one should
not remain standing, but "go further." So regard her ethically, and the thing becomes a jest. Even Plato and Aristotle
take it that woman is an incomplete form, that is, an irrational quantity, which perhaps some time in a better existence might be brought back to the male form. In this life
one must take her as she is. What this is will soon appear,
for she too is not satisfied with the aesthetic sphere, she
"goes further," she would be emancipated—that she is man
enough to say. Let that come to pass, and the jest will be
beyond all bounds.[14]

14. *Ibid.*, 61, 67.

Victor Eremita arose to express gratitude to the gods that he was born a man and not a woman. Women are inferior creatures, he said, which is illustrated by the gallantry that is shown them:

> Now gallantry consists quite simply in construing by means of fantastic categories the person to whom one is gallant. Hence gallantry showed toward a man is an insult, for a man deprecates the application of fantastic categories to him. . . . On the other hand, woman instinctively accepts this homage . . . , and the fact that she accepts it may be explained as an instance of nature's tender care for the weak, for those who have had a hard deal, to whom illusion gives more than adequate compensation. And woman's great misfortune is that she is never able to free herself from "the illusion with which life has consoled her." She lives by the power of the fantastic.[15]

For this reason, a man should steer clear of any encumbering relationships with women. Because of the fantasy inherent in their lives, they can easily become despots under whom a man becomes an adoring and servile suitor. On the other hand, if a purely negative relationship to woman is maintained, a man can approach the highest reaches of ideality:

> It is quite true, therefore, as I said: through woman ideality came into the world—what would man be without her? Many a man became a genius through a girl, many a man became a hero through a girl, many a man became a poet through a girl, many a man became a saint through a girl— but he didn't become a genius through the girl he got, for through her he became only Privy-Councillor; he didn't become a hero through the girl he got, for through her he only became a general; he didn't become a poet through the girl he got, for through her he only became a father; he didn't become a saint through the girl he got, for he didn't get any, and he wanted only the one he didn't get, just as each of the others became a genius, became a hero, became a poet, through the girl he didn't get. If the ideality of a woman were in itself inspiring, then surely the inspiration must be the woman to whom a man is united for life. But actual

15. *Ibid.*, 68–69.

existence gives a different account of it. That is to say, in a negative relationship woman makes a man idealistically productive. . . . So long as the man does not have her she is an inspiration.

Thus marriage is to be avoided and the negative relationship to woman nurtured. If one should unwittingly become married, the best one can hope for is unfaithfulness, which, again, constitutes a negative (and therefore productive) relationship to woman: "It is true, this second ideality is bought with the sharpest pain, but it is also the greatest bliss; it is true, he cannot by any means wish it before it has come to pass, but afterwards he thanks her for it; and since after all, humanly speaking, he has no great reason for being so very grateful, all is for the best. But woe unto him if she remains faithful.[16]

Victor's speech is followed by that of the Ladies' Tailor, whose attitude toward women is even more unflattering:

Everything in life is a matter of fashion, the fear of God is a matter of fashion, and love, and hoop-skirts, and a ring in the nose. So with all my might I will abet the lofty genius who desires to laugh at the most ludicrous of all animals. Since woman has reduced everything to fashion, I by the aid of fashion will prostitute her as she deserves. I give myself no rest, I, the Ladies' Tailor; my soul chafes when I think of my task, she must yet come to the point of wearing a ring in her nose. Therefore seek no sweetheart, forego love as you would shun the most dangerous neighborhood, for also your sweetheart would have to come to the point of wearing a ring in her nose.[17]

Finally, Johannes the Seducer speaks. He claims to have no fear of women; in fact, he likes them. Is this too much of a concession? His answer is telling:

The fact that I undo the wire of this champagne bottle is also a concession, the fact that I let its foam spurt into the goblet is also a concession, that I raise the goblet to my lips is also a concession—now I have drained it—*concedo*. Now, however, the goblet is empty, so I make no more conces-

16. *Ibid.*, 73–74.   17. *Ibid.*, 80.

sions. Thus it is with the girls. If some unlucky lover has bought a kiss too dearly, that only proves to me that he knows neither how to help himself to a dish nor to abstain from it. I never buy it too dearly, I leave that to the girls.

Love, then, is a game. No promise is ever given or taken. The aesthetical pose is maintained to the last, and Johannes's peroration closes the banquet as he says of woman:

> Oh, marvellous Nature, if I did not admire thee, she would teach me to do so, for she is the *venerabile* of existence. Gloriously has thou fashioned her, but still more glorious for the fact that thou didst never make one woman like another. In the case of man the essential is the essential and therefore always the same; in the case of woman the accidental is the essential, hence the inexhaustible variety. Brief is her glory, but the pain I quickly forgot as if I had not even sensed it, when the same glory is proffered to me again. Yes, I too perceive the uncomeliness which may make its appearance later, but she is not thus with her seducer.[18]

Clearly, Johannes could be called "a collector of interesting experiences." He has skillfully and deliberately transformed his existence into an exquisite work of art.

Kierkegaard's own summary estimate of the banquet is illuminating: "The Young Man comes closest to being merely a possibility, and therefore he is still a hopeful case. He is essentially melancholy of thought. Constantine Constantius is case-hardened understanding. Victor Eremita is sympathetic irony. The Fashion Tailor is demoniac despair in passion. Johannes the Seducer is perdition in cold blood, a 'marked' individuality in whom life is extinct. All are consistent to the point of despair."[19]

THE BANKRUPTCY OF THE AESTHETICAL

We see, then, that the person who lives exclusively within the aesthetical modality is headed on a course that will eventually lead to despair. Judge William warns his young friend:

> You still have in your power all the factors requisite for an aesthetic life view, you have wealth and independence, your

18. *Ibid.*, 81, 88.   19. *Postscript*, 264.

health is unimpaired, your mind is still vigorous, nor have you yet become unhappy for the fact that a girl would not love you. And yet you are in despair. It is not despair about any actual thing but a despair in thought. Your thought has hurried on ahead, you have seen through the vanity of all things, but you have got no further. Occasionally you plunge into pleasure, and every instant you are devoting yourself to it you make the discovery in your consciousness that it is vanity. So you are constantly beyond yourself, that is, in despair. This is the reason why your life lies between two prodigious contradictions; sometimes you have enormous energy, sometimes an indolence just as great.[20]

Despair, then, is that state one chooses to live in when the immediate and the finite are conceived to be all there is. Or, as Kierkegaard says, "to despair is to lose touch with the eternal."[21] But because the moment perpetually vanishes into nothingness, a total investment in it will eventually lead to existential bankruptcy. It promises so much more than it can deliver, and no one of us has the power to sustain ourselves forever within it.

When Kierkegaard speaks of despair, he is not just talking about an emotional state or a case of severe disappointment. He is describing a condition involving the total person. He contrasts doubt with despair to make his point. Doubt, he says, is "an expression for thought" and hence only a partial thing, but despair is absolute. Talent is required for doubt—an intellect keen enough to make doubt possible—but there is no talent required for despair. It reaches across the spectrum of society and fells anyone who loses touch with the Eternal.[22] Accordingly, we find varying degrees or stages of despair, and the mildest form is displayed by the individual who has *never* been aware of his relation to the eternal: "This is pure immediacy, or else an immediacy which contains a quantitative reflection. —Here there is no infinite consciousness of the self, of what despair is, or of the fact that the condition is one of despair; the despair is passive, succumbing to the pressure of the outward circumstance, it by no means comes from within

20. *Either/Or*, II, 198–99.   21. *The Sickness unto Death*, 185.
22. *Either/Or*, II, 216–17.

as action." Kierkegaard goes on to say that insofar as this type of person is without self-reflection, he is psychically determined. He is in harmony with his environment; his existence is completely dependent upon the outside; he uses the pronoun *I* in an equivocal way. His dialectic is "the agreeable and the disagreeable"; his concepts are "good fortune, misfortune, fate." Even despair is something that *happens* to him. It cannot come about in any other way, because he does not possess the ability to think about his destiny. Thus, when a "stroke of fate" deprives him of the agreeable, he receives such a shock that he has no other course but to despair. He speaks of his loss as though it were the loss of the finite. In a sense this is true, but not in the way that he believes it to be. He has lost the earthly, because he has no relation to the eternal, which is another way of saying that he has lost his self: "This form of despair is: despair at not willing to be oneself; or still lower, despair at not willing to be a self; or lowest of all, despair at willing to be another than himself, wishing for a new self. Properly speaking, immediacy has no self, it does not recognize itself, so neither can it recognize itself again, it terminates therefore preferably in the romantic." [23]

One step away from the despair of immediacy is the despair that is qualified by reflection. Here there is a dim awareness of what it means to be a self. Here one is capable of choosing and is not totally dependent upon the decrees of Fate. This individual is able to discriminate between himself and his environment. Thus when despair comes, it is partly the result of his reflection. But in the process of self-reflection, he inevitably stumbles upon imperfections within himself which are distressing. He shudders under the experience and balks at choosing this imperfect self. "So he despairs," Kierkegaard concludes. "His despair is that of weakness, a passive suffering of the self, in contrast to the despair of self-assertion." His next tactic, instead of choosing the self, is to try to defend it, but this is a hapless task. There is so much more to contend

23. *The Sickness unto Death*, 184, 186.

with than he had bargained for. Indeed, he might have to deal with the presence of the infinite in the self, which would demand a complete break with immediacy, something he is not prepared to do. "So then he despairs, and his despair is: Not willing to be himself." [24]

In another and yet more sophisticated stage of despair, the individual is in despair over his relation to eternity:

> This despair is now well in advance. If the former was the despair of *weakness*, this is *despair over his weakness*, although it still remains as to its nature under the category "despair of weakness," as distinguished from defiance. . . . So there is only a relative difference. This difference consists in the fact that the foregoing form has the consciousness of weakness as its final consciousness, whereas in this case consciousness does not come to a stop here but potentiates itself into a new consciousness, a consciousness of its weakness.

From this brief outline, then, we can discern a definite principle at work: "Despair must be viewed under the category of consciousness: the question whether despair is conscious or not, determines the qualitative difference between despair and despair. . . . The more consciousness, the more self; the more consciousness, the more will; and the more will, the more self. A man who has no will at all is no self; the more will he has, the more consciousness of the self he has also." The serious cases of despair would seem to be those who are unaware of their plight, while conversely, the more intensely aware one is of his despair, the nearer salvation will be.[25] For the person who readily acknowledges despair as a part of his existence is better prepared to receive the solution for his predicament than the person who remains in the unreflective state of the aesthetical. In this vein, Judge William counsels his young companion: "So then choose despair, for despair itself is a choice; for one can doubt without choosing to, but one cannot despair without choosing. And when a man despairs he chooses again—and what is it he chooses? He chooses

24. *Ibid.*, 186–88.   25. *Ibid.*, 195, 162, 196.

himself, not in his immediacy, not as the fortuitous individual, but he chooses himself in his eternal validity." [26] On the other hand, the despair that is "the sickness unto death" seems to have a firmer grip on one than the despair that the Judge seems to think he can break by facing it. This despair has the effect of shutting up the individual within his predicament in such a way that he sees no way out at all. Whereas we ordinarily think of death as the end, "the sickness unto death" is precisely the opposite: "Not to be able to die." It is an unending end to one's desperation; it is the permanent attachment to despair. Thus "facing up," as Judge William suggests, is a plainly inadequate solution to such an extreme problem. That is because, "when I despair, I use myself to despair, and therefore I can indeed by myself despair of everything; but when I do this, I cannot by myself come back." Something much stronger is needed, and this "something" is religiousness.[27]

26. *Either/Or*, II, 215.   27. *Postscript*, 230, 231.

10

The Romantic Horace Benbow

HORACE BENBOW is a man whose very bearing exudes an "air of fine and delicate futility." Throughout *Sartoris* and *Sanctuary*,[1] we are struck by his inability (or unwillingness) to escape this fatalistic aura. There are, of course, moments of brightness and comic relief scattered here and there throughout the two novels, but our general and lasting impression is one of hopelessness. Because Benbow's mood so poignantly reflects what Kierkegaard means by the aesthetical, a detailed analysis of his modality of existence is called for.

But one cannot begin this discussion without first calling attention to the fact that *Sartoris* (1929) marks the beginning of Faulkner's most significant and prolific phase as a writer. Whereas the earlier works *Mosquitoes* and *Soldier's Pay* clearly showed that he possessed talent, it was with *Sartoris* that he found his real subject and his own language. The

1. William Faulkner, *Sartoris* (New York: The New American Library, 1964); and *Sanctuary* (New York: The Modern Library, 1958). The consistency of characterization from one novel to the next lends credence to the proposition that Horace Benbow lived on in Faulkner's imagination and possessed a kind of independent existence all his own.

brittle, biting, staccato style of the earlier works is moderated into the flowing and majestic language of the mature Faulkner. Though *Sartoris* is not one of the great novels, it does have moments of brilliance. Most important, the outlines of the Yoknapatawpha epic are set down. The great families are mentioned and even some of the Snopes clan find their place here. Perhaps the only major defect is the inept and stereotypical handling of Negroes. But in this book we are introduced to Jefferson and its people, and we enter one of the most evocative and profoundly moving fictional worlds ever created:

> The hill flattened away into the plateau on which the town proper had been built these hundred years and more ago, and the street became definitely urban presently with garages and small shops with merchants in shirt sleeves, and customers; the picture show with its lobby plastered with life, episodic in colored lithographed mutations. Then the square, with its unbroken low skyline of old weathered brick and fading dead names stubborn yet beneath the scaling paint. . . . The courthouse was of brick too, with stone arches rising amid elms, and among the trees the monument of the Confederate soldier stood, his musket at order arms, shading his carven eyes with his stone hand.[2]

"THE AIR OF FINE AND DELICATE FUTILITY"

The first mention of Horace Benbow suggests that he wanted to remain detached from others in order to avoid the problems and pain that inevitably accompany commitment in inter-personal relationships. If he did not deliberately obfuscate his relations with others, there is certainly a strong unconscious tendency to remain enigmatic and mysterious in typical aesthetical fashion. The novel opens in 1918, immediately after World War I. Horace had wired his sister, Narcissa Benbow, that he had landed safely in New York from France but that he would not be home for a week or so. Why he would delay the trip to Jefferson is not made clear: "It was

2. *Sartoris*, 142–43.

such an incoherent message. . . . Horace could never say anything clearly from a distance." [3] But as it turns out, he could never say anything with great clarity at close quarters either. He simply wished to remain aloof under any circumstances.

His tendency toward confused abstract language is variously alluded to by others. Miss Jenny, for example, said Horace had "spent so much time being educated that he never learned anything." Mrs. Marders called him a poet and remarked "poets must be excused for what they do." [4] Ruby Lamar thought of him as "a man given to much talk and not much else." [5] Indeed, it is possible to see the contours of Horace's existence from his use of speech; his rhetoric, like Othello's, is highly inflated and romantic. Or, as "A," the author of the first volume of *Either/Or*, notes:

What is a poet? An unhappy man who in his heart harbors a deep anguish, but whose lips are so fashioned that the moans and cries which pass over them are transformed into ravishing music. His fate is like that of the unfortunate victims whom the tyrant Phalaris imprisoned in a brazen bull, and slowly tortured over a steady fire; their cries could not reach the tyrant's ears so as to strike terror into his heart; when they reached his ears they sounded like sweet music. And men crowd about the poet and say to him, 'Sing for us soon again'—which is as much as to say, 'May new sufferings torment your soul, but may your lips be fashioned as before; for the cries would only distress us, but the music, the music, is delightful.' And the critics come forward and say, 'That is perfectly done—just as it should be, according to the rules of aesthetics.' Now it is understood that a critic resembles a poet to a hair; he only lacks the anguish in his heart and the music upon his lips. I tell you, I would rather be a swineherd, understood by the swine, than a poet misunderstood. [6]

3. *Ibid.*, 41–42.   4. *Ibid.*, 169, 156.   5. *Sanctuary*, 13.
6. Søren Kierkegaard, *Either/Or*, trans. David F. Swenson and Lillian Marvin Swenson with revisions by Howard A. Johnson (2 vols.; Princeton: Princeton University Press, 1959), I, 19.

The Structure of Existence

Although we shall see later on that language and self-declaration are important indexes to the ethical modality of existence, for the time being it is only important to understand that one can deliberately obscure oneself with language as Horace certainly does. Instead of revealing himself, he remains hidden. We listen to the sound of his words rather than to him. In this connection, Judge William states that "a poet existence as such lies in the obscurity" which is the result of not having overcome the power of despair by having chosen it. Instead of soaring into the realm of the ideal and making the strenuous either/or decision as the ethical man does, a poet-existence is contented to remain "midway and rejoices in the pictures reflected in the clouds and weeps that they are so transitory."[7] A poet-existence is therefore lost, neither finite nor infinite. A person inhabiting a poet-existence cannot live in the real world because he has not made the ideal decision about it. He cannot bear to be in the midst of the confusions of everyday life because he has no eternal reference point to guide him through the confusion. And so he retires, withdraws behind whatever barrier he can erect. In Horace's case, it is language. Instead of using language to make himself known to others, he hides himself behind the melodic and languorous quality of his speech.

If, as Kierkegaard says, the perfect medium for the aesthetical is music, then Horace attempts to make his speech into music. He frequently lapses into a kind of melodic prose that "sounds" good, although its meaning escapes us. Horace's mode of expressing himself thus affords a natural outlet for Faulkner's own penchant for phrase and poetry. It is as if the author stands expectantly in the wings of a stage, waiting for the florid and sentimental phrases to flow from Horace's mouth in a mellifluous and shimmering stream in order that it might be recorded on the page:

. . . and since the essence of spring is loneliness and a little sadness and a sense of mild frustration, I suppose you do

7. *Ibid.*, II, 214.

118

get a keener purification when a little nostalgia is added in for good measure. At home I always found myself remembering apple trees or green lanes or the color of the sea in other places, and I'd be sad that I couldn't be everywhere at once, or that all the spring couldn't be one spring, like Byron's ladies' mouths. But now I seem to be unified and projected upon one single and very definite object, which is something to be said for me, after all.[8]

Horace's wish to encompass and embrace everything at once is typical demoniac desire. Don Juan wants to seduce, not one, but all women. Faust wants to conquer, not a part of knowledge, but the whole realm of intellectuality. Horace wants to be everywhere at once, or alternatively, wants everywhere to be concentrated in a single place. This desire, which is energy (*and* inertia), is aroused by dread, which is the sympathetic antipathy and the antipathetic sympathy to the nothingness which lurks at the base of human existence. Dread posited before or anterior to the either/or dichotomy is sensuousness expressed in the aestheticism of characters like Faust, Don Juan, and Horace Benbow.

Horace said of himself one time, "I have always been ordered by words."[9] If he meant that he had been passively related to words as they might have helped to shape and determine his life, that is so. But if he meant that there was a kind of neatness and order to his existence, then he was only fooling himself. The only intentionality he expressed was purely diversionary: to remain enigmatic and aloof. Hearing, after all, Kierkegaard noted, is the most spiritual of the senses. If one only hears sounds so that the meaning is negated or depressed, one has gained the realm of the sensuous.[10]

Benbow's aestheticism is revealed in other ways as well. The fact that he went to war as a civilian with the YMCA is indicative of his basic modality of existence. He chose the YMCA, not so much because he was a moral coward—though he claimed to be that, too[11]—but because he was basically fas-

8. *Sartoris*, 281.   9. *Ibid.*, 282.   10. *Either/Or*, I, 66.
11. Benbow once said, "I lack courage: that was left out of me. The machinery is all here, but it wont run" (*Sanctuary*, 18).

119

tidious. He simply wished to live as far as possible above all the clamor and strife of a world that, in his estimation, was uncontrollably evil. Even his choice of law as a vocation and his commitment to that calling was fundamentally aesthetical: "He was a lawyer, principally through a sense of duty to the family tradition, and though he had no particular affinity to it other than a love for printed words, for the dwelling-places of books, he contemplated returning to his musty office with a glow of . . . not eagerness, no: of deep and abiding un-reluctance, almost of pleasure. The meaning of peace. Old unchanging days; unwinged perhaps, but undisastrous, too."[12] Thus, toward the end of *Sanctuary*, when he makes a falter-ing but at times gallant attempt to become engaged with existence during the murder trial of the bootlegger Lee Good-win, the perjured testimony of Temple Drake and the lynch-ing of Goodwin by the mob are too much for him to bear. Rather than being catapulted into action, he retreats as a broken and dejected old man at forty-three by returning to Belle and her relentless domination. In a word, he gave him-self over to Fate, to the external forces that impinged upon his life, and could (or would) not make the leap to the ethical. Indecisiveness becomes the basic shape of his *lebenswelt*, and it plagues him from beginning to end.

Nor is it surprising to learn that he wants to make all human (potentially ethical) relationships into aesthetical experiences. Faulkner develops one of the major images of *Sartoris* around a glass-blowing set Horace had bought in Italy during the war. For a time it assumes an excessively important role in his life, for he not only wants to create *objets d'art* with his recently acquired equipment and skill, but he also wishes to make all of his relationships with people into artistic creations—especially his relationship with Nar-cissa. He equates her with the "one almost perfect vase" that he eventually blew and appropriately addresses her, "O Serene."[13] So far as he is concerned, Narcissa and his vases are, indistinguishably, Keats's "still unravished bride of quiet-

12. *Sartoris*, 149.   13. *Ibid.*, 152, 153.

120

ness." [14] At the end of his first day with her following the war, we are told that he lay down to sleep "while that wild, fantastic futility of his voyaged in lonely regions of its own beyond the moon, about meadows nailed with firmamented stars to the ultimate roof of things, where unicorns filled the neighing air with galloping, or grazed or lay supine in golden-hoofed repose." He was home at last, reunited with his love, from whom he had been separated by the War, "a stupid mischancing of human affairs." [15]

Narcissa's name is almost too obvious. It indicates, along with her actions, that she was just as prone to the aesthetical as he. Like Horace, she skirted close interpersonal relationships—especially those involving men—and thought "that there would be peace for her only in a world where there were no men at all." And yet there was, deep within her, a wild impulse that drove her to the opposite sex. When Horace first got home and asked about the Sartoris boys, she retorted hotly, "I hate Bayard Sartoris. . . . I hate all men." Horace immediately read the situation correctly: "What's the matter? What's Bayard done to you? No, that's backward; what have you done to Bayard?" [16] Horace recognized the wild and incoherent urge behind her apparent indifference to men and marriage. It would therefore be entirely consient for her to be attracted to yet repelled by the hot-headed young flying ace, over whom she would attempt to gain control. Horace knew that if she were to fall in love it would be violent and would have to be with someone who was at least her equal.

But the most dialectically potentiating factor in her life

14. Not only does Benbow use this word with reference to Narcissa, but the omniscient author does also. He uses "serene" in much the same way that Homer uses his well-known epithets. After awhile the reader comes to expect "serene" to be used conjointly with Narcissa. Faulkner also uses this word and other imagery from Keats's ode in the Lena Grove passages of *Light in August,* though Lena and Narcissa are poles apart in every respect. Narcissa's is a serenity of aloofness (and in *Sanctuary,* of heartlessness), whereas Lena's is a serenity of composure. She is the one pool of quietness in an otherwise turbulent and wild sea. It seems that the "Ode on a Grecian Urn" was one of Faulkner's favorites. See chapter fifteen below.
15. *Sartoris,* 152, 153.   16. *Ibid.,* 201, 144.

was the dread and excitement she derived from the clandestine letters she received from the depraved Byron Snopes. Though she never knew his identity, it is clear that she was able to reap the most patently sexual stimulation from them. But it is important to note that this stimulation takes place only in the realm of the fantastic, and her fantasizing about sex with an unknown partner carries her aesthetic titillation to its extreme. She wants to avoid incarnate sex, while enjoying the *eidos* of sexuality. Miss Jenny sums it up well when she observes that Narcissa would not want "anybody to know that any of her folks could know people that would do anything as natural as make love." [17]

None of Narcissa's relationships with men, then, were natural, or—in the terms of this essay—ethical. Consequently the intricate and delicately balanced relationship with Horace had to be carefully guarded. Nothing must be allowed to disturb it. Therefore, when Horace first returns home and wants to know about Belle Mitchell, we can understand Narcissa's defensiveness. Her closeness to Horace is threatened. She calls Belle "dirty" and claims she has "a backstairs nature." [18]

An investigation of Horace's alliance with Belle shows that it is no more filled with ethical content than his relationship to Narcissa. During the War, Horace and Belle had corresponded frequently in spite of the fact that Belle was married. Under ordinary circumstances this kind of arrangement would be ideal for the aesthete: he can enjoy feminine contact without having to commit himself because of the implied previous commitment on the part of his modern-day Laura. But we soon learn that her union with Harry Mitchell was more a marriage of convenience than of conviction, so that its value as a barrier is changed. It is no longer absolute but something that can be bargained. Divorce is tentatively thrust forward and then withdrawn as a means of further excitation and stimulation. Romance, as such, has taken hold.

Next, we see that Belle treats Horace with the same con-

17. *Sanctuary*, 141.   18. *Ibid.*, 167, 209.

tempt with which she has treated her first husband. He is little more than a toy:

> "Come," she said, rising. Horace rose, and Belle preceded him and they crossed the lawn and entered the house . . . they went on through the house, where all noises were remote and the furniture gleamed peacefully indistinct in the dying evening light. Belle slid her hand into his, clutching his hand against her silken thigh, and led him on through a dusky passage and into her music room. This room was quiet too and empty and she stopped against him half turning, and they kissed. But she freed her mouth presently and moved again, and he drew the piano bench out and they sat on opposite sides of it and kissed again. "You haven't told me you love me," Belle said, touching his face with her finger tips, and the fine devastation of his hair, "not in a long time."
> "Not since yesterday," Horace agreed, but he told her, . . . They sat thus for some time while the light faded, Belle in another temporary vacuum of discontent, building for herself a world in which she moved romantically, finely, and a little tragically, with Horace sitting beside her and watching both Belle in her self-imposed and tragic role, and himself performing his part like the old actor whose hair is thin and whose profile is escaping him via his chin, but who can play to any cue at a moment's notice while the younger men chew their bitter thumbs in the wings.[19]

What an exercise in futility! And yet Horace seems to welcome his romantically masochistic role in the presence of Belle, which means that their marriage, when it does take place, will never bear fruit, because it possesses this basically self-denying rather than self-affirming quality.

Within the compass of several moments Belle reveals her utter scorn for him. She says, "Now, sit over there," and he does. They talk for awhile about the desirability of Belle's divorcing Harry, but then she says, " 'You'd make a rotten husband.' 'I won't as long as I'm not married,' Horace answered." Then, " 'Sit over there,' she hissed at Horace. 'What

---

19. *Ibid.*, 163.

do you want, Belle?' " But she does not know. Again, " 'Sit over there,' Belle repeated. Horace resumed his chair." [20] And so it went: Belle ordering and Horace submitting. The relationship was bound to suffer.

The opening pages of *Sanctuary*, of course, make us acutely aware of the poverty of the then ten-year-old marriage. Predictably, we discover how unsatisfactory things have been. When Ruby Lamar asks him why he left Belle, she gets a most pathetic yet comical answer:

> "Because she ate shrimp," he said. "I couldn't—You see, it was Friday, and I thought how at noon I'd go to the station and get the box of shrimp off the train and walk home with it, counting a hundred steps and changing hands with it, and it—"
> "Did you do that every day?" the woman said.
> "No. Just Friday. But I have done it for ten years, since we were married. And I still dont like to smell shrimp. But I wouldn't mind the carrying it home so much. I could stand that. It's because the package drips. All the way home it drips and drips, until after a while I follow myself to the station and watch Horace Benbow take that box off the train and start home with it, changing hands every hundred steps, and I following him, thinking Here lies Horace Benbow in a fading series of small stinking spots on a Mississippi sidewalk." [21]

And so he left Belle and ran, stumbling along through the countryside, spending "one night in a sawdust pile at a mill, one night at a negro cabin, one night in a freight car on a siding." This, for a man who had degrees from those strongholds of respectability—Sewanee and Oxford! The flat lands of the Delta, where Belle and he had lived, had got to him, he said. If he could just return to Jefferson, all would be all right: "I just wanted a hill to lie on, you see." Nothing had been right in Kinston: "When you marry your own wife, you start off from scratch . . . maybe scratching. When you marry somebody else's wife, you start off maybe ten years

20. *Ibid.*, 163, 164.   21. *Ibid.*, 18–19.

behind, from somebody else's scratch and scratching. I just wanted a hill to lie on for a while." [22]

There are several indexes to Horace's modality of existence in these passages. He considers his basic problems to be external: he needs a hill to lie on, he has inherited someone else's problems in marriage, the shrimp detail is just too much to bear. He also uses a highly reflective way of talking about himself and has assumed an objective and rather abstract stance in relation to himself. That is to say, he talks about himself in the third person and sees himself as an object of derision and ridicule. For example, he feels himself so abused by his life in Kinston that he begins to think of himself as "a fading series of small stinking spots on a Mississippi sidewalk." This raises the whole question of reflectiveness. Is he purely aesthetical, or does self-reflection give him a vantage point from which to make the either/or choice?

Benbow is, throughout his life, a mildly ironic person, and with some bitter humor he is capable of considerable self-effacement. But even with this distance from himself, he is still unable to secure the kind of grasp on himself that would make it possible to choose himself. His self is, in the words of Kierkegaard, "perpetually vanishing." That is because he considers his problem to be outside himself: Belle, Little Belle, Kinston, and so on. He is so accustomed to assuming a fundamentally passive attitude toward his environment that he cannot act in the presence of Popeye. He tells the gangster:

"My name is Horace Benbow. I'm a lawyer in Kinston. I used to live in Jefferson yonder; I'm on my way there now. Anybody in this country can tell you I am harmless. If it's whiskey, I dont care how much you all make or sell or buy. I just stopped here for a drink of water. All I want to do is get to town, to Jefferson."

Popeye's eyes looked like rubber knobs, like they'd give to the touch and then recover with the whorled smudge of the thumb on them.

22. *Ibid.*, 17.

"I want to reach Jefferson before dark," Benbow said. "You cant keep me here like this."

Without removing the cigarette Popeye spat past it into the spring.

"You cant stop me like this," Benbow said. "Suppose I break and run."

Popeye put his eyes on Benbow, like rubber. "Do you want to run?"

"No," Benbow said.

Popeye removed his eyes. "Well, dont, then." [23]

And he did not, because he did not know how to choose.

Indeed, his whole life may be seen as a submission to Fate in the form of the women who surround him. During the Goodwin trial, Narcissa twice browbeat him into not taking Ruby Lamar home to the Benbow house as he had wanted to. She accused him of just "meddling" in the affairs of others and having no consideration for the good name and reputation of his family. She taunted him for leaving Jefferson and running off to Kinston with Belle, a divorcee. In every case Horace protested, but in every case he did nothing to back up his words. Moreover, Narcissa intervened in the trial and wanted to help the district attorney in order to remove Horace from the embarrassing position in which he had placed them all. Although it is never clear that she makes any overt contribution to the outcome of the trial, it is clear that she would do anything to accomplish her ends.[24] But what is most distressing of all is the letter she wrote to Belle after her visit to the district attorney's office. When it was apparent that Horace would lose the case, she wrote to Belle telling her that Horace would, for sure, be back in Kinston within a few days. Or, in so many words, she was saying that Horace would once again capitulate to his fate/her domination. When the trial was over and Horace was defeated, Narcissa waited for him outside the courthouse, because she knew—even if he did not—that he was finished.

23. *Ibid.*, 4.
24. See, for example, the means she used to retrieve the Snopes letters in "There Was a Queen."

His pathos is raised to its highest pitch when he returns meekly to Belle at the end of the novel: " 'I came back,' Horace said. She looked at him across the magazine. 'Did you lock the back door?' she said." He does and thereby submits finally and tragically to his fate. It is the last word about the romantic Horace Benbow in the Faulkner canon.

THE DESPAIR OF THE AESTHETE

Horace's despair is therefore "the despair of weakness," which is the despair of the aesthetical or the passive.[25] This is in fundamental contrast to the despair of self-assertion or defiance, which is the despair of the ethical. That is to say, Horace is in despair at not willing to be himself, whereas the ethical person is in despair at willing despairingly to be himself, which is, basically, a form of sin.

The general category "the despair of weakness" comes in a variety of forms. It ranges all the way from the despair of pure immediacy (in which one gives oneself over to external determination) to the despair of self-reflection and introversion. In seeking to develop a program of the modalities, it will help to note forms of despair that grip the various types of aesthetes.

Joe Christmas. Among the characters dealt with so far, Joe Christmas best represents the despair of pure immediacy. Insofar as he possessed reflection, it was only a quantitative, not a qualitative, reflection. That is, he had absolutely no conception of himself as a self. Instead, "he believed with calm paradox that he was the volitionless servant of the fatality in which he believed that he did not believe." [26] Thus, his despair was purely passive, "succumbing to the pressure of outside circumstance" with little or no awareness of what was happening to him. He "cohered immediately" with *the*

25. Kierkegaard, *The Sickness unto Death*, in *Fear and Trembling and The Sickness unto Death*, trans. with introduction and notes by Walter Lowrie (Princeton: Princeton University Press, 1954), 184.
26. *Light in August*, 244.

other [27] "wishing, desiring, enjoying," but doing all of these
as a passive agent. Accordingly, when despair entered his
life, it "happened" to or "fell upon" him from the outside.
This relation to despair is markedly different from the ethical
exemplar, Judge William, who tells us to *choose* despair in
order to overcome it.

Joe Christmas did not know that he despaired. He only
knew that events are either fortunate or unfortunate, because
everything was external to him. He did not understand that
he had lost touch with the eternal. Instead, he thought that
he despaired because he had lost his grasp on the temporal
or the earthly. In a sense, what he said was true, but it was
not true in the way that he thought it was. That is to say, he
despaired when he lost Bobbie Allen. He did not know his
despair as despair but as loneliness, and believed himself to
be lonely *because* he had lost her. But it is truer to say that
he was in despair because the self that was so deeply attached
to Bobbie Allen depended on that relationship for its sus-
tenance in such a way that when the relationship was removed, the self began to shrivel up. Had the self been reliant
upon itself as grounded transparently in the Power that
originally posited it, it would have been able to withstand
the "blow" of Fate—namely, the loss of Bobbie Allen. When
she turned her back on Joe, his reaction, though violent, was
essentially passive, completely lacking in self-reflection. For
months afterward, he wandered aimlessly from city to city
and "thought it was loneliness he was trying to escape and
not himself." [28] He did not understand that he despaired because he had no self.

But no matter where he ran down that seemingly interminable street of *Light in August*, Christmas never made the
leap into a higher modality. Several years after the Bobbie
Allen affair, he met another and stronger woman, Joanna
Burden, who also became his lover. For awhile life returned
to Joe, and he began roughly where he left off with Bobbie.

27. *The Sickness unto Death*, 184.   28. *Light in August*, 197.

128

He still "had no self, and a self he did not become, but he continued to live on with only the quality of immediacy." [29] He was alternatively repelled and attracted to something outside himself—the demoniac sensuality expressed in Joanna Burden:

> At first it shocked him: the abject fury of the New England glacier exposed suddenly to the fire of the New England biblical hell. Perhaps he was aware of the abnegation in it: the imperious and fierce urgency . . . which she appeared to attempt to compensate each night as if she believed that it would be the last night on earth by damning herself forever to the hell of her forefathers, by living not alone in sin but in filth. She had an avidity for the forbidden word-symbols; an insatiable appetite for the sound of them on his tongue and on her own. She revealed the terrible and impersonal curiosity of a child about forbidden subjects and objects; that rapt and tireless and detached interest of a surgeon in the physical body and its possibilities. . . .
> But something held him, as the fatalist can always be held: by curiosity, pessimism, by sheer inertia. Meanwhile the affair went on, submerging him more and more by the imperious and overriding fury of those nights. Perhaps he realised that he could not escape. Anyway, he stayed, watching the two creatures that struggled in the one body like two moongleamed shapes struggling drowning in alternate throes upon the surface of a black thick pool beneath the last moon. Now it would be that still, cold, contained figure . . . who, even though lost and damned, remained somehow impervious and impregnable; then it would be the other, the second one, who in furious denial of that impregnability strove to drown in the black abyss of its own creating that physical purity which had been preserved too long now even to be lost. Now and then they would come to the black surface, locked like sisters; the black waters would drain away. Then the world would rush back: the room, the walls, the peaceful myriad sound of insects from beyond the summer windows where insects had whirred for forty years. She would stare at him then with the wild, despairing face of a stranger; looking at her then he paraphrased himself: "She wants to pray, but she dont know how to do that either." [30]

29. *The Sickness unto Death,* 186.   30. *Light in August,* 225–28.

Later on, when Joanna sought to force Christmas to accept the grotesquely conceived Calvinism she held, he resisted, because he intuited the emptiness there. Again, it was not a reflective reaction; it was immediate. He only knew that he would not stand for it and in fact would have to destroy it because of the threat it represented. He had plenty of opportunities to escape but did not. "Something" held him there, and they became hopelessly locked in mortal combat, not by choice but by acquiescence: "neither surrendered; worse: they would not let one another alone; he would not even go away." [31]

The resolution of the conflict between these two demon-ridden people would therefore have to be violent and apocalyptic. Though Faulkner doubtlessly saw fire and murder-*cum*-castration as the artistically logical conclusion to this distorted affair, it must be admitted that the energy and power so precariously contained within these persons would eventually have to burst out of bounds in rage and destruction. Neither of them were really in control of their destinies. Joe Christmas did not "decide" to kill Joanna Burden; he only felt the implacable urge to perform an act, the shape of which he could not even formulate in his own consciousness: *"Something is going to happen. Something is going to happen."* [32]

Thus, we see how pure immediacy, when given full range, can not only impel people into the unreal dreamworld of a character like Don Juan, but it can also become so highly charged with power that the power unleashed results in disaster and tragedy. Such is the case with Joe Christmas. His despair was so fierce that he was driven to remove what he believed the cause of it was: not the eternal (himself), but the external, the "other," encountered in the realm of the earthly.

Flem Snopes. The pseudonymous author of *The Sickness unto Death* says that the only way the immediate man thinks

31. *Ibid.*, 244.   32. *Ibid.*, 103.

he can help himself is to try to become someone else. He defines the despair of immediacy as "despair at not willing to be oneself; or still lower, despair at willing to be a self; or lowest of all, despair at willing to be another than himself, wishing for a new self." [33] We often see such people. Because they are so unhappy with themselves (but are not aware of it), they want to become someone else or something other than themselves. Such a person is "infinitely comic"; he is not aware of the contradiction within himself but thinks of contradiction only as a condition existing outside himself. Flem Snopes, with all his skullduggery, falls within this category. In his immediacy, he thinks that he can make himself "respectable" by acquisition but does not realize that acquisitiveness is the very thing that cuts him off from Jefferson's uppercrust. He only knows that he intends to leave behind him the meanness and grossness of Frenchmen's Bend. V. K. Ratliff is correct:

> When it's jest money and power a man wants, there is usually some place where he will stop; there's always one thing at least that ever—every man wont do for jest money. But when it's respectability he finds out he wants and has got to have, there aint nothing he wont do to get it and then keep it. And when it's almost too late when he finds out that's what he's got to have, and that even after he gets it he cant jest lock it up and set—sit down on top of it and quit, but instead he has got to keep on working with ever—every breath to keep it, there ain't nothing he will stop at, aint nobody or nothing within his scope and reach that may not anguish and grieve and suffer.[34]

Horace Benbow. When self-reflectiveness begins to enter the realm of the aesthetical, as it does with Horace Benbow, "despair is somewhat modified." He "talks" of being in despair, because he has begun to have some awareness of the nature of his predicament, but his is still "the despair of weakness, a

33. *The Sickness unto Death,* 186.
34. Faulkner, *The Town* (New York: Vintage Books, 1957), 259.

passive experience; its form is . . . despair at not wanting to be oneself." [35]

Horace's progress from the level of despair indwelt by someone like Joe Christmas is evidenced by the fact that his despair does not always come as "a blow" or as a result of something that has happened to him externally. Rather, he realizes that despair may be occasioned by mere reflection within himself, so that his "despair is not a purely passive defeat by outward circumstances." [36] On the contrary, it results from self-reflection, for on those occasions when Horace turns toward himself to seek some sort of understanding, some stable standpoint from which to act, he encounters *nothing*. Such was his experience after having interviewed Temple Drake at Miss Reba's in Memphis. Following that disturbing episode he found just how poverty-stricken his inner self really was—a condition that had existed for years simply because he had sought stability outside himself rather than within himself. But after Memphis, he felt nothing but desperation. He was repelled, not only by the degradation he was made to feel by hearing Temple's "confession" ("suddenly Horace realised that she was recounting the experience with actual pride, a sort of naive and personal vanity"), but he was repelled by the emptiness he found within himself. For a moment, he contemplated suicide, "thinking how that were the only solution. Removed, cauterised out of the old tragic flank of the world." Then, when he eventually arrived home in Jefferson, he reached the absolute low point of this grave personal crisis: "he knew suddenly that it was a friction of the earth on its axis, approaching that moment when it must decide to turn on or to remain forever still: a motionless ball in cooling space, across which a thick smell of honeysuckle writhed like cold smoke." [37] His first impulse was to take up little Belle's photograph in hopes of finding some solace there. But none was to be had. All he felt was a profound sense of loss, of non-being. He vomited.

35. *The Sickness unto Death*, 187.   36. *Ibid*.
37. *Sanctuary*, 259, 265, 267.

At this point, Horace had discovered himself as "something different from the environment, from the externalities," and it was too much for him. He was frightened by what he saw, and retreated toward immediacy. For one brief moment he was confronted by the possibility of the leap, but backed off. That is, his imagination discovered "a possibility which, if it were to come to pass, would . . . cause a breach with immediacy." [38] This breach the aesthete does not want to chance at all.

Horace's despair, then, is the despair of weakness, which is contrasted with the despair of defiance or self-assertion, "but by the aid of the relative self-assertion which he has, he makes an effort (which again distinguishes him from the purely immediate man) to defend his self." He does this by attempting to convince himself that he would be better off without Belle, that Little Belle is as much a vixen as her mother, that injustice must be overcome in the Goodwin case, that he is not emotionally dependent upon Narcissa, and so on and on. He understands, to a degree, what it means to be at the beck and call of every whim of Fate, how "apoplectically muddled" the immediate person can become, and yet he cannot make the strenuous effort to gain self-sufficiency and ethical reflection. He does *not* possess "consciousness of a self which is gained by the infinite abstraction from everything outward," which is the first step "in the whole process whereby a self infinitely accepts its actual self with all its difficulties and advantages." [39] He lapses deeper into aestheticism; his despair is the despair of not willing to be himself.

On the other hand, he does *not* possess the "ludicrous" desire to be someone else as Flem Snopes does. Horace, along with Gavin Stevens and other Jefferson patricians, is able to maintain a relation to himself, however tenuous and fragile it may be. But he does not want to be something other than what he is. He merely keeps on thinking that things will change and get better; that if he gets away from all his

38. *The Sickness unto Death,* 188.   39. *Ibid.*

problems they will evaporate. Periodically he returns to himself to see "how things are doing," but he still finds his inner condition pretty much as it was, which is the signal to pick up and leave again. And he always does. Horace, in sum, dwells in the despair of weakness.

Quentin Compson. Benbow's type of aestheticism, if carried to its extreme, will lead to suicide. And there were moments when he contemplated such self-destruction. But it was Quentin Compson who demonstrated this highest potentiation of despair.

Quentin's despair was *over* something earthly but *about* the eternal; or, to put it in explicit terms, he was in despair *over* Caddy, her loss of virginity and the subsequent damage to Compson honor, but *about* his own inability to deal with his feelings of repulsion toward Caddy's action. He stands in contrast to Joe Christmas who did not understand what was really happening to him, who always attributed his predicaments to external circumstance. He is also contrasted with Horace, but not as sharply. Horace *did* have moments of self-reflection and partially understood that he was, himself, the source of his despair. Quentin, on the other hand, saw himself for what he was and could not abide what he saw. His imaginary conversation[40] with Mr. Compson is particularly revealing, and a close reading of the last several pages of his section in *The Sound and the Fury* will illustrate how he drove himself to make the either/or decision in full view of the abyss of nothingness.

Quentin, until the very last day of his life, was convinced

40. When asked if Quentin "actually" had that conversation with his father, Faulkner answered: "He never did. He said, if I were brave, I would—I might say this to my father, whether it was a lie or not, or if I were—if I would say this to my father, maybe he would answer me back the magic word which would relieve me of this anguish and agony which I live with. No, they were imaginary. He just said, Suppose I say this to my father, would it help me clarify, would I see clearer what it is that I anguish over?" *Faulkner in the University*, ed. Frederick L. Gwynn and Joseph L. Blotner (New York: Random House, 1965), 262–63.

that Caddy was not only worth despair but was the source of his desperation. When he finally discovered "that she was not even worth despair,"[41] he had no recourse but to make the leap into a higher modality or fall more deeply into despair and perhaps suicide. He, of course, chose the latter.

One of Kierkegaard's minor pseudonyms, who likewise chose suicide, wrote:

> I do not regard suicide as a praiseworthy thing. It is not out of vanity that I have resolved upon it. On the contrary, I believe in the correctness of the proposition that no man can bear to behold the infinite. That once became evident to me in an intellectual respect, and the expression for this is [Socratic ignorance]. That is to say, ignorance is the negative expression for infinite knowledge. Suicide is the negative expression for infinite freedom. It is a form of the infinite freedom, but the negative form. Hail to him who finds the positive form.[42]

It is clear that Quentin could not "bear to behold the infinite." He could not bear to contemplate the infinite freedom that was his when he no longer could attribute his despair to extreme circumstances. He was cut loose from all moorings and thrown into the limitless ocean Kierkegaard speaks of as the spiritually determined universe of the modern West created when the Infinite Spirit irrupted in time.

At the beginning of the imaginary conversation, Quentin taunted his father, "you dont believe i am serious" about suicide, and Mr. Compson replied, on the contrary, "i think you are too serious." Otherwise, Mr. Compson said, "you wouldnt have felt driven to the expedient of telling me you have committed incest" with Caddy. What Quentin was trying to do, according to his father, was "to sublimate a piece of natural human folly into a horror and then exorcise it with truth." Or, to be more precise, Quentin was trying to cover up for Caddy by claiming he had committed incest and then

41. *The Sound and the Fury,* in *The Sound and the Fury and As I Lay Dying* (New York: Random House, Inc., 1946), 221.
42. *Either/Or,* II, 251 n.

confessing it to his father. Or, to put it still another way, he was trying to be the scapegoat for Caddy's sin. Mr. Compson called her extramarital sexual intercourse an act of "natural human folly"; but in Quentin's mind it was the unforgiveable sin.

However, this was all imaginary, and it is noteworthy that the real Quentin would not permit his imaginary self or the imaginary Mr. Compson to engage in such falsehoods. There was no incest, and Quentin knew it. There was only the desire for it, perhaps. Therefore, the fantasy conversation had to take a different turn. Mr Compson (conscience?) tells Quentin he is still blind to what is in himself, "to that part of general truth the sequence of events that shadows every mans brow even benjys." According to his father, Quentin "cannot bear to think that someday" Caddy's loss of virginity—*an external blow of circumstance*—will not also be a loss for Quentin; that he will be put in a position of *not* having something on which he can place the blame for his despair; that he will have to face up to the fact that he, Quentin, is responsible for his own black despair. It is as if Mr. Compson is saying "As long as you can blame Caddy, you will not commit suicide, but when you can no longer place the responsibility on her shoulders for your despair but must accept it yourself, you are then at the most extreme position of your existence."

The point is *not* that Mr. Compson says this but that Quentin seems to *imagine* Mr. Compson says this, which means that Quentin grasps it within his own consciousness.

Mr. Compson continues by saying that no man ever kills himself "under the first fury of despair or remorse or bereavement"; he does that "only when he has realised that even despair or remorse or bereavement" are in themselves of no significance. Or, more precisely, the absence of any *legitimate* reasons or causes for "despair or remorse or bereavement" mean that we are faced with the dialectic: nothing/God.

In Kierkegaardian terms, then, we can say that Quentin has come to "a consciousness of himself." His despair is *about* the eternal and "to despair about the eternal is impossible without having a conception of the self." [43] And when he discovers that this self in its aloneness has been so weak in its dependence on Caddy and her folly, then he is absolutely repelled by his self and wishes to disinherit it. In his despair he cannot forget his weakness and hates himself, and instead of humbling himself in faith in order to regain himself, he refuses to know anything about the self he so deeply despises. Thus, he becomes more and more introverted and alone, and, as the author of *The Sickness unto Death* points out, suicide is the danger nearest him. If he should try to talk with anyone else about his predicament, this may throw him further into despair simply because it is an added manifestation of his weakness. Or, it may be that continued aloneness is preferable.

Aptly enough, the section on the despair of aestheticism in *The Sickness unto Death* ends this way: "It would be the task for a poet to represent this agonizing self-contradiction in a demoniac man who is not able to get along without a confidant, and not able to have a confidant, and then resolving it in such a way as this." [44] Quentin Compson is such a creation by one of the great poet-novelists of our era.

43. *The Sickness unto Death*, 195.   44. *Ibid.*, 200.

11

The Ethical According to Kierkegaard

THE USEFULNESS of Kierkegaard's schema for a study of this kind is nowhere more clearly evident than in his discussion of the ethical. Though he never attempted to write systematically or dogmatically about ethics and obviously never wanted anyone to think of him as an ethicist in the traditional sense of that word, he was trying to discover how people can live within an infinite universe. Some live transcendentally or above the world by never becoming involved in it in any important way. Others attempt to fix boundaries to this ever-expanding universe in order to subdue it. Still others are *in* but paradoxically not *of* this world. That is, people inhabit the world aesthetically, ethically, or religiously. His utterances about *ethics* are descriptive of the ethical modality rather than prescriptive for a system of ethics. As Collins notes, "Kierkegaard does not attempt to settle any question by means of this phenomenological analysis of contrasting viewpoints." He frequently asserts, instead, that he is simply setting forth the various modalities in order that the reader might better grasp the meaning of his own personal existence. Collins further points out:

The Ethical According to Kierkegaard

"Kierkegaard never tires of warning his readers that he is to be taken as a corrective rather than a norm, . . . This warning should be kept in mind during the investigation of his ethical stand . . . , since the latter is quite evidently conditioned by, and in some respects limited to, his historical situation."[1]

THE ETHICAL MODALITY

There are a number of places in which the ethical stage is discussed in the Kierkegaardian canon, but there is no obvious and consistent thesis that we can confidently point to as Kierkegaard's. But why? First, his ideas, like those of any seminal artist or thinker, are not fixed. We find his notions shifting and being modified from place to place. This is true of the *Journals* as well as the works. At every stage of his creative effort he employs his dialectical strategy so that he might lift his exposition to increasingly higher levels of refinement. This means that from *Either/Or* to the last of the *Edifying Discourses* he is constantly bringing under judgment previous statements by himself or his pseudonyms. In fact, the second complicating factor is that he chose to write pseudonymously. He deliberately warns us *not* to accept the attitudes of the pseudonyms as his, a request we must seriously heed. The desirability of following his request is borne out when we realize that Judge William's ethical notions, which have some merit on their own, are successfully critized by Johannes *de silentio*, the author of *Fear and Trembling*, and *both* are competently evaluated by Johannes Climacus in the *Postscript*. However, the fact that no consistent Kierkegaardian point of view can be identified becomes the real value of his work for this particular essay. His approach allows us to deal more succinctly and directly with the concrete problems of existence as they arise and are exhibited by characters such as those he creates or by those selected from Faulkner's novels. What we are concerned with,

1. James Collins, *The Mind of Kierkegaard* (Chicago: Henry Regnery Co., 1953), 42, 68.

then, is methodology more than content. We do not have to agree with any of his findings about the ethical life in order to appreciate what he is driving at. But we must so insinuate ourselves into the Kierkegaardian methodology—which *is* consistent—that we may be able to see the world in his dialectical way. This will help pry open the secret of existence as it stands concretely before us. He does not attempt to construct a theory about existence, but tries to give a description of existers. And the first step in approximating his technique is once again to admit the Infinite within our range of view. This is what makes him so obstinately manic in the dialectical manipulation of his material. In Kierkegaard's comparison between the psychically determined cosmos of antique thought and the pneumatically determined infinite universe of Western culture after the proclamation of the incarnate *logos*, he emphasizes the restlessness and dread of a Don Juan, suspended over an abyss and hurrying in a state of perpetual vanishing. The question posed by the irruption of infinity becomes "Within what medium is human existence possible?" It cannot be the medium of the aesthetical, as we have already seen. What then of the medium of speech and self-declaration?

The person who dwells in the aesthetical modality is ultimately volatilized by his relative or even total indifference toward the concrete, but the person who dwells in the ethical modality seeks to find some reference point, some stopping place in the infinite movements of existence. It is an awesome spectacle to see anyone attempt the ethical. Anti-Climacus writes, "The Christian heroism (and perhaps it is rare to be seen) is to venture wholly to be oneself, as an individual man, this definite individual man, alone before the face of God, alone in this tremendous exertion and this tremendous responsibility." [2] The ethical man wants to bring life down to

2. Søren Kierkegaard, *The Sickness unto Death*, in *Fear and Trembling and The Sickness unto Death*, trans. with introduction and notes by Walter Lowrie (Princeton: Princeton University Press, 1954), 142.

the manageable, the pedestrian, the daily round of duty and responsibility—all of which require prodigious effort.

The ethical may also be thought of as the most humanistic of the stages. It is the attempt fully to realize human potentiality. The author of the *Postscript*, for instance, echoes the entire Western humanist tradition when he says that, "for the study of the ethical, every man is assigned to himself." [3] But this advice is not stated in the balanced and moderate eighteenth-century atmosphere evoked by Pope's couplet about "the proper study of mankind." This is an atmosphere in which rationalism has been a colossal failure and in which the terrors of an infinite universe become increasingly evident.[4] It is now more imperative than ever for the individual to find a way to be himself in this kind of world—a world that continues to elude him. It is no longer a question of "nothing in excess." It is a question of finding some place to stop and take hold of something permanent and lasting. Everyone suddenly sees how difficult it is for the individual to order his life in such a way that the "universal" is actually made concrete within the course of daily living, and the ethically serious person knows that nothing should be spared in making the attempt. Judge William, Kierkegaard's spokesman for the ethical way, shows how life without the attempt is virtually no life at all:

> There comes at last an instant when there no longer is any question of an either/or, not because he has chosen but he has neglected to choose, which is equivalent to saying, because others have chosen for him, because he has lost his self. . . . For to think that for an instant one can keep one's personality a blank, or that strictly speaking one can break off and bring to a halt the course of the personal life, is a delusion. The personality is already interested in the choice

3. Kierkegaard, *The Concluding Unscientific Postscript*, trans. David F. Swenson and Walter Lowrie (Princeton: Princeton University Press, 1941), 127.

4. The *locus classicus* for this terror is Pascal's fragment 72 of the *Penseés*.

before one chooses, and when the choice is postponed the personality chooses unconsciously, or the choice is made by obscure powers within it.[5]

What Judge William wants to talk about more than anything else, then, is the formation of the self through choice and the despair of the aesthetical in the infinitized world of the modern West.

In the first place, the Judge holds that the self, so chosen, is the most abstract and yet the most concrete of concepts. By this he means that the self may be equated with freedom. He explains this apparent conundrum by the simple psychological observation that we rarely ever want to be someone else.[6] That is, an individual may be discontented with his own lot, he may wish to have someone else's mind or money or good looks, but he never desires to become that other man. The individual furthermore believes (incorrectly) that, even when his most cherished wishes are granted, he nevertheless is still substantially the same person he was all along. The self is concrete; it is grounded in history. Judge William then observes that we can remain what we are only because we are free to choose to do so. Thus, the self is only abstract until chosen. The self is concrete in that it is situated in history, but it does not come into being until it is chosen. Therefore, the person who knows freedom on the deepest level is he who is continually willing to choose himself in an absolute sense. That is, he chooses himself and not someone else: "This self which he then chooses is infinitely concrete, for it is in fact himself, and yet it is absolutely distinct from his former self, for he has chosen it absolutely." The point here is that the aesthetical man or the man who has not chosen absolutely has chosen relatively or finitely. On the other hand, the absolute self did not exist until it was chosen, "for it came into

5. Kierkegaard, *Either/Or*, trans. David F. Swenson and Lillian Marvin Swenson with revisions by Howard A. Johnson (2 vols.; Princeton: Princeton University Press, 1959), II, 168.
6. As we have seen, only the purely immediate man—Flem Snopes— is that un-*self*-conscious.

existence by means of the choice, and yet it did exist, for it was in fact 'himself.'" Judge William then sums it up by saying that one has performed two dialectical movements simultaneously when one has chosen one's self absolutely:

> That which is chosen does not exist and comes into existence with the choice; that which is chosen exists, otherwise there would not be a choice. For in case what I chose did not exist but absolutely came into existence with the choice, I would not be choosing, I would be creating; but I do not create myself, I choose myself. Therefore, while nature is created out of nothing, while I myself as an immediate personality am created out of nothing, as a free spirit I am born of the principle of contradiction, or born by the fact that I choose myself.

Because the act of choosing is what shapes and forms our selves, the selves can wither away for lack of exercise and use if we do not continually choose or act. Because that which is to be chosen (the self) lies closest to the chooser, the longer we put off making this concrete choice, the greater danger we run of becoming alienated from our selves. Or to put it the other way around: to allow one's self to be pushed and directed by outside forces means that one becomes less and less a self and more and more an object. Too much contemplation can destroy subjectivity.[7]

Since the end of all ethical striving is *self*-realization, one is to seek a *telos*, not outside, but within oneself. Here the Judge is not talking abstractly but most concretely. That is, an individual must choose himself absolutely in his environment, for to do otherwise would be to slip back into aestheticism. Anyone who relates himself negatively to the environment therefore abstracts himself out of existence: "His self must be opened in due relation to his entire concretion; but to this concretion belong also the factors which are designed for taking an active part in the world. So his movement, then, is from himself through the world to himself. Here the movement is a real movement, for it is a work of freedom, but at

7. *Either/Or*, II, 219–20, 167–68.

the same time it is immanent teleology." [8] The point is that if I am married, I must find myself *in* marriage, *in* that particular context and not another. And so it is *in* the context of my work, my vocation, my station in life, and so forth.

It is not surprising to find that the Judge is an advocate of duty. For he holds that the most direct way to self-realization and achievement of the ethical stage is through obedience to the imperatives of duty. The indecisiveness of the aesthetical is brought to a stop when the individual responds to its call: "When with all his energy a person has felt the intensity of duty he is then ethically mature, and in him duty will emerge of itself. The chief thing is, not whether one can count on one's fingers how many duties one has, but that a man has once felt the intensity of duty in such a way that the consciousness of it is for him the assurance of the eternal validity of his being." [9] The inner coherence and clarity of the ethical life may be sought and won by the exertion of effort and will. While the aesthetician gives himself over to instability and anarchy, the ethicist is he who can order and form his life along the lines of duty.

The actions of the ethicist are more than blind adherence to the demands of some autocratic God, however. Duty lies within us all. It is our *telos*. We are not subject to some capricious and unbearable heteronomy. Instead, we are subject to the law of our own inner selves:

When duty is viewed thus it is a sign that the individual is in himself correctly oriented. For him, therefore, duty will not split up into a congeries of particular definitions, for that is always an indication that he stands in an outward relation to it. He has clad himself in duty, for him it is the expression of his inmost nature. When he has thus oriented himself he has become absorbed in the ethical and will not chase breathlessly after the fulfillment of his duties. The genuine ethical individual therefore possesses calmness and assurance because he has not duties outside himself but in himself. The more profoundly a man has planned his life

8. *Ibid.*, 279.   9. *Ibid.*, 270–71.

ethically, the less will he feel the need of talking every instant about duty, of being fearful every instant as to whether he has fulfilled it, of taking counsel every instant with others about what his duty is. When the ethical is rightly viewed it makes the individual infinitely secure in himself, when it is not rightly viewed it makes the individual insecure, and I cannot imagine a more unhappy and agonizing existence than that of a man who manages to put duty outside himself and yet would endeavor to realize it.[10]

Another benefit to be derived from doing one's duty is victory over the philosophical dichotomy that exists between the universal and the particular:

Duty is the universal, what is required of me is the universal; what I am able to do is the particular. . . . But this must be more closely defined. It is to be noted that language itself emphasizes this scepticism. I never say of a man that he does duty or duties, but I say that he does *his* duty, I say, "I am doing *my* duty, do *yours*." This shows that the individual is at once the universal and the particular. Duty is the universal which is required of me; so if I am not the universal, I am unable to perform duty. On the other hand, my duty is the particular, something for me alone, and yet it is duty and hence the universal. Here personality is displayed in its highest validity. It is not lawless, neither does it make laws for itself, for the definition of duty holds good, but personality reveals itself as the unity of the universal and the particular.[11]

The achievement of personal unity and integrity therefore becomes the Judge's goal. He is saddened by the apparent aimlessness in the aesthetical life. One must "choose one-self" in all of one's finiteness and particularity in order to achieve that goal. The Socratic maxim "Know thyself" is fine insofar as it goes; it is a worthwhile object for anyone's life; "but it is equally certain that it cannot be the goal if it is not at the same time its beginning." And the way to make a beginning toward self-knowledge is to choose oneself absolutely. This

10. *Ibid.*, 259.   11. *Ibid.*, 268.

is an action, whereas knowing oneself could become a form of passivity or contemplation.[12]

There are, however, certain problems which arise when one is enjoined to choose oneself. The question could obviously be raised about the purely accidental and fortuitous, both of which are inimical to the ethical stance. If the whole purpose of self choice is to prevent oneself from becoming dissipated into multifariousness, would the individual not have to be selective about what in himself he is to choose? The Judge answers this quandary: "He who lives ethically abolishes to a certain degree the distinction between the accidental and the essential, for he accepts himself, every inch of him, as equally essential." The accidental is not "wiped out" but is incorporated fully into one's life by the act of choice. The ethical man therefore ennobles accidentality by deliberately choosing it.[13]

The crux of the matter is that personality—that which has been resolved into being by choice—is seen by the ethicist as the one constant or absolute factor in an otherwise structureless world. By choosing oneself, one establishes the unity between the universal and the particular and thereby overcomes the apparent relativity of the historical. To those who suggest that ethical norms vary from culture to culture, Judge William replies that they have simply "allowed themselves to be dazzled by the external; for in the ethical realm there is never any question about the external but only the internal." The skeptic, of course, sees that the quickest way to "volatilize the ethical" is to posit historical infinity:

And yet there is something true in his position, for in the last resort, if the individual is not himself the absolute, empiricism is the only road open to him, and this road has with respect to its issue the same peculiarity as has the river Niger with respect to its source, that no one knows

12. *Ibid.*, 263.
13. *Ibid.*, 265, 266. It is significant that the phrase "to a certain degree" is used by the Judge, for it is precisely the admission of this qualification which will be the ultimate flaw in his position.

where it is. If finiteness is my lot, it is arbitrary to come to a stop at any particular point. On this road, therefore, one never gets to the point of beginning, for in order to begin one must have got to the end, but this is an impossibility. If personality is the absolute, then it is itself the Archimedean point from which one can lift the world.[14]

The ethicist must assert over and over again that the human personality is indeed the absolute, because the act of choosing this absolute will halt the never-ending flux within the pneumatically qualified universe. Limits and boundaries are established, because the self is established absolutely. (Again, a flaw in the Judge's position is apparent: can one really choose oneself in one's eternal validity?)

Sin is another enduring problem for those who inhabit the ethical stage. If one chooses oneself absolutely, is there not a sense in which one might be choosing evil since it is such a part of existence? Judge William attempts to pull the sting of the question by suggesting that, as one chooses oneself, one is in effect repenting oneself out of the whole of existence: "For repentance is the expression for the fact that evil belongs to me necessarily, and at the same time the expression for the fact that it does not necessarily belong to me. If the evil in me did not belong to me essentially, I could not choose it, but if there were something in me which I could not choose absolutely, I would not be able to choose myself absolutely at all, so I would not myself be the absolute but only a product." The act of choosing the whole self absolutely is in the Judge's estimation the most courageous act one can perform. One is even under obligation to repent his father's and his society's sin. Thus, he repents himself "back into himself, back into the family, back into the race, until he finds himself in God. Only on these terms can he choose himself, and he wants no others, for only thus can he absolutely choose himself."[15]

At first, repentance sounds strangely like recollection, a movement which other pseudonyms regard as essentially pa-

14. *Ibid.*, 270.   15. *Ibid.*, 229, 220–21.

gan. Repentance, as it is defined here, is concerned with things past and is a process of being thrust "back into" the substantial categories of family, nation, race and ultimately to God. In *The Sickness unto Death*, for example, the God-factor is introduced in such a way that it infinitizes and potentiates the whole matter of sin. One cannot purify oneself before God; it is impossible to choose oneself "back into" God. Moreover, in the *Postscript* we are told that repentance is essentially contradictory and hence comical. It is only in confrontation with the God-Man that one can make the double movement of giving up and getting back all that one has. Repetition, not recollection, is the movement to be made—an action that cannot be performed by the guilty party on his own. He is drawn forward by the power of the Infinite and responds in faith. This is the opposite of repenting oneself back into the Infinite.[16]

THE ETHICAL PARADIGM

The one human act that most profoundly illustrates what is meant by the ethical in Kierkegaardian terms is marriage. This is especially true for his ethical pseudonym, Judge William. The Judge sees marriage as an expression of the universal that puts limits on the irregularity and multifariousness of "romantic love" or what he sometimes calls "first love." Marriage is the paradigm, in fact, for all ethical behavior, for it is within the marital state that one can achieve selfhood in the deepest possible way. When one says "I will" in the wedding ceremony and sincerely promises to live faithfully with a spouse, one is performing the ultimate ethical act. Nothing can be higher; nothing can be more exhaustive. It is asserting one's individuality in universal terms.

In this vein Judge William sets out to explain to his young friend the difference between marriage and romantic love: "Marriage contains an ethical and religious factor, as love does not; for this reason marriage is based upon resignation,

16. See *The Sickness unto Death*, 268ff., and *Postscript*, 467 and elsewhere.

as love is not." [17] Not the resignation of stoical indifference, but the resignation of absolute choice: *either* aesthetical detachment and the frantic flight from despair, *or* resignation in which despair is chosen because the self is chosen. The romanticist continually evades life; the ethicist constantly pursues it, flaws and all. Accordingly, to resign oneself is to make the final choice, and in doing so, to pull the fangs of despair. Resignation is, therefore, the act in which the absolute self is chosen absolutely; it is created; it comes into being.

Next, one has a peculiar opportunity in marriage to follow the demands of duty. The Judge tells the young man:

> You regard duty as the enemy of love; I regard it as its friend. . . . If duty, once it has appeared in consciousness, is an enemy of love, then love must do its best to conquer it; for you, after all, would not think of love as being so impotent that it cannot vanquish every opposition. On the other hand, you think that when duty makes its appearance it is all over with love . . . the truth is that you are afraid of conjugal love because it has in it duty to such a degree that when it makes its appearance you cannot run away from it. In romantic love, on the other hand, you think this is all right, for as soon as the instant arrives when duty is mentioned, love is over, and the arrival of duty is the signal for you, with a very courtly bow, to say farewell. If duty is the enemy of love, and if love cannot vanquish this enemy, then love is not the true conqueror. The consequence is that you must leave love in the lurch. When once you have got the desperate idea that duty is the enemy of love, your defeat is certain, and you have done just as much to disparage love and deprive it of its majesty as you have done to show despite of duty, and yet it was only the latter you meant to do. You see, this again is despair, whether you feel the pain of it or seek in despair to forget it. [18]

In another passage, the Judge asks the young man to compare the "Mine!" pronounced by the married man with the "Mine!" uttered by the erotic. He claims that the married man is better prepared than the romantic to enjoy the pleas-

17. *Either/Or*, II, 37.   18. *Ibid.*, 149–50.

ures and seductions of the instant, because marriage possesses ethical validity. That is to say, it is impossible for one
protected by the boundaries of matrimony to be dislodged by
the allurements of the purely aesthetical. Anyway, why would
one want to give up everything for nothing? All human possibilities and dreams can be realized within marriage and
with all the benefits of marriage in addition. This does not
mean, however, that the aesthetical is automatically excluded.
It only means that the aesthetical "is excluded as the absolute,
but relatively it is still left." [19]

In fact, the Judge wants to make it quite clear that there is
aesthetical as well as ethical validity to marriage, and he
claims that the pleasures of the instant are more readily enjoyed within marriage than in some aesthetical modality.
There, one runs the risk of having pleasure perpetually vanish from one's presence, while in marriage the pleasure may
be repeated time and again and all the "beauty inherent in
the erotic" may be enjoyed just so long as it is combined
with marriage. If left to itself, then, pure eroticism is self-
defeating, but when nurtured within the structure and
framework of marriage, eroticism has its rightful place.

Romantic love or reflective love—love that is not founded
on choice—is not satisfactory because "it stops arbitrarily
now at this point, now at another." It cannot hold fast to any
one spot or any one person; volatilization is its logical end.
Nor can it point beyond itself to anything higher, such as
duty or the ethical stage. It is too busy trying to capture the
elusive instant. Therefore, if an individual ever hopes to live
with purpose, he must allow his romantic love to give way
to choice. Again, this does not mean that romantic love is
to be destroyed; instead, it is transfigured and becomes the
primary ingredient of marriage. Indeed, love constitutes marriage and gives it its substance: "If this is lacking, the life
in common is either satisfaction or a carnal lust, or it is an
association, a partnership, for the attainment of one aim or

19. *Ibid.*, 59–60, 181–82.

another. But love has in it precisely the characteristic of eternity, whether it be the superstitious, romantic, chivalrous love, or the deeper moral and religious love which is filled with a mighty and lively assurance." [20]

What is the difference between the love experience in the aesthetical and that in the ethical stage? One is at the mercy of Fate, the other has within it a "law of motion." That is to say, romantic love remains "an unreal *an-sich* which never acquires inward content because it moves only in an external medium," whereas marriage is free and responsible. The person who lives in marriage has the possibility of an "inner history," but the romanticist is at the mercy of every extraneous whim that might strike him. Although romantic love appears to be "strong, stronger than the whole world, . . . the instant doubt occurs to it, it is annihilated." Marital love, however, really is strong, because it lies in wait for internal as well as external threats. The inward man has been so cultivated in marriage that despair, doubt, or any other potentially destructive agent is neutralized because they are chosen when the self is chosen absolutely.

The heart of the matter, according to the Judge, is that in marriage the Church requires a vow, while in romantic love no promise is given or received. The Judge believes that by reciting the words of the marriage ceremony, he can, in effect, validate his own being absolutely and eternally. He believes that he can enter into the marriage contract with the purest intentions and fully endorse the words by the strength of his own personality. For him, marriage is the place where one can exhaustively and finally demonstrate what "choosing oneself" really means. Marriage is therefore the place where the self can become absolutely transparent to the beholder. The romanticist clings to enigma and intrigue up to the very last, for he fears that all love will disappear if his inner self is revealed. But, according to Judge William, the contrary is true: it is precisely because the romanticist holds onto a

20. *Ibid.*, 31, 33.

dream of immediacy and mystery that his self is dissipated into nothingness. One must seek candor and sincerity; one must hope to pour one's life totally into the promise of marriage; only then will one know the meaning of real love.

THE INSUFFICIENCY OF THE ETHICAL

The difficulty with Judge William's enthusiasm for the ethical may be described in one word: "extravagance." He puts such an inordinate amount of confidence in human nature and invests marriage with such an aura of heroism that we can only wonder what world he lives in: "Marriage I regard as the highest telos of the individual human existence, it is so much the highest that the man who goes without it cancels with one stroke the whole of earthly life and retains only eternity and spiritual interests—which at the first glance seems no slight thing but in the long run is very exhausting and also in one way or another is the expression of an unhappy life." Marriage, for him, is the goal and perfection of a normal and happy life, and all other considerations, including one's religious convictions, are to be subordinated to it. Collins marvelously sums up the Judge's case: "Judge William likes to consider himself as a kind of anointed priest; he gives his belief to marriage and worships the miracle of love; it provides him with the wedding garment, which alone enables him to sit undisturbed at the banquet of existence. In his wife he finds a renewal of the principles of esthetic life, apart from its selfishness and despair. Thus the married state alone can resolve the tension between the various aspects of human life." [21]

If we consider the Judge's position from a purely pragmatic point of view, we can dismiss all his rhetoric about marriage as highly inflated and unrealistic. We know tacitly and explicitly that marriage cannot be all that good. We might well wonder, however, what Kierkegaard thought of the

21. Kierkegaard, *Stages on Life's Way,* trans. Walter Lowrie (Princeton: Princeton University Press, 1945), 107; Collins, *The Mind of Kierkegaard,* 107.

Judge's notions. This, of course, is impossible to discern completely, but it is not insignificant that other Kierkegaardian pseudonyms were able to make some rather trenchant and perceptive criticisms of the ethical stage. Just as the aesthetical was successfully "dethroned" by Judge William, so the ethical is successfully "dethroned" by others.

Frater Taciturnus in *Stages on Life's Way*, for example, speaks of the ethical as a transitional stage on the way to the religious. It is transitional because its requirement is "so infinite, the individual always goes bankrupt." He cannot possibly live up to the rigorous demands of the universal. Then Vigilius Haufniensis, another pseudonymn, says rather pointedly: "Ethics points to ideality as a task and assumes that man is in possession of the conditions requisite for performing it. Thereby ethics develops a contradiction, precisely for the fact that it makes the difficulty and the impossibility clear. What is said of the Law applies to ethics, that it is a severe schoolmaster, which in making a demand, by its demand condemns, does not give birth to life." [22] This does not mean, however, that ethics should ever be compromised, for "the more ideal ethics is, the better." In this way the individual will be more accurately apprised of the depth of his own intransigence.

It seems, therefore, that Kierkegaard's overall strategy is first to show how the aesthetical founders upon the demands of ethics and then how the ethical founders on its own demands. Religiousness, "which is precisely the ideality of reality and therefore is just as desirable as that of aesthetics and not impossible like that of ethics," bursts on the human scene just at the moment when the limits of the ethical are reached. Religiousness greets us with the affirmation: "Behold, all things become new!" Just at that moment one is freed from the impossible burden of attempting to fulfill the insatiable requirements of the ethical. [23]

22. *Stages*, 430; *The Concept of Dread*, trans. with introduction and notes by Walter Lowrie (Princeton: Princeton University Press, 1946), 15.   23. *The Concept of Dread*, 16.

The most serious charge that may be levelled at the ethical, especially as it is espoused by someone like Judge William, is that it ultimately has no place for the concept of sin. Haufniensis says, "If ethics must include sin, its ideality is lost." That is to say, the ethicist cannot fit sin into his scheme, because he really does believe that one can choose oneself absolutely. With the introduction of sin into the picture, however, human capability is compromised, the ethical stumbles, and the only way out of the dilemma, according to the ethicist, is to increase the requirement. Haufniensis notes:

> Now all is lost for ethics, and it has contributed to the loss of all. There has come to the fore a category which lies entirely outside its province. *Original sin* makes everything still more desperate—that is to say, it settles the difficulty, not, however, by the help of ethics but by the help of dogmatics. As all ancient thought and speculation were founded upon the assumption that thought had reality, so also all ancient ethics upon the assumption that virtue is realizable. Scepticism of sin is entirely foreign to paganism. For the ethical consciousness, sin is what an error is in relation to knowledge, it is the particular exception which proves nothing.[24]

For the religious consciousness, however, sin (or the exception) proves everything. It proves that one's eternal happiness is not dependent upon achieving the universal. It proves that the exception (the individual) who has committed the exceptional act (sin) has put himself in a position where he must suffer perdition or make the paradoxical movement of faith. By admitting the depth and power of sin, the individual automatically makes himself "higher," though in another sense he is certainly lower, than the universal. That is to say, he has moved out of the ethical into the religious modality when sin is posited, for sin may only be posited, as such, before God. He now understands that it is not by virtue that sin is overcome; it is by faith. For the opposite of sin is faith.[25]

24. *Ibid.*, 16–17.
25. *Fear and Trembling and The Sickness unto Death*, 108, 213.

Or, seen from a slightly different angle, the Judge simply does not grasp the nature and seriousness of sin, although he makes mention of it. His version of repentance turns out to be little more than an acknowledgment that one has not measured up. But sin, according to Kierkegaard, is to be *"in despair at* willing *to be oneself.* Thus sin is . . . potentiated defiance: sin is the potentiation of despair." The Judge does not understand that. It is indeed necessary to choose oneself in order to consolidate oneself in the fact of the aesthetical, but one must not stop at this level, for it is inevitably self-defeating. For despair, instead of being overcome by one's having chosen oneself, is in fact increased "in proportion to consciousness of self." The individual simply does not have the power to overcome his own despair even if he chooses it. Johannes Climacus therefore notes, "When I despair, I use myself to despair, and therefore I can indeed by myself despair of everything; but when I do this, I cannot by myself come back. . . . In this moment of decision . . . the individual needs divine assistance."[26]

But more than all this, the Judge has not yet comprehended what it means to live in dread before the face of the holy God. Thus, another pseudonym writes:

> The earlier dogmatic was right in asserting that the fact that the sin was before God infinitely potentiated it. Their fault lay in regarding God as something external, and in assuming that it was only now and then men sinned against God. But God is not something external in the sense that a policeman is. What we need to emphasize is that the self has the conception of God, and that then it does not will as He wills, and so is disobedient. Nor is it only now and then one sins before God; for every sin is before God, or rather it is this which properly makes human guilt to be sin.[27]

According to the *Postscript*, what we must emphasize is the notion, "before God." He is "the factor which dialectically, ethically, religiously, makes 'qualified despair' (to use a ju-

26. *Ibid.*, 208, 211; *Postscript*, 230.
27. *The Sickness unto Death*, 211.

ridical term) synonymous with sin." The ethical therefore *must* be considered a transitional stage; otherwise, one continues in a state of radical contradiction to God. With this agonizing discovery the sinner learns that it is his sin which will prevent him from reaching God. He cannot make the infinite movement "backward," through recollection, to God, for sin stands in his way. He may only move "forward" toward God. Eternal truth is out in "front," so to speak, "through its being in existence or having existed, so that if the individual does not existentially and in existence lay hold of truth, he will never lay hold of it." [28]

This way of talking is, of course, thoroughly absurd to the ethicist. He simply keeps on saying that the solution to the problem is to relate oneself to the absolute by relating to the universal. Because he cannot fit exceptions into consciousness (whether it be the exception of sin or the exception of the Infinite becoming enfleshed in time), he will continue to be frustrated in his attempts to validate himself eternally. His best hope would be to discover his own exceptionableness, his own incommensurability with the universal, so that he might be enabled to make the leap of faith in which the exception is embraced. By excluding the exception, he unwittingly excludes himself and the God-Man as well, both of whom are exceptions.

This, of course, is what *Fear and Trembling* is all about. Here the Abraham story is brilliantly examined and interpreted by Kierkegaard through the pseudonym, Johannes *de silentio*. The Father of Nations is shown to be "the prototype of the exception," [29] for he was called to perform a task which would have been abhorrent to the ethical mind but which was of the essence of the religious. He was asked to give what he loved most. Moreover, he was called by direct communication from God; there were no intermediaries. He had to bear his burden alone and at the risk of appearing to

28. *Postscript*, 187.   29. Collins, *The Mind of Kierkegaard*, 91.

156

deceive those he loved most. Although he was tempted to call the whole thing off as a violation of the moral law—a very attractive possibility—he nevertheless felt bound to obey the will of God. In complete and total isolation, Abraham gave up his most prized possession, only to get it back again, greatly enriched.

The nub of the matter is that the ethical founders upon religiousness. Ethically speaking, it would have been wrong to murder his son; religiously speaking this was required of him—except that now it is called "sacrifice." And it is the contradiction between the ethical and the religious which constitutes the problem for Abraham, one who dwells within the religious modality. By contrast, the problem for one dwelling in the ethical modality is viewed in an entirely different light. The author of *Fear and Trembling* explores the consciousness of Agamemnon to make this point. Here was a man who was asked to offer up his own daughter, Iphigenia, on behalf of the safety and well-being of the state—a tragic request, to say the least. But Agamemnon could seek the consolation of infinite resignation, for his conflict was between two ethical norms. His task—dreadful though it might be—was to decide which moral act was highest and then do it. Because the conflict was between two universals—love of daughter and love for the state—he becomes the tragic hero, not the knight of faith. He is magnificent in his sorrow, admired by his fellowmen, even reconciled to his daughter who is able to grasp the nature of the ethical demand upon her father. Now the difference between the knight of infinite resignation and knight of faith becomes clear: "The tragic hero still remains within the ethical. He lets one expression of the ethical find its *telos* in a higher expression of the ethical; the ethical relation between . . . daughter and father he reduces to a sentiment which has its dialectic in its relation to the idea of morality. . . . With Abraham the situation was different. By his act he overstepped the ethical entirely and possessed a higher *telos* outside of it, in relation

157

to which he suspended the former." [30] Abraham, then, can at no point in his life be called a tragic hero; he is either a "murderer or a believer." The middle-way—the way of resignation—was reserved for the ethical modality entirely.

In what has been said thus far, it is evident that the focus on the ethical has begun to shift. It has begun to assume a different role than that advocated for it by Judge William. In the Abraham story, the ethical is relativized. That is to say, love of God causes "the knight of faith to give his love to his neighbor the opposite expression to that which, ethically speaking, is required by duty." The ethical has become paradoxical:

> In the story of Abraham we find such a paradox. His relation to Isaac, ethically expressed, is this, that the father should love the son. This ethical relation is reduced to a relative position in contrast with the absolute relation to God. To the question, "Why?" Abraham has no answer except that it is a trial, a temptation (*Fristelse*)—terms which . . . , express the unity of the two points of view: that it is for God's sake and for his own sake. In common usage these two ways of regarding the matter are mutually exclusive. Thus when we see a man do something which does not comport with the universal, we say that he scarcely can be doing it for God's sake, and by that we imply that he does it for his own sake. The paradox of faith has lost the intermediate term, i.e., the universal. On the one side it has the expression for the extremest egoism (doing the dreadful thing it does for one's own sake); on the other side the expression for the most absolute self-sacrifice (doing it for God's sake). Faith itself cannot be mediated into the universal, for it would thereby be destroyed. Faith is the paradox, and the individual absolutely cannot make himself intelligible to anybody.

Thus it appears to everyone else that, by following the duty imposed on him by God, the knight of faith "hates" the universal. This is not so at all. Abraham obviously never stops loving Isaac, though the ethical understanding of what he does is that he *apparently* hates his son in order to perform

30. *Fear and Trembling*, 69.

such a reprehensible act. Nothing could be further from the truth. He loves his son totally, for only in this way does sacrifice, as a religious act, make sense. Indeed, it is precisely his love for Isaac, which "by its paradoxical opposition to his love for God, makes his act a sacrifice." [31]

At the heart of the matter is the Kierkegaardian notion of the "teleological suspension of the ethical." That is, though the ethical is present and in force at every moment and under every circumstance, the religious individual is always under the more profound compulsion to obey the will of God, which may on occasions be in conflict with moral law. Indeed, there are moments in Abraham's life when the ethical constitutes the temptation and becomes a more appealing way to deal with a troublesome dilemma. As Eliot's Becket says: "The last temptation is the greatest treason: To do the right deed for the wrong reason."

For most people, the ethical has a more negative (but dialectically more positive) connotation. It is always in force and bears down upon us at every point in our lives, but as it becomes more and more demanding, we eventually realize that it is more than we can accomplish. Not so much because of our weakness or imperfection, but because we are absolutely heterogeneous to the ethical. If the suspension took place because of our infirmity, then it would be out of pity for our inadequacies. It would be like suspending a public official from office when he doing a moderately good job, says Johannes Climacus, for we are doing a moderately good job ethically. But the suspension occurs when the individual finds that he is existing in exactly the opposite state from what the ethical demands of him, "so that far from being able to begin, each moment he remains in this state he is more and more prevented from beginning. He is not related to the task as possibility to actuality, but as impossibility." Thus when suspension comes, it comes in the most dreadful way, for the individual then discovers how absolutely out of touch he is

31. *Ibid.*, 80, 81, 84.

with the ethical. It is not merely a separation by distance, but a qualitative distinction. This position is *sin*, a religious term. It is from sin that we are delivered in faith, and it is precisely this fact that Judge William could not see. Sin is more than the discrepancy between the finite and the infinite. It is more than imperfection or weakness. It is the decisive expression for the whole existential sphere, which is in absolute defiance of God. Johannes Climacus says "the inwardness of sin . . . , is the greatest possible and most painful possible distance from the truth when truth is subjectivity."[32] This is a long way from the world of Judge William.

In sum, the Judge had too great a confidence in the whole ethical enterprise. The individual *cannot* choose himself in his eternal validity, he *cannot* reveal himself completely, he *cannot* choose despair in such a way as to overcome it, he *cannot* realize the universal in his own life—all because of sin, which infinitizes his dilemma. The ethical falters because it does not understand religiousness, a modality which is the quintessence of irregularity. The religous paradigm expresses, not the universal, but the particular in all its scandal. Judge William never was able to grasp this, for in his mind to be a paradigm of the religious is to be a pattern for all times and places, to be the universal. And yet the religious paradigm is exactly the opposite of the universal: it is the particular, the exceptional, the irregular.[33]

32. *Postscript*, 238–40.   33. *Ibid.*, 231.

12

The Ethical Courage of Charlotte Rittenmeyer and Harry Wilbourne

THE HEURISTIC QUALITY of the Kierkegaardian modalities is dramatically revealed when they are applied to Faulkner's characterizations in *The Wild Palms*.[1] By most standards, the torrid love affair between Charlotte Rittenmeyer and Harry Wilbourne would be judged unrealistic and immoral, the desertion of her husband and children irresponsible. Only the most romantically inclined would attempt to build a case *for* Charlotte and Harry. And yet it is clear that no matter how extravagant and wrongheaded their actions appear to be, they believed they were operating from what Kierkegaard would have considered a profoundly ethical base.

What Charlotte and Harry hoped to accomplish was the perfect love relationship; they "sacrificed everything for love."[2] For Judge William, marriage alone is the paradigm of the ethical, but Harry and Charlotte wanted to carry the

1. William Faulkner, *The Wild Palms* (New York: Vintage Books, 1964). All in-text references in this chapter apply to this edition.
2. Faulkner's description of the story to Jean Stein in "William Faulkner: an Interview," *William Faulkner: Three Decades of Criticism*, ed. Frederick J. Hoffman and Olga W. Vickery (New York: Harcourt, Brace & World, Inc., 1960), 75.

logic one step further and say, "No, there is something higher and more ideal, and we shall have it." Indeed, the purity and power of their love made it possible for her to leave her children, but with a slight wince: "I wasn't thinking of them. I mean, I have already thought of them. So now I dont need to think of them any more because I know the answer and I dont think I can change me because the second time I ever saw you I learned what I had read in books but I never had actually believed: that love and suffering are the same thing and that the value of love is the sum of what you have to pay for it and any time you get it cheap you have cheated yourself. So I dont need to think about the children" (48).

Charlotte and Harry believed that most married couples do not make the kind of commitment to one another that is required; that most people settle for hopelessly bourgeois standards in marriage; that whereas holy matrimony should be the *entrance* into the modality of self-declaration, it has in fact become an *exit* to aesthetical conventionality. By contrast, they wanted an unsullied yet ravishing love, unencumbered by the institution of marriage, and they believed their special relationship would forever protect them from the despoiling encroachments of a sick society.

For this reason, they sought a place, a situation, a condition in which they could be alone, free from the hypocrisy of ordinary life. They fled New Orleans and its middle-class respectability and for months were continually on the move, seeking to establish that perfect relationship they so desperately wanted. They went first to Chicago where Charlotte worked for awhile as a department store artist and Harry did odd jobs around the hospitals and clinics. Predictably, Chicago palled on them because they had not yet realized that the externals (the *place* in which they resided) had little or nothing to do with their *mode* of living. They left the rough and tumble existence of Chicago for a secluded spot on a Wisconsin lake. There they lived as twentieth century Adam and Eve until the snows came, when they were forced to move back to Chicago (they had run out of food and money).

Charlotte returned to her work with the department store, and Harry started a brief career as the author of "true confessions" stories he easily sold to the pulp magazines. But one day Harry woke up to the fact that they were betraying their ideal:

> "I had turned into a husband," he said. "That was all. . . . At first I used to have to watch myself, rehearse myself each time so I would be sure to say 'my wife' or 'Mrs. Wilbourne', then I discovered I had been watching myself for months to keep from saying it; I have even caught myself . . . thinking 'I want my wife to have the best' exactly like any husband with his Saturday pay envelope and his suburban bungalow full of electric wife-saving gadgets and his table cloth of lawn to sprinkle on Sunday morning that will become his actual own provided he is not fired or run down by a car in the next ten years—. . . . I had even stopped being ashamed of the way I earned money, apologising even to myself for the stories I wrote; I was no more ashamed of them than the city employee buying his own bungalow on the installment plan in which his wife can have the best is ashamed of his badge of office, the rubber plunger for unstopping toilets, which he carries about with him." (132)

The only way left was another withdrawal—to pick up and leave again and attempt once more to establish the ideal love relationship in remote surroundings. He took a job as a mining camp doctor in Utah.

The curiously ethical character of this relationship was established as soon as the two met. Harry rather clumsily arranged an assignation at an old, run-down New Orleans hotel. When they got to their room, Charlotte felt something was wrong. Not that she was running out on her husband and children but that there was something basically dishonest and deceptive about *their* going to a hotel under the guise of man and wife:

> "Oh, God, Harry," she said. She beat her clenched fists on his chest. "Not like this. Jesus, not like this."
> "All right," he said. "Steady, now." He caught her wrists and held them, still doubled into fists against his chest while

she still wrenched at them to free them to strike his chest again. *Yes,* he thought. *Not like this and never.* "Steady now."

"Not like this, Harry. Not back alleys. I've always said that: that no matter what happened to me, whatever I did, anything, anything but not back alleys. If it had just been hot pants, somebody with a physique I just leched for all of a sudden so that I never looked nor thought higher than his collar. But not us, Harry. Not you. Not you." (46–47)

Furthermore, it turns out that Charlotte had already told her husband about the affair, a clear indication of her determination to try to be absolutely transparent to others, and she did not want to begin her relationship with Harry aesthetically—in an aura of mystery and fraud.

But that was not all; there was "one other thing" that momentarily impeded her decision to leave Francis Rittenmeyer: money. Wilbourne, as a medical intern, was practically speaking, a pauper, and it seemed, for one brief moment, to be an insurmountable obstacle. "Listen," Charlotte said. "Tell me again you haven't got any money. Say it. So I can have something my ears can listen to as making sense even if I can't understand it. . . . Come on. Say it." "I have no money," he said. "All right. It makes sense. It must make sense. It will have to make sense" (49). So they left one another—Charlotte with the intention of breaking off the relationship for good, and Harry returned to the hospital, which in Kierkegaardian terms became a symbol of the aesthetical for him: *"I can hide behind my white jacket again, draw the old routine up over my head and face like niggers do the quilt when they go to bed"* (51). In the hospital, he became a mere "cipher in the crowd."[3]

But the affair was off again and running when Harry *accidentally* found a wallet on the street containing twelve hundred dollars. It gave them the financial independence they needed to break from New Orleans. But one independence

3. Søren Kierkegaard, *The Sickness unto Death,* in *Fear and Trembling and The Sickness unto Death,* trans. with introduction and notes by Walter Lowrie (Princeton: Princeton University Press, 1954), 167.

only led to another enslavement. Precisely the accidentality of finding the twelve hundred dollars and their consequent dependence on money was an aesthetical feature of their relationship that they would have to deal with. The novel is set during 1937 and 1938. Hunger for food was a problem for the masses, but Charlotte pointed to a more fundamental hunger in their fastidiously ethical relationship: love. Money could only be of relative importance in their scale of values: " 'That's just whether it's steak or hamburger. And hunger's not here—' She struck his belly with the flat of her hand. 'That's just your old gut growling. Hunger's here.' She touched his breast. 'Don't you ever forget that' " (86). He promised not to.

In Charlotte's terms the only cost worth taking an accounting of was the cost of love and sacrifice for each other, and no cost was too great: "You stole the money we've got now;" she said, "wouldn't you do it again? Isn't it worth it, even if all busts tomorrow and we have to spend the rest of our lives paying interest?" "Yes," he said. "Only it's not going to bust tomorrow. Nor next month. Nor next year—" "No. Not as long as we are worthy of keeping of it. Good enough. Strong enough. Worthy to be allowed to keep it. To get what you want as decently as you can, then keep it" (88).

Later on Harry realized that it was simply not enough to subordinate the power of money to that of love; one must forget about money altogether. It is dehumanizing. It makes objects of people. He even uses typically Kierkegaardian language to talk about money. He calls it "volatile"—so "volatile" that those people whose lives become caught up in financial transactions soon find themselves translated into monetary terms and consequently volatilized themselves. Money is a medium of exchange; people become a medium of exchange. Harry told McCord: "I was in eclipse. It began that night in New Orleans when I told her I had twelve hundred dollars and it lasted until the night she told me the store would keep her on" (137). They had somehow become seduced by money. Indeed, it was so abstracting in its power

that Harry felt himself to be "outside of time," which is another way of saying that he felt himself to be "volatilized
into multifariousness." He was so emotionally attached to
money, he felt his continued *existence* depended on it: "I
was still attached to it, supported by it in space as you have
been ever since there was a not-you to become you . . . —
supported by it but that's all, just on it" (137). He was saying
that he allowed money to give him his being: "You know:
I was not. Then *I am*, and time begins, retroactive, is was
and will be." But money is fraudulent; what it promises,
never comes to be. If one hopes for life from money one can
never get caught up to the present. One is always in time
past: "*I was* and so I am not and so time never existed." It
was all a hoax. Harry said that as long as money had this
kind of grip on him he could never become reflective enough
to see the danger of his situation:

> "I wasn't afraid then because I was in eclipse but I am
> awake now and I can be afraid now, thank God. Because
> this Anno Domini 1938 has no place in it for love. They used
> money against me while I was asleep because I was vul-
> nerable in money. Then I waked up and rectified the money
> and I thought I had beat Them until that night when I found
> out They had used respectability on me and that it was
> harder to beat than money. So I am vulnerable in neither
> money nor respectability now and so They will have to find
> something else to force us to conform to the pattern of hu-
> man life which has now evolved to do without love—to con-
> form, to die." (140)

He then told McCord that "They" would find a way; that he
and Charlotte were "doomed." Why go on? Because everyone has to. Harry despairingly and romantically willed to be
himself in the face of what he considered to be the ineluct-
able forces of Fate.

Charlotte was, in some ways, the stronger of the two.
Harry, for example, thought, "*Maybe I'm not embracing her
but clinging to her because there is something in me that
wont admit it cant swim or cant believe it can*" (84). And

this is not an altogether inaccurate picture of himself. By comparison, we see Charlotte, for page after page, heroically attempting to establish herself in the face of circumstances that would have overwhelmed a lesser person. First of all, she told "Rat," her husband, that she was leaving him for Harry. This was not merely an impulsive act with her, if we can believe her account of the break-up. She knew the pain it would cost to leave her children. She refused to take any money from Rat, because she wanted to be completely on her own—able to face Harry squarely with no entanglements with her previous life. One of the many poignant scenes in the book occurs when she tells Harry how *she* must sever the connection with Rat and the children. "It's not finished. It will have to be cut." "Cut?" he asked. " 'If thine eye offend thee, pluck it out, lad, and be whole.' That's it. Whole. Wholly lost—something. I've got to cut it" (59). And she did.

Harry admired her determination. By simple might and effort, he thought, Charlotte would take the ingredients of a totally aesthetical experience and would try to make it ethical without destroying the aesthetical value in it: "Listen: it's got to be all honeymoon, always. For ever and ever, until one of us dies. It cant be anything else. Either heaven or hell: no comfortable safe peaceful purgatory between for you and me to wait in until good behavior or forbearance or shame or repentance overtakes us" (83). Moreover, it was she who made Harry understand what money and respectability had done to him—how he had succumbed to their enrichment: "My God, I never in my life saw anybody try as hard to be a husband as you do. Listen to me, you lug. If it was just a successful husband and food and a bed I wanted, why the hell do you think I am here instead of back there where I had them?" (116–17).

Then, there were times—especially in their sexual encounters—when she seemed to take on a curiously masculine way of being in the world. She was extremely aggressive and Harry passive: " 'Stand up. . . . Stand up like a man.' He rose, she put her arms around him, wrestling him against her with restrained savage impatience. 'Why dont you grow up, you damned home-wrecking boy scout? Dont you know yet that we just dont look married, thank God, even to brutes?' She held him hard against her, leaning back, her hips against him and moving faintly while she stared at him, the yellow stare inscrutable and derisive and with that quality which he had come to recognize—that ruthless and almost unbearable honesty. 'Like a man, I said' " (109).

Finally, it was she who on the last few days before her death sat in "complete immobile abstraction from which even pain and terror are absent" because she *willed* it to be that way. It is difficult to conceive of a more heroical stance than hers.

THE DESPAIR OF THE ETHICIST

Despair accompanies the ethical modality as well as the aesthetical. The despair of the aesthetical, it should be recalled, is the despair of weakness—of not willing to be oneself. In the ethical stage, it is the despair of self-assertion—of willing despairingly to be oneself. "In order to will in despair to be oneself," Kierkegaard writes, "there must be consciousness of the infinite self. This infinite self, however, is really only the abstractest form, the abstractest possibility of the self." [4] Certainly Charlotte Rittenmeyer and Harry Wilbourne are talking about their infinite selves when they describe their love. They wish to abstract themselves right out of the concrete realm of husbands, children, medical practices, money, and all the other finite concerns of existence. And they want to do it on their own, without the help of the Power that posited those selves in the first place. Indeed, they will be the selves they project for themselves without any aid of any sort from any outside force or agency, human or divine. They are governed by an inner *telos*. And, as Kierkegaard would say, although a man's concrete self consists of perfectly definite components, Harry and Charlotte expect to create their

4. *Ibid.*, 201.

ideal form of existence by distinguishing within themselves what they will accept and what they will reject. In short, they will to refashion their selves in such a way as to suit themselves.

Now, the basis for calling their despair "defiance" is obvious enough: they are choosing to be the kinds of selves they want to be *in defiance* of the original selves posited by God. Hence, in the final analysis, they become no selves at all because they ultimately deny some of the most basic ingredients of their existence. Kierkegaard writes of this kind of person: "The self is its own lord and master, so it is said, absolutely its own lord, and precisely this is despair, but it also is what it regards as its pleasure and enjoyment. However, by closer inspection one easily ascertains that this ruler is a king without a country, he rules really over nothing; his condition, his dominion, is subjected to the dialectic that every instant revolution is legitimate. For in the last resort this depends arbitrarily upon the self." [5]

Indeed, defiance despair becomes the theme of the novel. Harry and Charlotte would not tolerate the ordinary, the concrete, the accidental in their lives but attempted to see everything in ideal perspective.[6] The moments of despair therefore naturally came. When they were up in the Wisconsin woods, Harry told McCord how much he looked forward to an idyllic existence there: "And then fall will come, the first cold, the first red and yellow leaves drifting down, the double leaves, the reflection rising to meet the falling one until they touch and rock a little, not quite closing. And then you would open your eyes for a minute if you wanted to, remembered to, and watch the shadow of the rocking leaves on the breast beside you." But the hard "realist," McCord, could see the despair lurking behind such idealistic hankerings:

5. *Ibid.*, 203.

6. It should be noted that Judge William's ethicism is considerably less strained, more pedestrian, but no less ideal than Harry's or Charlotte's. The Judge professes to choose the accidental, but only "up to a point." See chapter eleven above.

"For sweet Jesus Schopenhauer," McCord said. "What the bloody hell kind of ninth-rate Teasdale is this? You haven't near done your share of starving yet. You haven't near served your apprenticeship to destitution. If you're not careful, you'll talk that stuff to some guy who will believe it and'll hand you the pistol and see you use it. Stop thinking about yourself and think about Charlotte for a while."

"That's who I'm talking about. But I wouldn't use the pistol anyway. Because I started this too late. I still believe in love." (100–101)

Harry is convinced of his and Charlotte's ability to transcend the mundane ways of ordinary existence. But after they got to Wisconsin, despair did come and come with a vengeance:

He would look about at his familiar surroundings with a sense of profound despair, not even knowing that he was worrying now, worrying so terribly that he did not even know it; he looked about with a kind of aghast amazement at the sunfilled solitude out of which she had walked temporarily yet still remained in and to which she would presently return and re-enter her aura which had remained behind exactly as she might re-enter a garment and find him stretched on the cot, not sleeping now and not even reading, who had lost that habit along with the habit of sleep, and said quietly to himself, *I am bored. I am bored to extinction. There is nothing here that I am needed for. Not even by her. I have already cut enough wood to last until Christmas and there is nothing else for me to do.* (112)

The strenuous effort expended at removing themselves from the boredom and hypocrisy of New Orleans or Chicago had only postponed a more profound boredom and despair. They had abstracted themselves right out of existence and out of one another's lives—the very thing they dreaded most. Indeed, their effort was so strenuous, so idealized, so fastidious that Faulkner managed in this brilliant gem of a novel to undercut and parody the ethical modality of existence. His comments to Jean Stein reveal what he thought he had accomplished: by using the comical and contrapuntal story of the tall convict in "Old Man" he succeeded in exposing the highly unrealistic and inflated romanticism of "The Wild Palms."[7] In doing so, he proved Kierkegaard's thesis that humor and irony are powerful tools with which to divest the ethical modality of all its pretensions and contradictions.

At Charlotte's death Harry's desperation was raised to its highest pitch, and Kierkegaard might have traced its development as follows. Harry, by virtue of being in the ethical stage, chose once again to be the ideal self he had been during his months with Charlotte, but her death was almost too much. He was deeply shaken by this tragedy and thought—momentarily, at least—that he would like to be able to forget her. But when Rittenmeyer first visited Harry in jail and offered him money to jump bail and the trial, Harry refused. Rat appealed to him: " 'Think of her.' 'I wish I could stop. I wish I could. No I dont. Maybe that's it. Maybe that's the reason—' Maybe that was; that was the first time when he almost touched it. But not yet: and that was all right too; it would return; he would find it, hold it, when the time was ready" (312). This enigmatic talk about the "something" that would return, that he would find and hold "when the time was ready" was a *memory* of Charlotte—an exquisitely painful one. Not the ghostly memory of the aesthete who uses memory as a way of avoiding hurt, but the aching memory that the ethicist chooses in his heroic way. Not a disembodied, transcendent memory, existing independently of the flesh, but a memory incarnate in one's own physical body and nourished by the emotions. It was not that he had the possibility of memory but memory as actuality: *"Not could. Will. I want to. So it is the old meat after all, no matter how old. Because if memory exists outside of the flesh it wont be memory because it wont know that it remembers so when she became not the half of memory became not and if I become not then all of remembering will cease to be.—Yes, he thought, between grief and nothing I will take grief"* (324). Harry despairingly wills to choose the painful memory of

7. Stein, "William Faulkner: An Interview," 75.

Charlotte rather than leave himself at the disposal of Fate. Kierkegaard could have been writing about Harry Wilbourne when he said:

> Precisely upon this torment the man directs his whole passion, which at last becomes a demoniac rage. Even if at this point God in heaven and all his angels were to offer to help him out of it—no, now he doesn't want it, now it is too late, he once would have given everything to be rid of this torment but was made to wait, now that's all past, now he would rather rage against everything, he, the one man in the whole of existence who is the most unjustly treated, to whom it is especially important to have his torment at hand, important that no one should take it from him—for thus he can convince himself that he is right. This at last becomes so firmly fixed in his head that for a very peculiar reason he is afraid of eternity—for the reason, namely, that it might rid him of his (demoniacally understood) infinite advantage over other men, his (demoniacally understood) justification for being what he is. It is himself he wills to be; he began with the infinite abstraction of the self, and now at last he has become so concrete that it would be an impossibility to be eternal in that sense, and yet he wills in despair to be himself. Ah, demoniac madness! He rages most of all at the thought that eternity might get it into its head to take his misery from him! [8]

Harry remains defiant and, in spite of Charlotte's death, has dedicated all his energies to willing despairingly to continue their relationship. Maybe with her death, half the relationship is gone because her flesh is gone, but he, as enfleshed being, will nevertheless remember her and carry on their ideal love. He chooses thus to torment himself, and lives out Kierkegaard's description. If the torment (the memory of Charlotte) were removed, Harry fears that he would lapse into a kind of aestheticism in which his self would be volatilized by the blows of circumstance. That he must avoid at all costs. He must continue to make the strenuous effort to choose himself daily, hourly, during every moment of consciousness.

8. *The Sickness unto Death*, 205–206.

The Ethical Courage of Charlotte and Harry

It takes the genius of a Faulkner to describe this kind of ethical modality—a modality which by its very extravagance discloses its own basic flaw and eccentricity: that the very ideality of the ethical project will eventually abstract the individual from the realm of the finite. In some ways, Harry and Charlotte, in their defiance, are as absurdly fantastic as anyone inhabiting the most highly refined aesthetical modality.

III

The Structure of Time:
Entr'acte

13

Kierkegaard's View of Time

TIME PLAYS an important role in all Kierkegaard's writing, but is brought into focus in *The Concept of Dread*. That focus, like the discussions of sensuousness and tragedy, further illustrates what Kierkegaard believes to be the essence of a civilization organized around the principle of the Incarnation.

He first urges that we define time as "infinite succession" but then immediately alerts us to the problems which arise when we attempt to divide time into past, present, and future. No matter how plausible this division may seem to be, it is false, because we are assuming that these distinctions exist within time itself. This cannot be so. Past, present, and future exist only when we try to see time purely in terms of our own finite experience. "If in the infinite succession of time one could in fact find a foothold which would serve as a dividing point," Kierkegaard writes, "then this division would be quite correct. But precisely because every moment, like the sum of the moments, is a process (a going-by) no moment is present, and in the same sense there is neither past, present, nor future."[1]

The question of the present arises, of course, as soon as we begin to think of one moment succeeding another. There is a past moment that preceded the moment that is just skittering by and so on. But the present "is not the concept of time unless precisely as something infinitely void, which again is the infinitely vanishing." The decisive notion here is the infinite, for, if one does not understand that infiniteness is a characteristic of the present, then one has posited the present as something finite—something that does apparently exist between past and future—a wholly untenable position. The point Kierkegaard makes is that the eternal is the present, or, better still, that the present is the eternal. If we try to put it in conceptual terms, we say that "the eternal is the annulled (*aufgehoben*) succession." Or, if we try to visualize it, we say that "eternity is a going-forth, yet it never budges from the spot, because for visual representation it is the infinitely void present."

What is Kierkegaard driving at here? He wants to show that in *an infinite series* there can be no finite quanta because each quantum is in turn infinitely divisible. This is especially evident when we consider *time*, for time has the quality of an infinite series in two ways. First, it makes an infinite allusion forward and an infinite allusion backward. Second, the "specious present" Kierkegaard talks about is specious precisely because it is infinitely divisible within itself. But another characteristic peculiar to time is that it seems to possess direction; it has a vectorial, "from-to" thickness which is succession.

Now, we can overcome the giddiness of existence within the infinite flight of succession in one of two ways. First, we can make (think of) the infinite flight of succession as fundamentally a *finite* flight of succession. That is, we can make

1. Søren Kierkegaard, *The Concept of Dread*, trans. with introduction and notes by Walter Lowrie (Princeton: Princeton University Press, 1946), 76–77.

time a moving image of eternity—*temporal* insofar as it is moving; a *mere* image of eternity insofar as it is temporal; nevertheless an *image* of eternity insofar as it is cyclical—which is to say, finite. (This is the way of the ancient pagan world.) In making this move, one endows each moment with finitude as a rhythmic beat finitizes the intervening periods. But one also gives each period an equal value (there are no "arhythms") which deprives them all equally of any singular or unique value. Moreover, there are no rhythmical climaxes. There is, in short, no moment.

Or alternatively, one may overcome the giddiness of existence within the infinite flight of succession by annulling the successiveness in the summing up of all time in the providential, fore-seeing, intentional, vectorially-oriented care of God—much as a man does when he at last grasps or completes his own projects. The vectorial character and "from-to" thickness of the will of God is represented in such phrases as "the Alpha and the Omega," "from age to age," and "thy kingdom come."

The Incarnation is that intersection of *mere successiveness* and *succession annulled* and is the earnest of this providential summing up. The eternity which is present is a summation *still thick with succession*, still heavy with the future, a plenum of realized expectations, hence a proper place for hope and faith (*fiducia*). So conceived, each moment has a value, but each moment has its own special and unique value. Time is a terrain of dramatic peaks and valleys. There can be moments because there is a Moment.

Don Juan is a creature of the destruction of the first solution, but for whom the second (whose ultimate ground is faith) is not yet a possibility.

The ramifications of this viewpoint are numerous, but one of the most illuminating has to do with personal existence. For example, Kierkegaard says, "The life which is in time and is merely that of time has no present." Moreover, if one insists on using the instant to define time and thinks of the instant as that purely hypothetical exclusion of past and future, "then the instant is precisely not the present, for that which in purely abstract thinking lies between the past and the future has no existence at all."[2] Or we might put it another way: one is never present (or one's life is never present to one) so long as one lives *only* for the moment and has no relation to the eternal end. Some of Faulkner's heroes and heroines live this way and suffer for it. We have already encountered a number of them and will meet others. They live only for the moment, but the instantaneity they so desperately seek continually eludes them precisely because it bears no relation to the eternal. Instead, the instant they seek is abstracted from the eternal, has no ultimate foundation, skitters on by, and becomes lost. The moment is therefore a specious moment, a parody of the present. It has no content at all, for it has no past or future. Paradoxically, the fact that "the present as the eternal" *also* has no past or future is exactly what constitutes its perfection. Therefore, when we say of someone that he has or shows *presence,* we mean that he is neither carried away by the flux of instantaneity nor is yet abstracted into "atemporality." He is not, in the popular jargon, "out of it" but "with it." For him, the past and future are in new dimensions of fullness, and he can choose the present because it has content.

In order to find the true present or instant, time must therefore be understood eschatologically. That is to say, the true present is discovered at that point where eternity and time intersect one another: "Thus understood, the instant is not properly an atom of time but an atom of eternity. It is the finite reflection of eternity in time, its first effort as it were to bring time to a stop. For this reason Hellenism did not understand the instant; for even if it comprehended the atom of eternity, it did not comprehend that it was the instant, did not define it with a forward orientation but with

2. This pure abstraction does not even resemble time, because the fundamental characteristic of time is its passing by. Kierkegaard therefore rightly says that time, "if it is to be defined by any of the characteristics revealed in time itself, is the passed time." *The Concept of Dread,* 77–78.

a backward, since for Hellenism the atom of eternity was essentially eternity, and so neither time nor eternity had true justice done it." [3]

The modern understanding of the instant, the true and authentic grasp of the present became possible, according to Kierkegaard, because of the irruption of the Spirit, which destroys the psychically determined cosmos of the ancient Greeks. He says. "No sooner is the spirit posited than the instant is there." Prior to that, man rested in nature or Fate and was not able to gain enough perspective on himself to grasp what is even meant by "the instant." He could not transcend the time within which he existed. Indeed, if the Greeks spoke of time in any way, it was as time past, by "defining it, like the definition of time in general, as a going-by." [4]

We are now in a position to appreciate the significance of the Hellenic notion of recollection, in which Plato tells us that we must move backwards into the past if we expect to get in touch with what is ultimately real. That is because, according to the *Dialogues*, eternity lies behind us. This, of course, stands in marked contrast to the Christian conception of eternity and to the Kierkegaardian category of "repetition." That is to say, eternity lies ahead of us and is the basis of our confidence; we pneumatically qualified people have been freed from the substantial categories of family, state, and destiny. Although repetition may not be strictly equated with the classical Christian understanding of the eschatological, perhaps we *can* say that repetition bears close affinities to what has recently been termed "realized eschatology." According to Kierkegaard's analysis, eternity is the present and has a forward thrust. In the opening paragraphs of the book entitled *Repetition* Constantine Constantius states it well:

> Say what one will, it is sure to play a very important role in modern philosophy; for *repetition* is a decisive expression for what "recollection" was for the Greeks. Just as they

3. *Ibid.*, 79.   4. *Ibid.*, 79–80.

taught that all knowledge is a recollection, so will modern philosophy teach that the whole of life is a repetition. . . . Repetition and recollection are the same movement, only in opposite directions; for what is recollected has been, is repeated backwards, whereas repetition properly so called is recollected forwards. Therefore repetition, if it is possible, makes a man happy, whereas recollection makes him unhappy.[5]

But just as "repetition" becomes a possibility when "the instant" is posited, so the distinctions between past, present, and future become possible. However ambiguous "the instant" may be, it is nevertheless a reference point by which past and future may be defined. We can begin to see the special significance of the future, for it appears to be saturated with power. The future, Kierkegaard says, may indeed be understood as "the whole of which the past is a part." For example, when we moderns talk about eternity, we are talking about something in the future, by and large, whereas the Greeks "recollected" eternity. Moreover, we see the future as the disguise in which the eternal will make its appearance, although it would of course be folly to confuse eternity with the future. For us, eternity has a relation to time, but a paradoxical relation, so that when we speak of the future as identical to or commensurate with eternity, we are speaking only metaphorically.[6] On the other hand, the Greeks could not have a concept of the eternal or the future. But we cannot reproach them for this—for losing time in the instant— nor can we even accuse them of having no sense of time whatsoever. All we have a right to say is that they merely thought of time in a simple and naive way, "because the category of the spirit was lacking." Infinity had not been opened up to them.[7] It was before what W. H. Auden called "the outrageous novelty" of the Incarnation had been intro-

5. Kierkegaard, *Repetition*, trans. Walter Lowrie (New York: Harper & Row, Publishers, Inc., 1964), 33.
6. But this entire discussion is, of course, metaphorical.
7. *The Concept of Dread*, 80.

duced into their childlike existence; they were still innocent children.

Kierkegaard's discussion of time and eternity forms a baffle against which Faulkner's work may be sounded. That, along with the great deal of criticism written on the subject of time in the Faulknerian canon, provides us with a convenient approach to the novels and stories.

14

Whose Time? Sartre on Faulkner

JEAN-PAUL SARTRE's now celebrated article on Faulkner examines time in *The Sound and the Fury* by first calling attention to the way in which this novelistic *tour de force* is constructed: "Faulkner did not think in terms of an orderly narrative and then shuffle the parts like a pack of cards." To think of it in this way is to miss the point entirely. Rather, the order of the novel reflects a way of perceiving the world. Faulkner told the Compson story as he saw and understood it and "could not have told the story in any other way."[1] He, of course, was seeking new fictional strategies and was following the lead of writers like Joseph Conrad and Ford Madox Ford who had experimented with the idea of writing novels with a deliberately confused and dislocated time sequence.[2]

1. Jean-Paul Sartre, "Time in Faulkner: *The Sound and the Fury*," in *William Faulkner: Three Decades of Criticism*, ed. Frederick J. Hoffman and Olga W. Vickery (New York: Harcourt, Brace, & World, Inc., 1963), 226.
2. Ford had written just five years before the appearance of *The Sound and the Fury*: "It became very early evident to us that what was the matter with the novel was that it went straight forward whereas in your gradual making acquaintanceship with your fellows you never

Many were at first "put off" by the narrative sequence in *The Sound and the Fury*. Recognition of the effectiveness of Faulkner's style came only after Conrad Aiken spoke up in 1939:

> If one considers these queer sentences not simply by themselves, as monsters of grammar or awkwardness, but in their relation to the book as a whole, one sees a functional reason and necessity for their being as they are. They parallel in a curious and perhaps inevitable way, and not without aesthetic justification, the whole elaborate method of *deliberately withheld meaning*, of progressive and partial and delayed disclosure, which so often gives characteristic shape to the novels themselves. It is a persistent offering of obstacles, a calculated system of screens and obtrusions, of confusions and ambiguous interpolations and delays, with one express purpose; and that purpose is simply to keep the form—and the idea—fluid and unfinished, still in motion, as it were, and unknown, until the dropping into place of the very last syllable.[3]

But Sartre's contention is that, with all its technical virtuosity, "nothing happens" in *The Sound and the Fury;* "the story does not progress." He attributes this suspension of forward action to what he calls Faulkner's "metaphysic of time," which he claims ends up destroying time. But this defect is not peculiar to Faulkner, according to Sartre. Most of the great artists of our day "have tried, each in his own way, to mutilate time." In addition to Faulkner he mentions Proust, Joyce, Dos Passos, Gide, and Virginia Woolf. He says that some of them have deprived time "of past and future and reduced it to the pure intuition of the moment; others, like Dos Passos, make it a limited and mechanical memory. Proust and Faulkner have simply decapitated it; they have taken away its future—that is to say, the dimension of free

do go straight forward. You must first get [your character] in with a strong impression, and then work backwards and forwards over his past. . . . We saw that life did not narrate, but made impressions on our brains." See Ford Madox Ford, *Joseph Conrad, a Personal Remembrance* (London: Gerald Duckworth & Co. Ltd., 1924), 180.

3. Conrad Aiken, "William Faulkner: The Novel as Form," in *William Faulkner: Three Decades of Criticism*, 138.

choice and act." [4] Sartre's criticism, then, has little to do with Faulkner's methods. What he does review is the metaphysic which informs *The Sound and the Fury.*

If we examine Sartre's essay carefully, however, we soon discover, as many recent critics have, that Sartre makes no distinction between Faulkner and his characters. As John W. Hunt puts it, "one need not deny that psychologically driven, haunted, and confused people populate [Faulkner's] novels, but it is a mistake to conclude that because his characters are confused he is himself confused." There is no doubt that violence, chaos, and decadence are themes which resonate throughout the Faulkner canon, but they are part of his grand strategy. And we must not conclude that they are there "because Faulkner himself is 'at home in this murkey, demonic world,' or because 'his psyche is completely out of control.'" [5] Instead, they are part of a total vision which gathers all kinds of attitudes toward time under the umbrella of his own understanding of the nature of time.

Sartre, however, does not see this. He takes hold of one particular attitude toward time that is displayed by a type of character that appears in the novels and calls that attitude Faulkner's. In one especially revealing passage in his essay he suggests that the theme of *The Sound and the Fury* is man's imprisonment in time:

> This is the true subject of the novel. And if the technique adopted by Faulkner seems at first to be a negation of time, that is because we confuse time with chronology. Dates and clocks were invented by man: ". . . constant speculation regarding the position of mechanical hands on an arbitrary dial which is a symptom of mind-function. Excrement Father said like sweating" (96). To reach real time, we must abandon these devices, which measure nothing: ". . . time is dead as long as it is being clicked off by little wheels; only

4. Sartre, "Time in Faulkner," 226, 230.
5. John W. Hunt, *William Faulkner: Art in Theological Tension,* (Syracuse: Syracuse University Press, 1965), 7.

when the clock stops does time come to life" (104). Quentin's breaking his watch has, therefore, a symbolic value; it forces us to see time without the aid of clocks.[6]

It may well be that "it is man's misfortune to be confined in time," but it does not necessarily follow that "this is the true subject of the novel." It is clearly one of the major motifs, but in the last or Dilsey section of the novel, there is yet another motif which contradicts the idea that man is enthralled in time. In this section we are led to believe that man is able to transcend time and to endure "the slings and arrows of outrageous fortune." Dilsey's language, her whole way of being in the world, is manifestly transcendent. For her, it is not a misfortune *to be* in time, because man's destiny (*her* destiny) is caught up in the "ricklickshun en de blood of de Lamb!" This must be considered of the essential Faulkner as much as the Quentin section, because one cannot arbitrarily choose one motif over another and identify it with the author. We can hear Sartre out, then, knowing that a sharp distinction between Faulkner and his characters must be kept in mind.

SARTRE'S COMPLAINT

The thrust of Sartre's complaint against Faulkner (as equated with Quentin) is felt in the analogy used to describe the Faulknerian vision of the world. Sartre says that that vision may be "compared to that of a man sitting in a convertible looking back." The road, as it stretches out behind the car, becomes time. Although the car speeds on down the road, the traveller never faces the front (or the future) but has his attention always directed to the road just travelled (or the past). Thus, the past begins to gain a "surrealistic quality; its outline is hard, clear, immutable. The indefinable and elusive present is helpless before it; it is full of holes through which past things, fixed, motionless and silent, evade it."[7]

6. Sartre, "Time in Faulkner," 226.   7. *Ibid.*, 228.

According to Sartre, the present that exists for Faulkner has two distinctive qualities. In the first place, it is irrational. In attempting to describe this quality, Sartre likens it to a thief who suddenly comes upon us and then disappears. Or, he says, "one present, emerging from the unknown, drives out another present," which means that we can never grasp any discreet moment as the "now." Or, to return to the image of the man riding in the car, the present is that slippery and unmanageable instant when "flickering and wavering points of light, which become trees, men, and cars," appear all at once, only to become fixed objects of the landscape stretching out behind.[8] Sartre attributes this flaw in Faulkner's present to his lack of a meaningful future, for our attention is exclusively directed to what has already happened. There are, of course, many passages in the novels that substantiate what Sartre says. For example, in *Light in August* we read quite unexpectedly: "The arm which she held jerked free. She did not believe that he had intended to strike her; she believed otherwise, in fact. But the result was the same. As he faded on down the road, the shape, the shadow, she believed that he was running. She could hear his feet for some time after she could no longer see him. She did not move at once. She stood as he had left her, motionless, downlooking, as though waiting for the blow which she had already received."[9] Here we are precipitately thrown into Bobbie Allen's consciousness. She and Joe Christmas have been talking, and the action of his striking her is not described until after it has happened and then only in the most indirect way.

The second characteristic of the present, which has already been hinted at, is what Sartre calls the sense of "suspension" that envelops Faulknerian time. He writes, "I use this word [suspension [10]], for lack of a better one, to indicate a kind of arrested motion in time." That is because the pres-

8. *Ibid.,* 226, 228.
9. Faulkner, *Light in August* (New York: Random House, Inc., 1950), 164.   10. The French word used here is "l'enfoncement."

ent does not contain within itself any hints of or motions toward the future: "Faulkner appears to arrest the motion at the very heart of things; moments erupt and freeze, then fade, recede and diminish, still motionless." [11] There is, for example, a passage in which Christmas seems not to be responsible for his own actions and views them from an anterior vantage point: "He seemed to watch his hand as if from a distance. He watched it pick up a dish and swing it up and back and hold it there while he breathed deep and slow, intensely cogitant. He heard his voice say aloud, as if he were playing a game: 'Ham,' and watched his hand swing and hurl the dish crashing into the wall, the invisible wall, waiting for the crash to subside and silence to flow completely back before taking up another one." [12]

Then in a later passage in the same novel, Christmas, in thinking about the murder of Joanna Burden before it actually happens, thinks of it in the past tense. He broods:

> Then he would leave. And before the door had shut and the bolt had shot to behind him, he would hear the voice again, monotonous, calm, and despairing, saying what and to what or whom he dared not learn nor suspect. And as he sat in the shadows of the ruined garden on that August night three months later and heard the clock in the courthouse two miles away strike ten and then eleven, he believed with calm paradox that he was the volitionless servant of the fatality in which he believed that he did not believe. He was saying to himself *I had to do it* already in the past tense; *I had to do it. She said so herself.*[13]

These revelations of Bobbie Allen's and Joe Christmas's mental processes illustrate Sartre's point about as well as anything. Their modes of existence seem to be curious combinations of determinism, on the one hand, and irrationality, on the other. They seem to be lashed about by Fate, which Kierkegaard says is "precisely the unity of necessity and

11. Sartre, "Time in Faulkner," 226–27.
12. *Light in August*, 208.   13. *Ibid.*, 244–45.

189

chance." [14] But still, what we have in these three passages just cited is a description of the way these particular characters, not Faulkner, inhabit time. They live for the "specious moment." They have lost touch with the eternal and have therefore lost touch with themselves. Instead of being able to transcend the categories of time, they become victims of time. Indeed, Joe Christmas becomes imprisoned by that past precisely because he *has* no past; he is driven to search for a past that will keep on eluding him. But in this process we have learned little or nothing about Faulkner's own attitude toward time. Although Satre's study sheds a great deal of light on the novels' preoccupation with the past, it is the characters, not Faulkner himself, who are entombed in this living death. A more balanced examination of the Faulkner canon will show a much broader and more comprehensive view of time than Sartre credits him.

14. Kierkegaard, *The Concept of Dread*, trans. with introduction and notes by Walter Lowrie (Princeton: Princeton University Press, 1946), 87.

15

Varieties
of Time
in the
Novels

OLGA W. VICKERY, a most astute critic, says that Faulkner's concept of time "constitutes a distinct facet of his concern with the truth about man. Time, as he sees it, is a necessary condition of existence."[1] Indeed, it is hard to think about any of the major characters of the novels without also thinking about the various ways in which they indwell time. Moreover, many make explicit comments about time: the reporter in *Pylon*, Dilsey, the Compsons, Ratliff, Mr. Hooper in *Mosquitoes*, just to mention a few. In addition, there is usually a time motif operating behind the incidents Faulkner describes.

TEMPLE DRAKE AND THE CLOCK MOTIF

One of the most effective symbolic devices Faulkner uses is frequent reference to clocks and watches—especially those that are broken and fail to keep proper time. How people respond to the various timepieces around them will tell us a great deal about the modalities of their existence. There are, of course, the many timepieces that appear in *The Sound and*

1. Olga W. Vickery, "Faulkner and the Contours of Time," *The Georgia Review*, XII (Spring, 1958), 191.

the Fury, already alluded to, but an equally brilliant use of the clock motif occurs in *Sanctuary.* In this novel, Temple Drake is abstracted from her normal surroundings and taken to Miss Reba's by Popeye. In this artificial situation, time (as well as space) takes on a fixed and almost claustrophobic quality for her: "The shades blew steadily in the windows with faint rasping sounds. Temple began to hear a clock. It sat on the mantel above a grate filled with fluted green paper. The clock was of flowered china, supported by four china nymphs. It had only one hand, scrolled and gilded, halfway between ten and eleven, lending to the otherwise blank face a quality of unequivocal assertion, as though it had nothing to do with time."[2] Temple has become an object among other objects. She is like the nymphs on the clock, like the prostitutes who work there at Miss Reba's place. She has lost almost all remnants of what Kierkegaard calls "subjectivity." Hence time becomes something that can be measured like all other objects. It is finite.

Just a few paragraphs later Faulkner further illuminates the consciousness of the prone Temple by slightly turning the many-faceted time metaphor: "The china figures which supported the clock gleamed in hushed smooth flexions: knee, elbow, flank, arm and breast in attitudes of voluptuous lassitude. The glass face, become mirror-like, appeared to hold all reluctant light, holding in its tranquil depths a quiet gesture of moribund time, one-armed like a veteran of the wars. Half past ten oclock. Temple lay in the bed, looking at the clock, thinking about half-past-ten-oclock." Two pages later the oppressiveness of time continues to push down on her: "She thought about half-past-ten-oclock in the morning. Sunday morning, and the couples strolling to church. She remembered it was still Sunday, looking at the fading peaceful gesture of the clock. Maybe it was half-past-ten-oclock. Then I'm not here, she thought. This is not me."[3] The cumulative effect is deadening. Nothing seems to happen, and she

2. William Faulkner, *Sanctuary* (New York: The Modern Library, 1958), 177.   3. *Ibid.,* 179–80, 182.

seems to be nobody. That is because she has abandoned all self-determination and has placed herself at the disposal of Fate. She does not attempt to make the infinite choice of the self, much less understand her self to be in any way related to the Power that originally posited it. She is completely at the mercy of circumstance and sees time to be nothing but successiveness. It is no wonder she acts and talks like a man-nequin much of the time. Her life, in Kierkegaardian terms, has become "objectified."

There are further references within the same episode at Miss Reba's which make us even more convinced that noth-ing has happened. They concern her own timepiece: "There was still a little light in the room. She found that she was hearing her watch; had been hearing it for some time. She discovered that the house was full of noises, seeping into the room muffled and indistinguishable, as though from a dis-tance. A bell rang faintly and shrilly somewhere; someone mounted the stairs in a swishing garment. The feet went on past the door and mounted another stair and ceased. She listened to the watch." But even with a new timepiece, time does not seem to advance. The author tells us that "for two hours she had lain undisturbed, listening," but nothing hap-pened: "Again time had overtaken the dead gesture behind the clock crystal: Temple's watch on the table beside the bed said half-past-ten." And as if that were not enough to give us the feeling of mechanization and objectification, Faulkner tells us that later on a "mechanical piano began to play." [4] Temple is under the sway of time. Or, in Kierkegaard-ian terms, she lives so much within the limits of time and time alone that she has no sense of the present. The moment or instant she so desperately has lived for has no content whatever, for it is a parody of the true present which is dis-covered only by those who stay in touch with the Eternal. Much to her bafflement, Temple's life failed to have any real excitement for her precisely because it was directed solely

4. *Ibid.*, 183, 189.

193

toward capturing the stimulation that was supposed to accompany the instant. The instant, so understood, is completely illusory. This is borne out by the fact that no matter
how sensual the circumstances are that surround her, she
seems either to be completely impassive or completely captive to a raging passion. In either case, she does not possess
herself in any significant way. Nothing happens to *her* because she has no self for anything to happen to. Or, alternatively, we could say that everything *happens* to her in that
she does not seek to control her own destiny. She has no
relish for the infinite or the eternal and has assigned herself
to finitude. When anyone attempts to tear her away from the
life of immediacy, she balks. Kierkegaard was describing her
type when he wrote:

> When [such] a man is supposed to be happy he imagines
> that he is happy (whereas viewed in the light of the truth
> he is unhappy), and in this case he is generally very far from
> wishing to be torn away from that delusion. On the con-
> trary, he becomes furious, he regards the man who does
> this as his most spiteful enemy, he considers it an insult,
> something near to murder, in the sense that one speaks of
> killing joy. What is the reason for this? The reason is that
> the sensous nature and the psycho-sensuous completely
> dominate him; the reason is that he lives in the sensuous
> categories agreeable/disagreeable, and says goodbye to truth
> etc.; the reason is that he is too sensuous to have the cour-
> age to venture to be spirit or to endure it.[5]

Temple is about as far as one can get from understanding
oneself as a spirit. The more she grasps for an emotional
"kick," the more it eludes her; the more she seeks to live for
the moment, the more it escapes her—all because she has no
concept of herself as a self.

In short, *time* is falsified when it is submitted to the mechanization of a clock just as *experience* is falsified when it is
submitted to any sort of objectification. That is why we have

5. Søren Kierkegaard, *The Sickness unto Death,* in *Fear and Trem-*
bling and The Sickness unto Death, trans. with introduction and notes
by Walter Lowrie (Princeton: Princeton University Press, 1954), 176.

to agree with Mr. Compson when he says to Quentin in the imaginary conversation, "Time is dead as long as it is being clicked off by little wheels; only when the clock stops does time come to life." [6] Professor Vickery well observes that all mechanical devices for measuring time in the novels merely "record history which consists of events in time, not time itself. If man confuses the two, the inventions meant to order his relation to time completely destroy it." Time, she says, is nothing more than the medium in which man lives; it is found not in some objectifiably measurable way, but in the actions of daily living. If a man "relies exclusively on the clock, he becomes, in the extreme case, a mechanical man, like Mr. Hooper of *Mosquitoes*, murmuring, 'Well, well. I must run along. I run my day to schedule.' " [7] But if one lives in the present as the eternal, then one's life is filled to the brim and overflowing.

JASON COMPSON AND TIME AS THE MAIN CHANCE

In the appendix to *The Sound and the Fury*, Faulkner made one last attempt to characterize Jason Compson: "the first sane Compson since before Culloden and (a childless bachelor) hence the last. Logical rational contained and even a philosopher in the old stoic tradition." [8] But in his "sanity" and "logic" he successfully steered clear of any entangling relationships with anyone else and used all the artfulness and skill he could muster to isolate himself from all the others in the Compson family who were caught up in the vortex of self-destruction. At bottom, Jason was an aesthete, whose aestheticism takes several different forms. [9]

6. Faulkner, *The Sound and the Fury*, in *The Sound and the Fury and As I Lay Dying* (New York: Random House, Inc., 1946), 104.
7. Vickery, *"Faulkner and the Contours of Time,"* 193.
8. *The Sound and the Fury*, 16.
9. Kierkegaard's Judge William notes, "Great as the differences within the aesthetical domain may be, all the stages have this similarity, that spirit is not determined as spirit but is immediately determined. The differences may be extraordinary, all the way from complete stupidity (Aandløshed) to the highest degree of cleverness

In the first place, what Faulkner calls the "rational" process in Jason places him in Kierkegaard's category of the aesthetical, for the person who "thinks about" life without making the either/or decision (the metaphysician) dwells in the most refined form of aestheticism. He is like the man who builds a castle but decides to live in a shack nearby. Jason's "rationality," however, was not so rarefied as the metaphysician's. He used his "sanity" to hold his own with the Snopses, to defraud his niece out of money rightfully hers, to fend off the accusing honesty of Dilsey—"his sworn enemy since his birth and mortal one" since the day she "divined by simple clairvoyance" that he was stealing Miss Quentin's monthly check. These were mostly "holding actions" and had no creative purpose to them. But then Jason also used his "sanity" to establish himself in the classic aesthetical posture—that of the bachelor. We have already seen how Judge William urges his young friend to marry, for marriage is the paradigmatic state.[10] But the Judge also makes an astute observation about bachelorhood and *time:* "The man who never marries is an unfortunate, either to an observer or to himself—in his eccentricity he will find time a burden."[11] One point is plain: time becomes a burden for the bachelor because he has to spend so much of it in avoiding commitments, which is precisely what Jason feels he has to do.

Thus, the aesthete may view time in one of two ways: *Either* one may be carried away so completely by time that one's life is volatilized to the point where time, as such, has no significance whatsoever (like one who is "out of it," not "present" to oneself, and so on), *or* time may be broken down into equal finite moments that begin to have value like other homogeneous measurable quanta (money, for exam-

---

(Aandrighed), but even at the stage where cleverness is evident the spirit (Aanden) is not determined as spirit but as talent. . . . Personality immediately determined is not spiritual but physical." *Either/Or*, II, 185.   10. See chapter eleven above.

11. Kierkegaard, *Stages on Life's Way*, trans. Walter Lowrie (Princeton: Princeton University Press, 1945), 121.

ple). Jason's view was primarily the latter. For him, time could be spent like money because it was interchangeable with money, which was interchangeable with people, who were interchangeable with time, and so on in a grinding circle. Therefore, when time is spent uselessly (in attempting to carry off a marriage, for example), one is wasting it, and wasting time, like wasting money, is the cardinal sin in Jason's book. It is no wonder the aesthete considers time a burden—one has to be so careful about the way one uses it— and it is no wonder that the aesthete wants so desperately to escape it.

Jason's method of escape was to attempt to gain time by planning for "tomorrow." Whereas Quentin was trapped by the past, Jason was enchanted by the future. He always had one eye cocked for "the main chance." Quentin was obsessed by the chivalric tradition inherited from his father, but Jason considered himself the epitome of practicality in that he was always on the lookout for a "good deal." He was concerned about "blood" and "family" only if there was some obvious benefit to be derived from them. He saw no intrinsic value in one's heritage as such. He had, of course, what he called "position" in Jefferson, and this had to be maintained. But position was important only because he felt it could give him control over others. As Hunt says, the meaning of his life lay in his ability to manipulate the lives of others for his own personal gain: "Benjy, Dilsey, Caddy, and Miss Quentin, certainly, but also Lorraine and Mrs. Compson as well as the pigeons and sparrows in the courthouse yard." [12] And the success of his manipulations was measured almost exclusively in terms of money. As Kierkegaard points out in *The Present Age*, when all else has failed, money is the one thing to be desired because it is only "representative, an abstraction." If people are dealt with in monetary terms, they become abstractions, and the individual does not have to become involved with them as persons. This, of course, was the

12. John W. Hunt, *William Faulkner: Art in Theological Tension*, (Syracuse: Syracuse University Press, 1965), 68–69.

way Jason treated almost everyone, and the section of *The Sound and the Fury* written from his point of view may really be considered an essay on avarice and greed, or, if we want to use Kierkegaardian terms, an essay on objectification and abstraction.

Because Jason thought of people as objects or quanta which can be bartered, Kierkegaard would say that Jason lived in a world that was fundamentally finite and determined. That he lacked appreciation for the Infinite or the Eternal is explicitly stated in the appendix: Jason thought "nothing whatever of God one way or the other." And in the novel proper when he gives any thought to ultimate powers, he believes he can manipulate them like he does people: "From time to time he passed churches, unpainted frame buildings with sheet iron steeples, surrounded by tethered teams and shabby motorcars, and it seemed to him that each of them was a picket-post where the rear guards of Circumstance peeped fleetingly back at him. 'And damn You too,' he said, 'See if You can stop me,' thinking of himself, his file of soldiers . . . dragging Omnipotence down from His throne." [13]

Jason dwelt in a world that was "desperately narrow-minded and mean-spirited" because he allowed himself to be entirely engulfed by finitude. Kierkegaard notes that a person like Jason, who is "worldly," ultimately refuses to escape the debilitating effects of time. He imagines himself too comfortable to give it up and to leap into the uncertainty of the infinite. But the worldly man is to be pitied, because the principal object of his life becomes "the indifferent" (the finite), and to be worldly means precisely to attribute infinite value to the indifferent: "The worldly view always clings fast to the difference between man and man, and naturally it has no understanding of the one thing needful (for to have that is spirituality), and therefore no understanding of the narrowness and meanness of mind which is exemplified in hav-

13. *The Sound and the Fury*, 322.

ing lost one's self—not by evaporation in the infinite, but by being entirely finitized, by having become, instead of a self, a number, just one man more, one more repetition of this everlasting *Einerlei*." This is exactly Jason Compson's dilemma. In his drive for control over others, he loses interest in himself as a self and becomes only one among the many. Everyone, including Jason himself, has become an object among objects. As Kierkegaard says, he "forgets what his name is (in the divine understanding of it), does not dare to believe in himself, finds it too venturesome a thing to be himself, far easier and safer to be . . . a cipher in the crowd." [14] That this passage from *The Sickness unto Death* is appropriate to Jason is revealed by the people outside his control who are unmoved by his claims to "power." This indifferent attitude reaches its climax on the fateful day of the chase after Miss Quentin. The sheriff is unimpressed with Jason's pleas and threats, the Negroes at Mottson are less than eager to drive him back to Jefferson, no one becomes wrought up about his plight: "Some looked at him as they passed, at the man sitting quietly behind the wheel of a small car, with his invisible life ravelled out about him like a wornout sock." [15]

This touch of pathos is, of course, not surprising when we consider Jason's modality of existence. He rages around the Compson place with apparent self-importance, but this represents more bluster than assurance, because he has no self to be assured of. He has given himself over to the dialectic: agreeable/disagreeable; good fortune/misfortune. A mild form of paranoia develops at the last so that even the natural environment seems hostile to him: "I had gotten beggar lice and twigs and stuff all over me, inside my clothes and shoes and all, and then I happened to look around and I had my hand right on a bunch of poison oak. The only thing I couldn't understand was why it was just poison oak and not a snake or something." [16] He is pathetic in that he *suffers* external forces to shape his life. He is therefore comical, in

14. *The Sickness unto Death*, 166–67.
15. *The Sound and the Fury*, 329.   16. *Ibid.*, 258.

Kierkegaard's terms, because of the many contradictions that crop up in his life.

It is of prime importance to notice that Jason is not the *purely* immediate man because he does possess a somewhat ironic view of himself. Though he always believes the contradictions to have originated outside himself (like the complete aesthete), he sometimes gains enough distance from himself to see the irony of his own situation. The comical way in which he expresses himself in the passage just cited is by no means an isolated phenomenon and is indicative of his ability to achieve a degree of self-consciousness. He has, for example, long resented the fact that his father had sold a large section of the Compson estate so that Quentin might be able to attend Harvard, but he can also see the humor in his own plight: "I says so I never had university advantages because at Harvard they teach you how to go for a swim at night without knowing how to swim and at Sewanee they dont even teach you what water is. I says you might send me to the state University; maybe I'll learn how to stop my clock with a nose spray and then you can send Ben to the Navy I says or to the cavalry anyway, they use geldings in the cavalry." [17] Underneath this harmless irony, however, is fright, hatred, and despair. Jason is never able to make the leap out of the border zone, irony, into the ethical. He is too attached to the finite. In the complaint about selling the pasture, it is his belief that the very source of existence (money) has been squandered; at least a portion of the proceeds should have been saved for him in order to reinforce his existence.

Jason's attachment to the finite world reaches its grossest proportions in his treatment of Caddy. In the years that he has resented the money spent on Quentin, he has also harbored ill feelings about the money spent on Caddy's "make-do" wedding. The most galling aspect of that whole episode is the fact that his one chance to become established in the

17. *Ibid.,* 213–14.

business world was thwarted when the marriage broke down and his connections with Herbert Head's bank were abruptly severed. He therefore gains his sweetest revenge when Caddy comes *incognito* to Mr. Compson's funeral and agrees to pay Jason $100 to let her see her baby. It is an excruciating scene:

> I told Mink to drive to the depot. He was afraid to pass the stable, so we had to go the back way and I saw her standing on the corner under the light and I told Mink to drive close to the walk and when I said Go on, to give the team a bat. Then I took the raincoat off of her and held her to the window and Caddy saw her and sort of jumped forward.
>
> "Hit 'em, Mink!" I says, and Mink gave them a cut and we went past her like a fire engine. "Now get on that train like you promised," I says. I could see her running after us through the back window. "Hit 'em again," I says, "Let's get on home." When we turned the corner she was still running.
>
> And so I counted the money again that night and put it away, and I didn't feel so bad. I says I reckon that'll show you.

Is this the work of a man who is "present"? Or is he so obsessed with something else (in this case, money) that he has removed himself from the sphere in which personal encounter might successfully take place? This man can *never* be present to himself because he is so desperately in search of the money with which to reinforce himself, and his desperation does not abate. He even manages to think of Benjy in monetary terms by suggesting that he either be rented to a sideshow—"there must be folks somewhere that would pay a dime to see him"—or perhaps he should be sent to the state asylum in order to derive some "benefit from the taxes we pay."[18]

Moreover, the one human attachment he attempts to maintain is to a Memphis whore, Lorraine, whom he visits once a month: "Last time I gave her forty dollars. Gave it to her. I never promise a woman anything nor let her know what I'm going to give her. That's the only way to manage them. If you

18. *Ibid.*, 222–23, 214, 329.

cant think of any other way to surprise them, give them a bust in the jaw." His relation to women is like his relation to time. Moments are numerable, interchangeable, all having the same value. The whore (time) does not even enjoy an "economic" contract. The relationship is more elusive than that, more tenuous. He "gives" her what *he* wants to give. But then his attitude toward Lorraine is nothing new. His misogyny is found throughout the novel. Indeed, the section written from his point of view begins and ends with the well-known remark, "Once a bitch always a bitch," and at another point he complains, "I have all the women I can take care of now if I married a wife she'd probably turn out to be a hophead or something." This aestheticism reminds one of the "In Vino Veritas" section of *Stages on Life's Way.* Jason's crudity would have excluded him from that fastidious little circle, but they doubtlessly would have applauded his basic attitude toward women.[19]

Naturally, the most devastating thing that could happen to an individual like Jason would be the loss of any of the quanta he attempted to hoard—whether people, money, or time. Faulkner is at his best when he writes of the two episodes in which money is pried from this tight-fisted, middle-aged miser. First, he is shown in his futile efforts to beat "a bunch of damn eastern jews" at cotton speculation and is confident he can: " 'I know I'm right,' I says. 'It's a sucker game, unless a man gets inside information from somebody that knows what's going on. I happen to be associated with some people who're right there on the ground. They have one of the biggest manipulators in New York for an adviser. Way I do it,' I says, 'I never risk much at a time. It's the fellow that thinks he knows it all and is trying to make a killing with three dollars that they're laying for. That's why they are in the business.' " But they get the best of him, and he is not even aware of it when it happens. Later in the afternoon, he receives a telegram from his New York "connections":

19. *Ibid.,* 211, 264. See also chapter eight above.

I opened it, just to see what kind of lie they'd tell me this time. They must be in one hell of a shape if they've got to come all the way to Mississippi to steal ten dollars a month. Sell, it says. The market will be unstable, with a general downward tendency. Do not be alarmed following government report."

"How much would a message like this cost?" I says. He told me.

"They paid it," he says.

"Then I owe them that much," I says. "I already knew this. Send this collect," I says, taking a blank. Buy, I wrote, Market just on point of blowing its head off. Occasional flurries for purpose of hooking a few more country suckers who haven't got in to the telegraph office yet. Do not be alarmed. "Send this collect," I says.[20]

The harder he tries to consolidate himself in the face of a highly volatilized existence by acquiring and hoarding, the more quickly the money (and hence his self) slips away from him. It reaches its culmination, of course, in Miss Quentin's theft of the $3000.

Jason's concern with money, it should be noted, was a lifelong characteristic. He and a childhood chum *"made kites on the back porch and sold them for a nickel a piece, he and the Patterson boy. Jason was the treasurer."* The Negro boy, Versh, put his finger on early signs of fascination with possessions. He noted that Jason, when a child, always walked around with his hands in his pockets: " 'Jason going to be a rich man,' . . . Versh said. 'He holding his money all the time.' " Even his physique revealed something of his rapacity: " 'If you keep them hands out your pockets, you could stay on your feet,' Versh said. 'You cant never get them out in time to catch yourself, fat as you is.' "[21] When asked what all this meant, Faulkner confirmed Versh's diagnosis: "That was a mannerism, keeping his hands in his pockets, to me that presaged his future, something of greediness and grasping, selfishness. That he may have kept his hands in his pocket to guard whatever colored rock that he

20. *The Sound and the Fury*, 210, 261.   21. *Ibid.*, 113, 55, 43.

had found that was to him, represented the million dollars he would like to have some day." [22] In sum, Jason was going to give time (existence) a meaning (neither the eternity of the Greeks nor the "present" of faith had any sort of claim on him) by hoarding instants, which are monetary tokens. He stood in no ethical relation to anyone or even to himself. He therefore decided he would overcome fugitive time by an absolute relation to an abstract and specious *telos*—accumulation. He would attempt to shore-up his existence by acquisition. The only difficulty was that his "possessions" were finally of no help: money, time as the "instant," people as objects (rather than subjects). Kierkegaard astutely observes: "Nowadays a young man hardly envies anyone his gifts, his art, the love of a beautiful girl, or his fame; he only envies him his money. Give me money, he will say, and I am saved . . . He would die with nothing to reproach himself with, and under the impression that if only he had had the money he might really have lived and might even have achieved something great." [23]

Because Jason possessed so little self-reflection, he was never really aware of his basic problem: despair. That is because he did not know himself to be "spirit" in Kierkegaard's terms. He did not know that he could choose the infinite as well as the finite in himself, or if he knew it, he did not do it. He was ignorant of the fact that he was *really* free to determine his destiny, that he was not entirely submerged in Fate. Judge William would have said that Jason's despair was "unfree" because he had sought "to gain the whole world," which did irreparable damage to his soul. But in the terms of *The Sickness unto Death* we might even wonder if he had a soul: "In unconsciousness of being in despair a man is furthest from being conscious of himself as spirit. But pre-

22. *Faulkner in the University*, ed. Frederick L. Gwynn and Joseph L. Blotner (New York: Random House, Inc., 1965), 263.

23. Kierkegaard, *The Present Age and Of the Difference Between a Genius and an Apostle*, trans. Alexander Dru (New York: Harper and Row, Publishers, Inc., 1962), 40–41.

cisely the thing of not being conscious of oneself as spirit is despair, which is spiritlessness—whether the condition be that of complete deadness, a merely vegetative life, or a life of higher potency the secret of which is nevertheless despair." We could not speak of Jason as being dead or vegetative, but we can say that he was unaware of himself as spirit. Kierkegaard writes:

> Every human existence which is not conscious of itself as spirit, or conscious of itself before God as spirit, every human existence which is not thus grounded transparently in God but obscurely reposes or terminates in some abstract universality [money] or in obscurity about itself takes its faculties merely as active powers, without in a deeper sense being conscious when it has them, which regards itself as an inexplicable something which is to be understood from without—every such existence, whatever it acomplishes, though it be the most amazing exploit, whatever it explains, though it were the whole of existence, however intensely it enjoys life aesthetically—every such existence is after all despair.[24]

Jason's kind is afraid of eternity and does anything to avoid it. He stakes his whole life on the proposition that he can quantify everything just as he quantifies time. Anytime anyone threatens to undo this finite world, he becomes most agitated—whether it is the Exception appearing in time or whether it is the irrational in time that threatens him. Our last glimpse of him reveals a frenzied and infuriated man jumping onto the running board of a moving surrey at the town square, shouting and hitting hysterically at the Negro driving the buggy: "Get to hell on home with him. If you ever cross that gate with him again, I'll kill you!" But he did not have to do that. Five years later, at his mother's death, he committed Benjy to the state asylum, discharged all the Negro servants, and sold the house. He moved "into a pair of offices up a flight of stairs above the supply store containing his cotton ledgers and samples, which he had converted into

---

24. *The Sickness unto Death*, 178, 179.

a bedroom-kitchen-bath." He entertained Lorraine there on the week-ends but still studiously avoided marriage. "He was emancipated now. He was free. 'In 1865,' he would say, 'Abe Lincoln freed the niggers from the Compsons. In 1933, Jason Compson freed the Compsons from the niggers.' " A paradigm of the aesthetic modality! [25]

THE REPORTER AND THE FOLKLORE OF SPEED

Faulkner was once asked what he had hoped to accomplish in *Pylon*. In reply he spoke of the characters who appear in the story:

> They were ephemera and phenomena on the face of a contemporary scene. That is, there was really no place for them in the culture, in the economy, yet they were there, at that time, and everyone knew that they wouldn't last very long, which they didn't. That time of those frantic little aeroplanes which dashed around the country and people wanted just enough money to live, to get to the next place to race again. Something frenetic and in a way almost immoral about it. That they were outside the range of God, not only of respectability, of love, but of God too. *That they escaped the compulsion of accepting a past and a future, that they were—they had no past. They were as ephemeral as the butterfly that's born this morning with no stomach and will be gone tomorrow.*[26] (Emphasis added.)

In effect, these people lived above or beyond time. They had no history; they saw no future for themselves; they had no sense of being an integral part of the present. Indeed, the airplane, which is central to the story, is almost too obvious a device to use in conveying the transcendent quality of the lives of those involved with "the folklore of speed." They were, in their relationship to time (existence), the precise opposite to Jason Compson, who had hoped to finitize time. By contrast, they wanted to infinitize it and remove themselves from any significant relation to the daily, hourly,

25. *The Sound and the Fury*, 336, 18.
26. *Faulkner in the University*, 36.

"timely" concerns of living. Their modalities were, at bottom, the type which Kierkegaard described as fantastical: "that which so carries a man out into the infinite that it merely carries him away from himself and therewith prevents him from returning to himself." [27] So in their aestheticism, they hovered above the finite, the concrete, the necessary, and remained transcendent to all of the concerns that would have engulfed Jason. His *telos* was accumulation, theirs was dissociation.

Because the major figures in the story had no feeling for time and had no roots in time, they were constantly referred to as waifs, an image which carries a great deal of freight in the novel. A cab driver, for instance, asked Jiggs where he was from. " 'Anywhere,' Jiggs said. 'The place I'm staying away from right now is Kansas.' " Jiggs was not able to commit himself to the demands of time and place with his wife and children and consequently joined the flying troupe. He had dissociated himself from finite things so that he could extend himself endlessly over the countryside. The constantly moving group was described vividly by the reporter:

> They aint human, you see. No ties; no place where you were born and have to go back to now and then even if it's just only to hate the damn place good and comfortable for a day or two. From coast to coast and Canada in summer and Mexico in winter, with one suitcase and the same canopener because three can live on one canopener as easy as one or twelve.—Wherever they can find enough folks in one place to advance them enough money to get there and pay for the gasoline afterward. Because they dont need money; it aint money they are after anymore than it's glory because the glory can only last until the next race and so maybe it aint even until tomorrow. And they dont need money except only now and then when they come in contact with the human race like in a hotel to sleep or eat now and then or maybe to buy a pair of pants or a skirt to keep the police off of them.[28]

27. *The Sickness unto Death*, 164.
28. Faulkner, *Pylon* (New York: Random House, Inc., 1962), 16, 46–47.

To Kierkegaard, the person who lives in this kind of world has a self that "leads a fantastic existence in abstract endeavor after infinity, or in abstract isolation, constantly lacking itself, from which it merely gets further and further away." So, Kierkegaard says, the quest for greater and greater speed infinitizes one, and this quest may become so intense that it becomes unendurable not to be able to personify in one's own body and mind the absolute speed—the pure instant. For this reason, a man's intentions are so dreadfully directed outward toward the achievement of the absolute, that he loses himself, cannot become himself. Such a fantastic and speed-demented individual pushes his chances closer and closer to the ultimate of speed—utter volatilization—like Roger Shumann, for whom it was unendurable not to leap over the last safety margin into death. To know that one has this capability and not to pursue it can drive one to distraction, momentary insanity.[29]

The most bizarre symptom of their incredible inability to live in time in any decisive way is illustrated by the "arrangement" between Roger, Laverne, and Jack. The reporter discovered that there was a child that belonged to the group, but it was not clear whose child the little boy was. Then the facts of the case surfaced:

> And so the kid was born on an unrolled parachute in a hangar in California; he got dropped already running like a colt or a calf from the fuselage of an airplane, onto something because it happened to be big enough to land on and then takeoff again. . . . Talk about your immaculate conceptions: born on the unrolled parachute in a California hangar and the doc went to the door and called Shumann and the parachute guy. And the parachute guy got out the dice and says to her 'Do you want to catch these?' and she said 'Roll them' and the dice come out and Shumann rolled high, and that afternoon they fetched the J.P. out on the gasoline truck and so hers and the kid's name is Shumann.[30]

29. *The Sickness unto Death,* 165.   30. *Pylon,* 48–49.

In this kind of world, all the normal human feelings are infinitized, which means that the self is simply "volatilized more and more, at last becoming a sort of abstract sentimentality which is so inhuman it does not apply to any [one] person."[31] So it was with these waifs. Their feelings were not concentrated enough to be directed specifically toward one another.

But the reporter's existence, it turns out, was more fantastical than that of the flyers. He is called a "patron (even if not guardian) saint of all waifs, all the homeless the desperate and the starved." His past is thoroughly ephemeral. At least we can learn where Roger hailed from, and we can date his death by the newspaper copy. But the reporter's origins are totally obscure:

> This was the man whom the editor believed (certainly hoped) to be unmarried, though not through any knowledge or report but because of something which the man's living being emanated—a creature who apparently never had any parents either and who will not be old and never was a child, who apparently sprang full-grown and irrevocably mature out of some violent and instantaneous transition like the stories of dead steamboatmen and mules. If it were learned that he had a brother for instance it would create neither warmth nor surprise anymore than finding the mate to be a discarded shoe in a trashbin. The editor had heard how a girl in a Barricade Street crib said of him that it would be like assessing the invoked spirit at a seance held in a rented restaurant room with a cover charge.[32]

The reporter's existence, like the flyer's, bore no essential relationship to the finite or the necessary; all of them existed in a dimension above time. We are told that the reporter "sprang full-grown" from out of nowhere and that his continued existence was just as tenuous. Such an existence, Kierkegaard says, freed from the definition given to it by necessity, becomes pure possibility. The result is deadening: "Now if possibility outruns necessity, the self runs away from itself, so

31. *The Sickness unto Death*, 164.   32. *Pylon*, 183, 41–42.

that it has no necessity whereto it is bound to return—then this is the despair of possibility. The self becomes an abstract possibility which tires itself out with floundering in the possible, but does not budge from the spot, nor get to any spot, for precisely the necessary is the spot; to become oneself is precisely a movement at the spot. To become is a movement from the spot, but to become oneself is a movement at the spot." [33] The reporter moves nowhere and achieves nothing.

Even the setting for the novel illustrates the rootlessness of modern society. The airfield, constructed under the auspices of the Sewage Board, was created out of a vast "waste land." The city of New Valois, which is celebrating Mardi Gras, has lost touch with the social as well as the religious dimensions of this pre-Lenten festival. The streets are decorated with "the cryptic shieldcaught (i n r i) loops of bunting giving an appearance temporary and tentlike to interminable long corridors of machine plush and gilded synthetic plaster running between anonymous and rentable spaces or alcoves from sunrise to sunset across America." The streets are strewn with "tortured and draggled serpentine and trodden confetti pending the dawn's whitewings—spent tinseldung of Momus' Nilebarge clatterfalque." [34]

This modern, urban society Faulkner so poetically portrays was foreseen by Kierkegaard as the one which would collapse into triviality. It would be an era "without passion," only "momentarily bursting into enthusiasm" (manufactured enthusiasm at that, like Mardi Gras) and then "shrewdly lapsing into repose." It would be a period when symbols—religious *and* secular—instead of conveying their true meaning would become mere decoration ("i n r i" no longer conveys "Jesus of Nazareth, King of the Jews," confetti no longer means "celebration"). For "an age without passion has no values, and everything is transformed into representational ideas" or abstractions. Moreover, it would be an era created by "the Press, which in itself is an abstraction." In this *milieu*, the

33. *The Sickness unto Death,* 169.   34. *Pylon,* 60, 77.

individual loses his identity and is overwhelmed by the power of "a monstrous abstraction, an all-embracing something which is nothing, a mirage—and that phantom is *the public*." [35] *Pylon* is set within such a society. We are told the story from the point of view of the Press (the reporter). It takes place when massive crowds (the public) push down the "tinseldung" strewn street to celebrate a synthetic festival. It is the wasteland described once more.

Within this context it is difficult for time to be much of a reality for anyone. More and more significant toward the end of the novel is the recurrent flash of the searchlight atop the control tower at the airport; it appears "for an instant in a long flick!" and then it is gone. As the reporter becomes particularly sensitive to the ephemeral character of the enterprise he has unwittingly become a part of, the searchlight takes on an eerie symbolic quality for him: "He began to think now. now. NOW. and it came: the long nebulous swordstroke sweeping steadily up from beyond the other hangar until almost overhead and then accelerating with that illusion of terrific strength and speed which should have left a sound, a swish behind it but did not." The major figures in this novel seek to focus their several existences on the "instant," and just as surely as the instant has no eternal reference point but in itself becomes the object of existence, so time becomes abstract, empty, fantastic. It is a time which coincides neither with the Eternal (succession annulled) nor with the finite (time as mere successiveness) but hovers between heaven and earth in a state of suspension. The time indwelt by the figures in *Pylon* is about as close to the time inhabited by Don Juan as we are likely to see in the whole of the Faulknerian canon. Even the news of Roger's fatal crash takes on an evanescent quality: "As they entered a newsboy screamed at them, flapping the paper, the headline: PILOT KILLED. SHUMANN CRASHES INTO LAKE. SECOND FATALITY OF AIRMEET as it too flicked away." And the newspaper is called "the dead

35. *The Present Age*, 33, 39–40, 59–60.

instant's fruit of forty tons of machinery and an entire nation's antic delusion." Time, in such an environment, is unreal: "As the [elevator] cage door clashed behind him, the editor himself reached down and lifted the facedown watch from the stack of papers, from that cryptic staccato cross-sections of an instant crystallised and now dead two hours, though only the moment, the instant: the substance itself not only dead, not complete, but in its very insoluble engima of human folly and blundering possessing a futile and tragic immortality:

FARMERS BANKERS STRIKERS ACREAGE
WEATHER POPULATION." [36]

Later the reporter entered the same elevator cage and was forced by circumstance to think about the day he had just passed through. It had about as much reality and substance as the "damp print of a lifted glass on a bar." But then he was really "not thinking about time," for time, as such, was beyond him. He did not think about "any angle of clockhands on a dial since the one moment of all the future which he could see where his body would need to coincide with time or dial would not occur for almost twelve hours yet." [37] Neither past, present, nor future gain credence in this man's consciousness.

In less than a year after Faulkner published *Pylon* he was asked to review a novel by Jimmy Collins, a newspaper reporter, entitled *Test Pilot*. In this article Faulkner revealed a great deal about what he had hoped to accomplish (but failed to do) in his own novel about the air. He said he had hoped to find in Collins's story the first symptoms of "a folklore of speed":

> It would be a folklore not of the age of speed nor of the men who perform it, but of the speed itself, peopled not by anything human or even mortal but by the clever willful machines themselves carrying nothing that was born and

36. *Pylon*, 247, 240, 111, 85.   37. *Ibid.*, 201.

will have to die or which can even suffer pain, moving without comprehensive purpose toward no discernible destination, producing a literature innocent of either love or hate and of course of pity or terror, and which would be the story of the final disappearance of life from the earth. I would watch them, the little puny mortals, vanishing against a vast and timeless void filled with the sound of incredible engines, within which furious meteors moving in no medium hurtled nowhere, neither pausing nor flagging, forever destroying themselves and one another.[38]

That was in November of 1935.

Although most critics look on *Pylon* as one of Faulkner's lesser accomplishments, it nevertheless is a remarkable piece of writing.[39] It shows how he is able so to insinuate himself into the lives of his characters that he can present the reader a modality of existence that is essentially outside of time. The folklore of speed is escape on a mythic scale. The characters in *Pylon*, as Faulkner himself said, were "outside the range of God, not only of respectability, of love, but of God, too. [They] escaped the compulsion of accepting a past and a future." That is to say, they existed outside time and place altogether—in utter transcendence. In Kierkegaard's terms, they lived almost entirely within the aesthetical stage.

LENA GROVE AND NATURAL TIME

Another prominent time motif in Faulkner's novels may be found in a close examination of his "primitives"—characters such as Lena Grove, the pregnant woman in "Old Man," Sam Fathers in "The Bear," and others whose modalities reflect a close kinship to soil and nature. Professor Vickery says they indwell a kind of time that can be "grasped intuitively as that vital impulse behind all things, manifesting itself in change

38. Faulkner, *Essays, Speeches & Public Letters*, ed. James B. Meriwether (New York: Random House, Inc., 1965), 192.

39. The discerning Professor Vickery is the only major commentator who is willing to concede that this book is something more than a splendid failure. See *The Novels of William Faulkner* (Baton Rouge: Louisiana State University Press, 1959), 145–55.

and yet to be identified in change." Theirs is a cyclical view of time, closely related to the seasonal ebb and flow in nature: "Endlessly, it moves through the recurrent cycles of creation and destruction, each of which is implied in the other, so that although there is continual change and destruction of particular objects and individuals, there is no end to the process itself." [40] Thus, the kind of natural time indwelt by the primitives bears a marked similarity to the time experienced in the psychically determined cosmos of the ancient Greeks. That is to say, it is a finite view of time, which makes no real distinction between succession annulled (eternity) and mere successiveness.[41] In short, eternity is commensurable with time (as would not be true in a pneumatically qualified world) and is continuous with it. Eternity has its ground in *this* world, which is thought to be eternal [42] and yet is obviously temporal (finite) in that time can be objectively measured by the

40. Vickery, "Faulkner and the Contours of Time," 192.

41. Neither does Professor Vickery. She writes that "natural time is characterized by its immediacy. Because its movement is cyclical and because it appears as a continuous process, all time exists in any one moment of it." She has confused the eternity of the Greeks (which is unending time) with the eternity of Christianity (which denotes the timelessness of existence). See Erich Frank, *Philosophical Understanding and Religious Truth* (London: Oxford University Press, 1945), 76, n. 14. His treatment of "Creation and Time" in chapter three is most illuminating.

42. See Frank, *Philosophical Understanding and Religious Truth*, 58: "For the Greeks, the world was god; nature itself was of divine character. The world had its beginning in itself. It had sprung from an original state, chaos or matter, which in a somewhat changed form, as its true 'nature,' remained inherent in it. To be sure, Plato in his transcendent Idea of Good visualized an absolute 'Principle' beyond this world. He even believed that this world had been created by a divine Being—anticipating in some measure the Jewish-Christian concept of creation. But the Platonic god did not really create the world out of nothing; he only transformed the chaos into cosmos. God was not a true creator, he was merely an artificer, an architect who had shaped the world out of the everlasting matter which was there, and which he had not created. This universe he built in conformity with the Idea—which again was an everlasting pattern independent of the artificer. The notion of true creation is only to be found in the Jewish-Christian religion."

ceaseless revolutions of the firmament. Or, as Kierkegaard says, in paganism "there is no historical starting-point. The individual merely discovers in time that he must assume he is eternal. The moment in time is therefore *eo ipso* swallowed up by eternity. In time the individual recollects that he is eternal." [43]

Because of their immediate relation to the eternal, the primitives of Faulkner's imaginary world possess the kind of vision by which the "intellectual sophistication and abstractions of modern society" are brought under judgment.[44] These are the people who can respond naturally and creatively to the abrasive effects of civilization. They do not resist the onslaughts of a technological society; instead, they render impotent the conditions they are in by submerging themselves in the natural and eternal processes, which in the Faulkner canon have rejuvenating and recreative powers. They serve as foils for the "sick" heroes of the novels. For Harry Wilbourne there is the convict of "Old Man," for Bayard Sartoris there are the McCallums, for Joe Christmas there is Lena Grove. They usually serve as correctives and palliatives for the "sickness" found in the novels. In fact, it is possible to argue, as one critic has, that Faulkner's conception of the primitives is "based largely on the very wants and needs of his sick protagonists." [45]

But of all the characters in the Faulknerian world, no one embodies the primitivism we have been describing better than Lena Grove. She not only is the recipient of the healing powers of nature; she becomes the symbol of the natural in its most luxuriant state. The very botanical quality of her name is suggestive. The procreative process going on in her belly sets in motion the narrative of *Light in August,* for she is look-

43. Kierkegaard, *The Concluding Unscientific Postscript,* trans. David F. Swenson and Walter Lowrie (Princeton: Princeton University Press, 1941), 508.

44. Peter Swiggart, "Moral and Temporal Order in *The Sound and the Fury,*" *The Sewanee Review,* LXI, 2 (1953), 234.

45. See Melvin Backman, "Sickness and Primitivism: A Dominant Pattern in William Faulkner's Work," *Accent,* XIV (Winter, 1954), 62.

ing in quiet confidence for the father of her unborn child. Not because she especially wants him, but because he is the biological parent of the foetus. It is not surprising, then, that she is frequently called "earth mother" by critics and is identified with oriental fertility deities. Melvin Backman says she is "like the unceasing murmur of the insects throughout the story, she is part of the never-ending placid current of life . . . ; like a serene goddess sojourning on earth she is served by all men as though they were administrants to Ceres." [46] Conception, birth, life, vitality, patience, endurance —the correctness of these subliminal relations is not important. Faulkner is neither preacher nor scholar; he is a novelist. But because he has drawn a figure of such strength and wealth in her associations with life as opposed to death, we will want to place her next to Dilsey in the list of Faulknerian saints, albeit she is a pagan saint. Even Samuel Yorks is willing to concede that she is different from most of the women found in the novels. He says Faulkner's women are usually destructive in their attitudes and actions toward life, but Lena is an exception. Indeed, the superiority of *Light in August* as a novel rests in its "greater ambivalence" at this point, for Lena represents salvation as well as peril. Hers is "an ironic innocence: by simply 'travelling' and accepting her role as tempter and consoler, lover and mother, she has denied evil." [47] The narrator of the last chapter of the novel sums it up well. In effect, he says that Lena's is a modality of ultimate trust and confidence, born of an almost unearthly wisdom: "I think she was just travelling. I dont think she had any idea

46. *Ibid.,* 68. Robert M. Slabey likens her to Ishtar, Astarte, Cybele, and Isis. She is a "primeval earth mother." See "Myth and Ritual in *Light in August,*" *Texas Studies in Literature and Language,* II, 3 (Fall, 1960), 333. Others associate her with the Blessed Virgin of Bethlehem because she gives birth to her child in an out-of-the-way place and for one brief moment is even linked with the name of Joe Christmas.
47. Samuel A. Yorks, "Faulkner's Woman: The Peril of Mankind," *Arizona Quarterly,* XVIII (Summer, 1961), 128.

of finding whoever it was she was following. I dont think she had ever aimed to, only she hadn't told him yet." But when the appropriate time came, she would be able to tell Byron. In the meantime, "she was just travelling." And at a very leisurely and unconcerned pace.

This tableau of Lena, her child, and Byron Bunch, which is found on the last page of *Light in August*, is merely a reiteration of what one first encounters in the novel: "Sitting beside the road, watching the wagon mount the hill toward her, Lena thinks, 'I have come from Alabama: a fur piece. All the way from Alabama a-walking. A fur piece.' Thinking *although I have not been quite a month on the road I am already in Mississippi, further from home than I have ever been before.*"

Between the placidity and patience which characterize the beginning and ending of the novel come the anguish and sorrow of Joe Christmas, Joanna Burden, Gail Hightower, Percy Grimm, and all the others who are swept up in the high drama of this remarkable work. It is as though Lena, the great earth mother, can absorb within her body the shocks and bruises of the civilization she meets. She is somehow involved in but at the same time above all the pain and travail that goes on around her. She is unmoved by the encroachments of the technological society she meets for the first time. She is, as Slabey points out, "a concrete personification of tranquility, the eternal renewal of life, and the triumph of the 'pure in heart.' " [48] Her modality of existence becomes one in which the temporal is swallowed up in the eternal.

The rhetorical devices Faulkner uses in the novel to describe Lena are of great significance. He frequently resorts to prodigious sentences in order to create the atmosphere of simultaneity. As he said, he wanted to "put everything into one sentence—not only the present but the whole past on which it depends and which keeps overtaking the present, second by second." He not only wanted to capture what hap-

48. Slabey, "Myth and Ritual in *Light in August*," 349.

pens in "the shifting moment" but also all the forces of the past which impinge on this moment.[49] The effect of his technique is powerful. Though certain images tend to come and go and make quick impressions, the general effect is one of fluidity. As Faulkner says in the first chapter after describing Lena's initial birth spasms, "The wagon has not stopped; time has not stopped. The wagon crests the final hill and they see smoke." [50] Even the use of the present tense here is an attempt to overcome the temptation to write exclusively of what has already happened. There are, of course, other figures in the book for whom time *is* a fixed reality. Joe Christmas and Joanna Burden do seem to be imprisoned by the past. But their stories are enclosed within the brackets of Lena's story, and what we are dealing with in her chapters is not a "was" but an "is" outside of time. Moreover, when we reach the end of the novel, time seems to keep on moving as infinite succession. For this reason, we can say that the novel ends, but the story does not.

It is significant that Lena's awareness of the processes that take place outside of her is, at best, limited. She never gains enough self-reflection to be conscious of the passage of time. She worries about neither the past nor the future. Darrel Abel says, "She is fully content with the moment which she occupies and with the bliss of being in it." If she does concern herself with what has already happened, it is only with the immediate past, because the immediate past is so much a part of the present which impinges on her life. At the beginning, Faulkner depicts her walking down the road, "swollen, slow, deliberate, unhurried and tireless as augmenting afternoon itself." Later, when she is not making her way on foot, she is riding in a wagon which "moves slowly, steadily, as if here within the sunny loneliness of the enormous land it were outside of, beyond all time and all haste." In this kind of setting

49. Malcolm Cowley, *The Faulkner-Cowley File* (New York: The Viking Press, 1966), 112.

50. Faulkner, *Light in August* (New York: Random House, Inc., 1950), 25.

and within her kind of consciousness, the measurement of time has no place. Clocks and calendars are superfluous. Abel aptly states that "the duration of things" is measured instead "by the elemental urges and responses of her nature to the immediate surroundings." [51] She feels a birth pang as "the implacable and immemorial earth, but without fear or alarm." She feels hunger and finally decides to buy a can of sardines by "waging a mild battle with that providential caution of the old earth of and with and by which she lives." If she has any awareness of abstract notions or theories, it is not apparent to the reader; instead, "she represents the ordinary naive mankind, inviolably innocent because it cannot enter the realm of ideas." Her simplicity and artlessness prevent her from fathoming even the rather self-centered anguish of old Mrs. Hines who insists on calling the baby "Joey." Lena tells Hightower about Mrs. Hines:

> "She is mixed up someway. And sometimes I get mixed up too, listening, having to . . ." Her eyes, her words, grope, fumble.
> "Mixed up?"
> "She keeps on talking about him like his pa was that . . . the one in jail, that Mr Christmas. She keeps on, and then I get mixed up and it's like sometimes I cant—like I am mixed up too and I think that his pa is that Mr—Mr Christmas too—" She watches him, it is as though she makes a tremendous effort of some kind. "But I know that aint so. I know that's foolish. It's because she keeps on saying it and saying it, and maybe I aint strong good yet, and I get mixed up too. But I am afraid. . . ."
> "Of what?"
> "I dont like to get mixed up. And I am afraid she might get me mixed up, like they say how you might cross your eyes and then you cant uncross . . ." [52]

It is all too complicated for her. Or maybe it would even be more correct to say that she is "too unsophisticated" to com-

---

51. Darrel Abel, "Frozen Movement in *Light in August*," *Boston University Studies in English*, III (Spring, 1957), 37.
52. *Light in August*, 359.

prehend the difference between good and evil. All life, for her, is to be luxuriated in. She does appear to be an epiphany of some exotic Eastern fertility goddess.

Moreover, these are the qualities that make her appear to be closer to the "silent stillness" of the art in the ancient pagan culture that Kierkegaard writes about than to the dynamic art found within the spiritually determined universe of the Christian West. She is caught up in the rhythms of nature. Early in the novel Faulkner says her consciousness is like "a long monotonous succession of peaceful and undeviating changes from day to dark and dark to day again, through which she advanced in anonymous and deliberate wagons as though through a succession of creakwheeled and limpeared avatars, like something moving forever and without progress across an urn." [53] The allusion to Keats's ode is too strong to overlook. She is "the still unravish'd bride of quietness," "the foster-child of silence and slow time" who makes her way across the pages of the frieze-like novel. Around her are the others in "mad pursuit" who "struggle to escape" their subservience to time and circumstance.[54] She does, in fact, seem to possess many qualities that throw her within a cosmos that precedes the liberated and infinite universe of Christianity. Her sensuousness is almost entirely innocent; it does not break out of the form of her body; it is in harmony and accord with its surroundings. Nor is her love concentrated on one object. She loves almost indiscriminately—Lucas, Byron, Hightower, her baby; she even has some feelings for the "nigger" Christmas, whom she has never seen. Her love is thus diffused in the mode of the ancient Greek culture. We would not be amiss to call her "the beautiful personality." And the

53. *Ibid.,* 6.
54. Faulkner had written of his admiration for Keats's poem some half dozen years prior to the publication of *Light in August:* "I read 'Thou still unravished bride of quietness' and found a still water withal strong and potent, quiet with its own strength, and satisfying as bread. That beautiful awareness, so sure of its own power that it is not necessary to create the illusion of force by frenzy and motion." See William Faulkner, "Verse Old and Nascent: A Pilgrimage," *The Double Dealer,* VII, (April, 1925), 130.

conception of time that surrounds her shows how definitely she dwells within a *lebenswelt* comparable to that of ancient Greece. It has been variously described as "natural time," "simultaneity," "the cyclical view," and other terms. It is a conception of time that is in no way assimilable to the eschatological time indwelt by the pneumatically qualified man, but is a time which bears an aesthetic relationship to the eternal, which in the last analysis is no relationship.[55] She inhabits an Edenic world—a world prior to the positing of the radical disjuncture, either/or.

The appropriateness of the close comparison of Lena with the antique Greek cosmos and Eastern fertility religions was borne out by Faulkner himself. In answer to a question about the meaning of the title *Light in August* he replied:

> Oh that was—in August in Mississippi there's a few days somewhere about the middle of the month when suddenly there's a foretaste of fall, it's cool, there's a lambence, a luminous quality of the light, as though it came not from just today but from back in the old classic times. It might have fauns and satyrs and the gods and—from Greece, from Olympus in it somewhere. It lasts just for a day or two, then it's gone, but every year in August that occurs in my country, and that's all the title meant, it was just to me a pleasant evocative title because it reminded me of that time, of a luminosity older than our Christian civilization. Maybe the connection was with Lena Grove, who had something of that pagan quality of being able to assume everything, that's—the desire for that child, she was never ashamed of that child whether it had any father or not, she was simply going to follow the conventional laws of the time in which she was and find its father. But as far as she was concerned, she didn't especially need any father for it, any more than the women that—on whom Jupiter begot children were anxious for a home and a father. It was enough to have had the child. And that was all that meant, just what luminous lambent quality of an older light than ours.[56]

55. "Let the reader remember that a direct God-relationship is aesthetic and is really not a God-relationship, any more than a direct relationship to the absolute is an absolute relationship, because the discrimination of the absolute has not been accomplished." Kierkegaard, *Postscript,* 497.   56. *Faulkner in the University,* 199.

16

Faulkner's
View
of Time

THERE IS, of course, no "official" Faulkner biography to which we may turn for help in understanding his view of time. It is well-known that he carefully avoided publicity and public appearances until long after his reputation was established. Indeed, his passion for privacy even led him to encourage fabrication about his life. What information we have is often inaccurate or whimsical and sentimental as in John Faulkner's *My Brother Bill*.[1] These data are not the kind that will help us discover much about Faulkner's attitude toward time. Just about the only reliable evidence we have are his literary remains—the poetry, the fiction, letters, speeches, and occasional essays. His recorded remarks at Nagano,[2] the University of Virginia, and West Point [3] add to the picture considerably.

As earlier sections of this essay show, there is a variety of

1. John Faulkner, *My Brother Bill* (New York: Trident Press, 1963).
2. Robert A. Jelliffe (ed.), *Faulkner at Nagano* (Tokyo: Kenkyusha Ltd., 1956).
3. Joseph L. Fant and Robert Ashley (eds.), *Faulkner at West Point* (New York: Random House, Inc., 1964).

attitudes toward time displayed by the various characters who appear in the novels. In one way or another we rather extensively examined the viewpoints of Quentin, Temple, Jason, the reporter in *Pylon*, and Lena Grove—each of whom live in time and space in their own highly individualized ways and none of whom could possibly be equated with Faulkner. Quentin and Jason are captives of time; one lives in the past, the other in the future. The reporter and the entourage of flyers in *Pylon* live above and beyond time in a kind of transcendent aestheticism in which no one ever becomes very much committed to anything. Lena, on the other hand, lives in a mythic time, imbued with pagan eternality. Lena's is a "natural time" within which eternity is continuous with temporality.

There are others who could have been dealt with as profitably. It is useful to know, for example, that Popeye has no past and in this sense resembles not only the reporter of *Pylon*, but also Januarius Jones of *Soldier's Pay* as well as Joe Christmas. And that Joanna Burden wishes to live down the past and yet spends hour upon hour remembering. And that Gail Hightower is so caught up in his reveries that at the end of *Light in August* he says, "I know that for fifty years I have not even been clay: I have been a single instant of darkness in which a horse galloped and a gun crashed." These are the people who forget that they not only can transcend the past but also appropriate it for themselves. They do not understand that the past may become part of the living present as one lives by faith.

All this suggests that one of the most fundamental Faulknerian principles has to do with the error of seeing time only in a rational or logical manner. An underlying theme of the novels seems to be that if we insist on seeing time as a purely sequential phenomenon that may be neatly divided into past, present, and future, then our attention may well become uncontrollably fixed on the past. That is because the past is the one aspect of time we think we can hold onto and fix in our field of perception. But, as Professor Vickery reminds us, each new present places the past in a new perspective and what we once *believed* to be static in the past turns out to be almost as fluid as the present. Moreover, the way the past is recalled by one person never seems to coincide with the way others recall it. The effect of attempting to establish oneself in a fixed past, then, is to isolate oneself from the present world:

> Those who make the act of remembering a consecration or a sacred duty gladly accept this isolation for the sake of gaining immunity from time and change for some cherished event or person. Thus, young Bayard Sartoris, Harry Wilbourne, Gail Hightower, and Rosa Coldfield, each in his own way lives in and through his memories. The latter two are, in addition, extreme representatives of a society which, as *Requiem for a Nun* observes, has turned its face "irreconcilably backward toward the old lost battles, the old aborted cause, the old ruined years whose very physical scars ten and twenty and twenty-five changes of season had annealed back into the earth." Clearly, an excessive concern with the past can destroy the continuity of time and paralyze the capacity for action not only in the individual but in society as a whole.[4]

Kierkegaard understands in a much better way what the problem is in this case. It is not just the fact that one lives in the past; it is that one lives outside himself. One of the pseudonyms writes, "The unhappy person is one who has his ideal, the content of his life, the fullness of his consciousness, the essence of his being, in some manner outside himself. He is always absent, never present to himself."[5] This means, then, that the unhappy people are not merely the ones like Quentin and Hightower who live in the past; they are also the principal characters of *Pylon* who never become reconciled to time, or figures like Jason Compson and Flem Snopes whose lives

4. Olga W. Vickery, "Faulkner and the Contours of Time," *The Georgia Review*, XII (Spring, 1958), 194.
5. Søren Kierkegaard, *Either/Or*, I, trans. David F. Swenson and Lillian Marvin Swenson with revisions by Howard A. Johnson (2 vols; Princeton: Princeton University Press, 1959), I, 220.

are lived almost exclusively in terms of the future. The "doomed" ones are those who are absent.

Although it would be somewhat dubious to credit Faulkner with precisely the same attitude toward past and future that Kierkegaard has made explicit, the similarity is remarkable. Any time anyone cannot be present to himself, he is lost; this is the problem for every major tragic figure in the Faulknerian canon. Time is the Enemy from which they flee. Only Dilsey, who lives in time as though it contains eternity, is able to "endure" or "prevail."

In addition to an investigation of the modalities of existence inhabited by the various characters, an analysis of Faulkner's narrative technique also helps reveal his own attitude toward time. The apparent disorderliness of more mature works has been shown to be more than merely perverse. Sartre, of course, says that this particular fictional strategy is used to demonstrate that the only real thing about man's time is the past. Günter Blöcker, however, makes exactly the opposite judgment: The apparent disorderliness is a clue to Faulkner's own way of perceiving the world.[6] It is a "mythical" perception, which is not subject to the customary cause-and-effect explanations of reality. We do not perceive the world and its events, of course, in any orderly fashion but in a confused and irregular way. True to that perception, Faulkner's picture of the world is not so much one of absurdity as it is of simultaneity, where everything is given at the same time. This is why the Benjy section of *The Sound and the Fury* is so brilliant a technique. It may not, in fact, accurately record what kind of thing actually goes on in the mind of an idiot, but it does give us the feeling that everything is happening at once. As Claude-Edmonde Magny says, "It restores for us the image of that synthetic universe of the 'whole of feeling,' . . . in which reality has not yet been broken up into a

6. Günter Blöcker, "William Faulkner," trans. Jacqueline Merriam, in *Faulkner: A Collection of Critical Essays*, ed. Robert Penn Warren (Englewood Cliffs: Prentice-Hall, Inc., 1966), 122f.

multiplicity of appearances by the intervention of clear consciousness."[7] This is why Faulkner tries to say it all "between one Cap and one period."

His view of the world may therefore be seen to be the primordial and primitive view of reality described by the phenomenologists. He is attempting to set forth on paper (in paradoxically a highly sophisticated way) what this preobjective view of the world is like. He is attempting to describe the, as yet, "unfalsified" character of human existence in all its vitality, ruggedness, and genuineness. Blöcker says that this desire accounts for the fact that most of Faulkner's important characters *at first* remain indistinct. They appear, rather, as "voices, as sound-emitting raw material" up and out of the depths of the primordial background and history in which they are imbedded. They are like "a vast whisper, a primeval groan, a rudimentary stammer in which the human, before taking form, is literally ex-pressed."[8]

The more one reads Faulkner, however, the more distinct these voices (characters) become, and we soon discover that we are confronted by a whole and complete world made up of a great many people and families who appear and reappear throughout the novels, whose lives are intertwined by circumstance and choice. What we have is a "total world" which, if it did not pre-exist in the author's mind, at least became clearer and more distinct the more closely he *attended* it.

Because he writes in the way he does, it is rather pointless to get bogged down in a debate about the symbolism in Faulkner. He never objected to the reader's attempt to interpret any part of the novels in any manner; on the other hand, Faulkner himself persistently refused to interpret what was there. He said if elements of the Christian tradition were used in his work, it was only because he found these elements readily available. Therefore, Blöcker is correct when he says that

7. Claude–Edmonde Magny, "Faulkner or Theological Inversion," trans. Jacqueline Merriam, in *Faulkner: A Collection of Critical Essays,* ed. Robert Penn Warren (Englewood Cliffs: Prentice-Hall, Inc., 1966), 77.   8. Blöcker, "William Faulkner," 123.

Faulkner did not have to try to worm his way into the collective subconscious; he found his natural habitat there. His real ability lay "on the other side of skimpy reason. . . . With him, dreaming and composing are one." [9] The way to read the novels, then, is to become a party to his reveries, his dreams, and allow him to move us as he will in and out of the various consciousnesses he exposes. After long association with this omniscient author, we eventually become sensitive to *his* views on the characters he has so carefully described for us, and *his* voice gains some distinction from all the others.

Faulkner tells his myth in a special language. It is, as Blöcker says, the sound neither of poetry nor of fiction; it is a "total language" which attempts to encompass the primordial viewpoint Faulkner has adopted. "It is the language of complete realism, enveloping all of reality, rather than the academic realism which mistakes the material, tangible surfaces of things for the things themselves." One therefore has no need to look for "the meaning" of this symbol or that; one has only to attend to what the author sets before us. Blöcker explains:

> As far as Faulkner is concerned, this means that the mythical creates its own categories, its own language—in short, that the mythical *is* its own language. The mythical point of view excludes any separation of the two; there is no within and without, no here and there, but only an entirety. Faulkner's digressive, violent lyricism is the resonance of the primitive, unhewn rock of humanity. Images and visions flow into one another, the fantastic mingles with the real, the abstract feeds on the blood of things, the senses fraternize in their joint sovereignty over the world, and objects assume personality.[10]

Time, then, for Faulkner is hardly a problem. It *is* for the Compsons, the Sartorises, the Harry Wilbournes, the Gail Hightowers, the fly-boys of *Pylon*, and all the others we have examined, but not for Faulkner. He sees it as probably the

9. *Ibid.*, 124.   10. *Ibid.*

most important ingredient of human existence; but he also understood that we are enslaved by time only if we allow ourselves to be. And he implies that those who "endure" or "prevail" are those who know this about themselves and their world and are willing to risk the pain of choosing themselves, rather than drift along aimlessly in the category of the aesthetical.

IV

*Modalities
of Religiousness*

17

The Religious According to Kierkegaard

THE LAST STEP prior to what Kierkegaard calls the leap into religiousness is infinite resignation. This is the act of concentrating the whole content of one's existence, the whole meaning of one's life into one single wish—that of becoming oneself. As Judge William said, the person who lacks this determination and power of concentration will find his life dissipated aimlessly. But then another of the pseudonyms, Johannes *de silentio*, unmasked the basic flaw of this strategy. He demonstrated that there is, ultimately, no way to choose oneself in one's eternal validity—that no matter how noble and strenuous our effort might be, we shall eventually fall into the profound despair of willing despairingly to be oneself. This Judge William failed to understand. Nor did he grasp the fact that we are potentiating our despair into sin the longer we persist in the will to be ourselves absolutely. Perhaps he should have known Charlotte Rittenmeyer and Harry Wilbourne—the prime examples of this form of defiance.

Resignation, then, requires no faith; it requires only courage and fortitude. What is gained by resignation is gained on one's own; it is an immanental movement, dependent upon what is within and not upon access to some power beyond the individual's sovereignty. It is the will to choose and constitutes the very act which prevents carelessly slipping back into the aesthetical. Johannes *de silentio* says he possesses this power: "This is a purely philosophical movement which I dare say I am able to make if it is required, and which I can train myself to make, for whenever any finiteness would get the mastery over me, I starve myself until I can make the movement." This movement is not the movement of faith, but many who write about religiousness have been content to reduce faith to these terms. Instead, this movement is an act of heroism in the first degree, fraught with resignation and renunciation. Faith, however, is much more positive: "By faith I make renunciation of nothing; on the contrary, by faith I acquire everything, precisely in the sense in which it is said that he who has faith like a grain of mustard can move mountains."[1] This is far from the sheer effort required to renounce the world in order to gain eternity. This puts the whole matter in a different perspective—not renouncing, but receiving all that is given. This, in itself, requires a kind of courage—the courage to accept graciously what is bestowed upon us, above and beyond our own deserts or desires. In sum, the ethical way is a system within which the individual is not dependent upon outward forces to shape his life but invariably determines it by his choice. (Or so he thinks.) The religious individual, by contrast, is open to the appearance and influence of the Infinite in history. He faces the external. As in the case of the aesthetical modality, the knight of faith puts himself at the disposal of the external (in the form of God) but this disposition comes *after* the reflection upon and the choice of the self in the ethical stage.

1. Søren Kierkegaard, *Fear and Trembling*, in *Fear and Trembling and The Sickness unto Death*, trans. with introduction and notes by Walter Lowrie (Princeton: Princeton University Press, 1954), 59. The association of the word "acquire" with "acquisitive" and "acquisition" may mislead here, taken out of context in the Kierkegaardian corpus. The expression "I receive everything" gives a sense more faithful to Kierkegaard's intention.

The difference between the knight of infinite resignation and the knight of faith becomes absolute: "The hero does the deed and finds repose in the universal, the knight of faith is kept in constant tension." That is because the knight of faith is constantly being tried and tested; at every moment there is the temptation to fall back into the ethical modality and to accept the comfort that is inevitably attached to the universal. But this he cannot do; he may only cling to himself in the midst of his dilemma and pray God that he is making the absolute choice as he goes along.[2] He now dwells in the realm of the absurd, which Johannes *de silentio* carefully describes.

The absurd, first of all, is not something merely illogical or irrational. It is much more than that. Indeed, it is not something that can be grasped by the human intellect; rather, it is something which itself grasps man. Moreover, it occurs when we least expect it, just when all seems lost. For example, Abraham was asked to give up Isaac, which he willingly did, and believed he would never see Isaac again—or even a substitute for Isaac. Abraham thus resigned himself with complete and utter finality. But then came the "prodigy": In spite of complete resignation, Abraham *believed* he would receive Isaac back again. Johannes says:

> The absurd is not one of the factors which can be discriminated within the proper compass of the understanding: it is not identical with the improbable, the unexpected, the unforeseen. At the moment when the knight [of faith] made the act of resignation, he was convinced, humanly speaking, of the impossibility [of ever receiving back his son]. This was the result reached by the understanding, and he had sufficient energy to think it. On the other hand, in an infinite sense it was possible, namely, by renouncing it; but this sort of possessing is at the same time a relinquishing, and yet there is no absurdity in this for the understanding, for the understanding continued to be in the right in affirming that in the world of the finite where it holds sway this was and remained an impossibility. This is quite clear to the knight of faith, so the only thing that can save him is the absurd, and this he

2. *Ibid.*, 89.

grasps by faith. So he recognizes the impossibility, and that very instant he believes the absurd; for, if without recognizing the impossibility with all the passion of his soul and with all his heart, he should wish to imagine that he has faith, he deceives himself, and his testimony has no bearing, since he has not even reached the infinite resignation.

Faith therefore is not an aesthetic emotion but something far higher, precisely because it has resignation as its presupposition; it is not an immediate instinct of the heart, but is the paradox of life and existence.[3]

So faith is paradoxical. It asserts that the particular is higher than the universal, but only as a result of progression *through* the universal. Or, to put it another way, faith cannot be achieved without first going through the transitional stage of the ethical. By means of the ethical movement, the individual consolidates himself in the universal against the multifariousness of the aesthetical, but then he must make the next movement into isolation as a particular in the realm of the religious. If the ethical should be counted the highest thing, as Judge William holds, and if sin only consists in asserting oneself as the particular against the demand of the universal, then all we would need under these circumstances is more will power to accomplish the universal. That, of course, was the Greek solution to the human dilemma, but we have already seen that there is a much more ominous ingredient in human nature, something that makes one not just incommensurate with the universal but in desperate conflict with himself, God, and the world—namely, sin. Sin is not simply the feeling that something might be out of harmony between oneself and the universal; sin is the full realization that at the base of one's existence there is a profound contradiction. It is, as Johannes Climacus says, our very *milieu:* "Sin is the new existence-medium. Apart from this, to exist means merely that the individual having come into the world is present and is in the process of becoming; now it means that having come into the world he has become a sinner; apart from this, 'to exist'

3. *Ibid.,* 57–58.

is not a more sharply defining predicate, but is merely the form of all the more sharply defining predicates: one does not become anything in particular by coming into being, but now, to come into being is to become a sinner."[4] Thus God calls the individual into being and proclaims him a "sinner." One cannot acquire this predicate in any other way; but "by coming into being the individual becomes another, . . . for otherwise the determinant, sin, is placed within immanence" —a wholly unsatisfactory way to account for sin. It cannot be synonymous with human nature. But just as it is the Deity who calls the individual into being, it is He who also prevents the individual from working his way back *out* of existence through the process of recollection. Instead, the sinner is called forward *into* existence, where God is and has been. We meet the Deity in time.[5]

This fact is what constitutes the absurd—namely, that "the eternal truth has come into being in time, that God has come into being, has been born, has grown up, and so forth, precisely like any other individual human being, quite indistinguishable from other individuals."[6] The absurd is therefore the center of the religious modality, for it is the only modality in which one can successfully establish an enduring relationship with the absolute. Indeed, it is an absolute relationship to the absolute and a relative relationship to the relative. That is, only *Christian* religiousness (or religiousness *B*) can make this distinction. The ethical and immanental religiousness (or religiousness *A*) speak of the absolute, but they do not see the absurdity, the paradox which rests at the core of the idea of the Eternal intersecting time. That is why they never do come to grips with sin in any profound way; they never see the individual in his singularity "before God" in such a way that his despair is potentiated into the category of sin. For the ethicist or the immanentalist, man is guilty, yes; but he has not found himself in outrageous conflict with God. That

4. Kierkegaard, *The Concluding Unscientific Postscript*, trans. David F. Swenson and Walter Lowrie (Princeton: Princeton University Press, 1941), 517.   5. *Ibid.*   6. *Ibid.*, 188.

discovery is left to the person who dwells in the religious modality:

> God and man are two qualities between which there is an infinite qualitative difference. Every doctrine which overlooks this difference is, humanly speaking, crazy; understood in a godly sense, it is blasphemy. In paganism man made God a man (the Man-God); in Christianity God makes Himself man (the God-Man)—but in the infinite love of His compassionate grace He made nevertheless one stipulation, He can do no other. This precisely is the sorrow in Christ: "He can do no other"; He can humble Himself, take the form of a servant, suffer and die for man, invite all to come unto Him, sacrifice every day of His life and every hour of the day, and sacrifice His life—but the possibility of the offense He cannot take away. Oh, unique work of love! Oh, unfathomable sorrow of love! that God himself cannot, as in another sense He does not will, cannot will it, but, even if He would, He could not make it impossible that this work of love might not turn out to be for a person exactly the opposite, to be the extremest misery! For the greatest possible human misery, greater than sin, is to be offended in Christ and remain offended.[7]

But it is precisely this offense which constitutes an individual's greatest hope. Sin or offense is in some sense necessary and preliminary to the full enjoyment of the religiousness of Christianity. Indeed, it is this fact which distinguishes Christianity from all other religions. It makes our condition the most desperate possible one to be in, because the Infinite is posited absolutely in time. "Before God" infinitizes our wrong, our despair. The only conceivable remedy for this situation is faith, which is the opposite of sin. Faith, like sin, is a religious category and participates in the potentiation that occurs in any human act "before God." It is the transaction which takes place between a particular sinner and the particular Christ, who is, in fact, the Deity in time. He is not some docetic Christ, nor some rationalistic Christ who may be fitted into the logical systems of man's invention. He is the Paradox, the God-Man. Sin, at its nadir, is the rejection of

7. *The Sickness unto Death,* 257.

the Paradox: "this is sin against the Holy Ghost. The self is here most despairingly potentiated; it not merely casts away from itself the whole of Christianity, but it makes it a lie and a falsehood. What a prodigiously despairing conception of itself that self must have!"[8] Faith, on the other hand, is the acceptance of the Paradox. When Johannes *de silentio* was trying to talk about Abraham's faith he described it as an acceptance of the finite. This sounds rather odd, at first, but then one realizes that it is of the essence of belief. If the Deity has come into time, the finite must, of necessity, be chosen: "Abraham believed, and believed for this life. Yea, if his faith had been only of a future life, he surely would have cast everything away in order to hasten out of this world to which he did not belong." But he did not fix his gaze on far-off things; he did not yearn for the universal; his heart and mind were directed toward what was immediately before him. His one concern was to receive his child back again. Accordingly, he "needed no preparation, no time to concentrate upon the finite and its joy," for the finite was his dwelling-place. But he indwelt the finite in such a way that he could willingly give it all up when it was required of him. He "sat loosely" to the world—was *in* it, yet not of it. The movements of faith are therefore made by virtue of the absurd, and yet they are made in such a way that "one does not lose the finite but gains it every inch"—the capstone of faith.[9] The knight of faith gives everything up by infinite resignation; he gets everything back by virtue of the absurd.

There is nothing akin to objective certainty in the realm of faith; it is primarily a matter of taking risks, which in itself makes inwardness more intense. The man who plays the game of life cautiously—who has it all "figured" ahead of time—is of little interest. His life is transparent to all. But the man of faith who takes risks "before God" is completely hidden—and therefore fascinating—because his *inwardness* has been in-finitely heightened. Johannes Climacus writes, "If I am ca-

8. *Ibid.*, 255–56.   9. *Fear and Trembling*, 34–35, 48.

pable of grasping God objectively, I do not believe, but precisely because I cannot do this, I must believe." Faith, then, is holding onto objective uncertainty with courage, "so as to remain out upon the deep, over seventy thousand fathoms of water, still preserving my faith." [10]

The risk "before God" is exactly what Abraham took. He started out on his journey with no objective certainty at hand. He only knew what he was commanded to do. As he rode up toward the crest of Mount Moriah, he kept believing. He "believed that God would not require Isaac of him, whereas he was willing nevertheless to sacrifice him if it was required." That is what is meant by the phrase "to believe by virtue of the absurd." It is ridiculous to explain that Abraham was somehow betting that God would relieve him of his awful task or that he was secretly trying to figure out how the demand for Isaac's sacrifice might otherwise be satisfied. But more than all this, it must have been absurd—in the profoundest sense of that word—for Abraham to discover at the crucial moment that God had reversed Himself. As Abraham "climbed the mountain, even at the instant when the knife glittered, he believed." Naturally, he was astonished at what eventually took place, but by his faith he was able to accept it. He was able to receive Isaac back again when God gave him back, *because* he believed, which in itself was a prodigious act.[11] Without that act of faith, there would have been no Isaac.

Silence is a symptom the believing individual manifests early; he discovers that speech is incommensurable with his new modality of existence. The ethicist, by contrast, is loquacious, sometimes to the point of pomposity, as in the case of Judge William. That is because talk expresses the universal; it is the very means of establishing communication, which must be carried on within a *universe* of discourse. But religiousness is idiosyncratic, irregular, unusual. Thus, Abraham could not have made himself understood even had he wanted

10. *Postscript*, 182.   11. *Fear and Trembling*, 46.

to. All he could do was to remain silent in the face of his task.[12]

In absolute solitude he made the infinite movement of resignation and gave up Isaac, but no one could have possibly grasped the significance of this act. Had he attempted to explain what he was up to, words would only have destroyed what he was trying to accomplish. But then he made the second movement of faith, whereby he accepted the fact that, if the sacrifice of Isaac *should* take place, God would give him a new son. This was his faith; he believed by virtue of this absolute absurdity. Johannes *de silentio* then notes the only words that Abraham was able to speak. Isaac asked his father, when they got to the mountain, where the sacrificial animal was. "And Abraham said, 'God will provide Himself the lamb for the burnt offering, my son!' "[13] And so he did, and Abraham, more than any other figure in our entire tradition, becomes the paradigm of faith.

RELIGIOUSNESS *A* AND *B*

Toward the end of the *Postscript* Kierkegaard, through Johannes Climacus, makes one of his more systematic analyses of the religious modality and devotes himself to a tightly argued discussion of the difference between religiousness *A* and religiousness *B*. The first of these is essentially the religion of immanence. It is the immediate religiosity which "rests in the pious superstition that it can see God directly in everything." The people who dwell in this modality believe they have some sort of privy access to the thoughts of God. They are what the author sarcastically calls the "awakened" people who apparently know a great deal more about God than anyone else does or anyone ever has. That is because "the 'awakened' individual has Him in his pocket."[14]

Religiousness *A* is the type of religion found in paganism.

---

12. Kierkegaard says that Christ was also silent in the face of his task. See *The Journals of Søren Kierkegaard*, ed. and trans. Alexander Dru (London: Oxford University Press, 1951), 306.
13. *Fear and Trembling*, 124–25.   14. *Postscript*, 452.

The pagan world was in immediate and constant touch with the divine realm, for sin had not yet been posited as the radical discontinuity between God and the individual.[15] But the trouble with this position is that paganism's practice of religion was in an essentially aesthetic modality: "Let the reader remember that a direct God-relationship is aesthetic and is really not a God-relationship, any more than a direct relationship to the absolute is an absolute relationship, because the discrimination of the absolute has not been accomplished. In the religious sphere the positive is recognizable by the negative. The most exuberant sense of well-being in the delight of immanence, which exults in joy over God and the whole of existence, is a very lovable thing but not edifying and not essentially a God-relationship." [16] It is therefore only after the immediate relationship with God is broken that a true God-relationship may be formed. A breach is needed in order that the self may be posited. This is "the first act of inwardness in the direction of determining the truth of inwardness." It would appear, from this argument, that the author of the *Postscript* subscribes to the notion of "the fortunate fall." Prior to sin, there is no selfhood, no inwardness. After sin, the self begins to take shape and express itself, albeit a disagreeable expression.

It is just too much to look at Nature and expect to see God: "Nature is, indeed, the work of God, but only the handiwork is directly present, not God." The only way to have a relationship with God is to be separated from him in order to face him, subject-to-Subject, sinner-to-Redeemer. Sometimes it appears that God is playing a game of cosmic hide-and-seek

15. Haufniensis consequently says: "It is remarkable that Christian orthodoxy has constantly taught that paganism lies in sin, whereas the consciousness of sin was nevertheless first posited by Christianity. Orthodoxy, however, is in the right, if it would explain itself a little more precisely. By quantitative definitions paganism, so to speak, procrastinates, never gets to sin in the deepest sense—but precisely this is sin." Kierkegaard, *The Concept of Dread*, trans. with introduction and notes by Walter Lowrie (Princeton: Princeton University Press, 1946), 84.   16. *Postscript*, 497n.

because of his elusiveness, but that elusiveness is precisely the essence of Deity. Because he is truth, he continues to be elusive so that men will not fall into the error of trying to make idols in substitute for him. Some may see God in Nature, but there are others who would just as quickly confine him to Creed, Sacrament, Ministry, Bible, or some other finite form. This kind of religiousness, then, is not exclusive property of paganism. It also exists in the Christian Church, where people are often quite sure they know all there is to know about the activities of God. But God will not be so confined; he must remain in a paradoxical relationship to the finite.[17]

Immanental religiousness, in its best forms, requires self-annihilation so that God might become more fully present in time. The individual must put himself out of the way, because he is the hindrance that prevents God's making himself known. When all the debris is cleared away, it is believed that God will then be found. This method is, of course, the *via negativa* of the mystics. Climacus observes in this case: "Aesthetically, the holy resting place of edification is outside the individual, who accordingly seeks the place; in the ethico-religious sphere the individual himself is the place, when he has annihilated himself."[18]

Religiousness *A* is essentially *aesthetical.* Religiousness *B*, on the other hand, is only *analogous* to the aesthetical; that is, the person who dwells in this modality finds meaning for his existence outside himself, but there is no talk of self-annihilation in order that God may appear. Rather, there is talk of being related in a dialectical way to that other Individual. It is both positive and negative: positive in that there is relation; negative in that we contradict the relation through sin. But it is nevertheless a relation and not an absorption into the divine life. In immanental religiousness, on the other hand, God is neither Subject who stands over against us nor is he outside the individual believer. He is the "All-in-All" and is found, most profoundly, by the individual within himself.

17. *Ibid.*, 218, 452. 18. *Ibid.*, 498.

But, for the person who dwells in religiousness *B*, existence is shaped precisely by the fact that God is the Individual. As the coming of Christ broke open the psychically-determined cosmos of the Greeks, so his coming into our lives breaks us out of our absolute commitment to the relative in order to be absolutely related to the absolute. Climacus says: "The paradoxical edification corresponds therefore to the determination of God in time as the individual man; for if such be the case, the individual is related to something outside himself. The fact that it is not possible to think this is precisely the paradox." [19] In other words, it is God who calls us *out* of the multifariousness of the aesthetical *through* the consolidation of the self in the ethical *to* the paradoxical stage of the religious, where the Infinite has come into time as Subject who stands over against us. Accordingly, the religious man is the one who can make the "double movement" between time and eternity—giving up everything and getting it all back again.

Religiousness *A* cannot deal in such traffic. For the immanentalist, the particular, time as such—that is, the finite—cannot be taken seriously. It has no "historical starting-point" as paradoxical religiousness does. It does not *need* a "historical starting-point," because one starts with one's own interior life when searching for God. The individual's one desire is to be swallowed up into eternity so that the matter of seconds, minutes, and hours will be annihilated and caught up in the eternal. His mode of seeking God is consequently recollection. By tearing off first one layer and then another he can find his way back to God through the process of recollection.

It is quite another matter, then, when the eternal is outside and remains outside and may be accounted for only in external terms. The way of religiousness *B* is not recollection, but repetition:

In truth, the love of repetition is the only happy love. Like that of recollection it has not the disquietude of hope, the

19. *Ibid.*, 498.

anxious adventuresomeness of discoverers, nor the sadness of recollection; it has the blessed certainty of the instant. Hope is a new garment, starched and stiff and glittering, yet one has never had it on, and hence one does not know how it will become one and how it fits. Recollection is a discarded garment, which beautiful as it may be, does not fit, for one has outgrown it. Repetition is an imperishable garment, which fits snugly and comfortably, neither too tight nor too loose. Hope is a charming maiden but slips through the fingers, recollection is a beautiful old woman but of no use at the instant, repetition is a beloved wife of whom one never tires. For it is only of the new one grows tired. Of the old one never tires. When one possesses that, one is happy, and only he is thoroughly happy who does not delude himself with the vain notion that repetition ought to be something new, for then one becomes tired of it. It requires youth to hope, and youth to recollect, but it requires courage to will repetition.[20]

The particular is seen to be higher than the universal, and it is so because one can enter the realm of the eternal only as an individual. Otherwise, as the immanentalist readily admits, the self (the individual) has to be annihilated. In religiousness *B*, then, the individual, subjectivity, the exceptional, the absurd—all of these are cherished and preserved, for they are of the kingdom of God.

20. Kierkegaard, *Repetition,* trans. Walter Lowrie (New York: Harper & Row, Publishers, Inc., 1964), 33–34.

243

18

They Endured

THE ONE FIGURE in the Faulknerian canon who stands clearly within the category of paradoxical religiousness is Dilsey in *The Sound and the Fury*. She is the heroine of faith whose *telos* is sacrifice. She is the "unrecognizable" who expresses the "law of her existence," not by telling or showing, but by suffering and helping "indirectly." [1]

The climax to Dilsey's existence occurs during the fourth section of *The Sound and the Fury*, which, appropriately enough, takes place on Easter Day, 1928. Those who have read the novel will recall that it was a cold and drizzly day. Luster, her grandson, says, "Always cold Easter. Aint never seen it fail." [2] Dilsey, who had not awakened on time, dresses and crosses over the windy backyard to the big house. As soon as she enters the house she discovers that Mrs. Compson is already up, complaining that, because Dilsey is late, break-

1. Søren Kierkegaard, *The Present Age and Of the Difference Between a Genius and an Apostle,* trans. Alexander Dru (New York: Harper and Row, Publishers, Inc., 1962), 82.
2. William Faulkner, *The Sound and the Fury,* in *The Sound and the Fury and As I Lay Dying* (New York: Random House, Inc., 1946), 291.

fast will be delayed and Jason will be upset. But, as one critic observes, by working with circumstance instead of against it, Dilsey manages to create "order out of disorder." She will not allow her existence to be shunted about by external circumstance. She instinctively knows how to accommodate herself to the needs of those around her in order to keep the Compson household from falling completely to pieces: "While occupied with getting breakfast, she is yet able to start the fire in Luster's inexplicable absence, provide a hot water bottle for Mrs. Compson, see to Benjy's needs, and soothe various ruffled tempers. All this despite the constant interruptions of Luster's perverseness, Benjy's moaning, Mrs. Compson's complaints, and even Jason's maniacal fury."[3] The question now becomes, what is the source of Dilsey's calm and endurance? Does she suffer and endure these and other indignities because she has despairingly willed to be herself in the face of the apoplectic blows of external forces? Or can she exist with such confidence because of her faith in God? But before trying to answer this question in detail, it is important to observe the pivotal event in "the Dilsey section" of the novel: the worship service at the Negro church.

Jason's "maniacal fury" was occasioned by the discovery that Miss Quentin sometime during the previous night had made off with the money he had stolen from her and hid. He storms out of the house in hot pursuit. But, significantly, the omniscient author does not have us follow Jason in his frantic search for the money; instead, he has us follow Dilsey and Benjy to the Church for the Easter sermon, the pivotal scene of the novel. Shegog, a slightly built man who looked something like a monkey, was to be the guest preacher for the day: "They were still looking at him with consternation and unbelief when the minister rose and introduced him in rich, rolling tones, whose very unction served to increase the visitor's insignificance. 'En dey brung dat all de way fum Saint Looey,' Frony whispered. 'I've knowed de Lawd to

3. Olga W. Vickery, *The Novels of William Faulkner* (Baton Rouge: Louisiana State University Press, 1959), 48.

245

use cuiser tools dan dat,' Dilsey said."[4] And so Dilsey, in her wisdom, knew that God could use even this frail vessel, absurd as it seemed to the more practical Frony. Dilsey's attitude toward Shegog was not something that she could have "figured out" or arrived at through some sort of intellectual or rational process. Rather, the notion that God might choose Shegog as a channel of grace was something that *possessed her* more than she possessed it. She was grasped by the validity and power of the historical—by the fact that Shegog (the particular) was indeed higher than the universal (the ideas conveyed by the abstract medium of language).

Viewed from a common sense perspective, Dilsey's trust in such an event would seem, at best, sentimental; at worst, sheer foolishness. As Kierkegaard says, "The contradiction first emerges in the fact that the subject [in this case, Dilsey] in the extremity of such subjective passion (in the concern for eternal happiness) has to base this upon a historical knowledge [Shegog's presence] which at its maximum remains an approximation." There is no way she can know for sure (with empirical certainty) that Shegog would be God's instrument. She *knows* it (with subjective passion), because the truth of it possesses her. But "the investigator" lives on dispassionately, looking for his kind of certainty and rejecting the approximation that is the foundation on which faith is built. Many readers of *The Sound and the Fury* will therefore remain untouched by the profound religious truth Faulkner has captured in this scene. They do not understand that "every Christian is such only by being nailed to the paradox of having based his eternal happiness upon the relation to something historical."[5]

What is even more scandalous than the appearance of the Infinite in time in the person of Shegog is his *manner* of

4. *The Sound and the Fury*, 309.
5. Kierkegaard, *The Concluding Unscientific Postscript*, trans. David F. Swenson and Walter Lowrie (Princeton: Princeton University Press, 1941), 510, 512.

preaching. When he started to speak, he sounded at first like a white man, which would make the experience seem all the more ambiguous and questionable to those present, because there could be no personal reinforcement of his words. But there was a magic to his voice that would not be denied. It gained the upper hand over the "white man's" language, and the congregation was soon captivated by his rolling rhetoric. Then he stopped speaking for a moment and silence filled the room. A leap had been made. Language as the incomparable vehicle for presenting "the universal" was abandoned. A new modality was entered. When he "spoke" again he used the dialect (existence medium) of the congregation: "It was as different as day and dark from his former tone, with a sad, timbrous quality like an alto horn, sinking into their hearts and speaking there again when it had ceased in fading and cumulate echoes. 'Brethren and sistern,' it said again. . . . 'I got the recollection and the blood of the Lamb!'" The magnetism of his voice and the majesty of his conviction overwhelmed those who listened: "And the congregation seemed to watch with its own eyes while the voice consumed him, until he was nothing and they were nothing and there was not even a voice but instead their hearts were speaking to one another in chanting measures beyond the need for words, so that when he came to rest against the reading desk, his monkey face lifted and his whole attitude that of a serene, tortured crucifix that transcended its shabbiness and insignificance and made it of no moment, a long expulsion of breath rose from them, and a woman's single soprano: 'Yes, Jesus!'"[6] There were no dogmas to accept, no rites to perform, no codes to adhere to; those who came to listen had only to accept the vision as given.

The religious experience Faulkner describes in this passage is *not* the "self-annihilation" characteristic of religiousness *A* but the unself-consciousness that accompanies the I-Thou

6. *The Sound and the Fury*, 310.

relation characteristic of paradoxical religiousness. *Christian* religious experience (even Christian mysticism) cultivates communion or marriage between the individual and God rather than the union or fusion of the individual with the One. In Christian religiousness the identity of the person is maintained in the relationship. Thus Shegog and his congregation do *not* retreat into realms isolated from one another, they do not lose themselves in "nothing." Rather, as the novel says, they "speak" to one another "in chanting measures beyond the need for words." In short, they have given up the abstractive communication of language for a more direct communication that theoretically should accompany *all* Christian worship, as, for example, in holy *communion*. The "nothing" gets in the way of this deep and primitive interpersonal communication.[7]

Then we read that Dilsey sat "bolt unright" as tears of joy streamed down her leathery face. Even Benjy remained "rapt in his sweet blue gaze," as if he, too, were caught up in the power of the moment—the moment filled with eternity. Thus Dilsey sees; she sees the point of it all, as each member of the congregation is lifted out of himself into rapport with his brothers. Isolation is replaced by communion. What a startling and effective contrast this worship service becomes to the objectification and alienation that runs throughout the rest of the novel.

What, for instance, does Jason know about communion? This man, who is not present to himself, can hardly be present to others. His eye is cocked on the main chance, and existence passes him by as he chases wildly about the countryside, attempting to recapture the last symbol of objectification—money. He complained before leaving for Mottson that, because Dilsey was allowed to go to Church, she would not be on hand to prepare the noon meal. He struck out viciously at his mother, who wanted to take the blame for the prospect of a cold Easter dinner: "I know it's my fault," Mrs. Compson

7. See Denis de Rougement, *Love in the Western World* (Garden City: Doubleday & Company, Inc., 1957), 154–72.

248

said. "I know you blame me." "For what?" Jason said. "You never resurrected Christ, did you?"[8]

Or what does Mrs. Compson know about communion or being present to others? She whines and pleads with Jason not to be cruel to Miss Quentin: "Cant you even let me have Sunday in peace?" When it appears that no one will listen to her she laments abstractedly, "But on Sunday morning, in my own house . . . when I've tried so hard to raise them Christians." There is no concern for others; she is entirely wrapped up in her own self-pity. Later on Mrs. Compson cannot understand why disaster has befallen her. "It cant be to hurt and flout me. Whoever God is, He would not permit that. I'm a lady. You might not believe that from my off-spring, but I am."[9] An open Bible lay on her bed, untouched and unread. Mrs. Compson is the opposite of Dilsey. Her despair is the despair of weakness, of not willing to choose herself. What she sees in herself is so disgusting, she would rather retreat into neurasthenia.

The sermon, then, furnishes us with a clue to Dilsey's endurance. She is able to face the world in contrast to Jason and Mrs. Compson, because she, along with Brother Shegog, "seed de power en de glory." Hers is not a stoical endurance, despairingly chosen, but an endurance begun and continued by the vision of God's manifest love for his creatures in "the blood of the Lamb." Somehow Dilsey is able to understand that God's actions are not to be "discriminated within the proper compass of the understanding"[10] but are merely facts of her existence. She does not know why, but in her view God has come, and this fact grasps her, absurd as it may be. Moreover, she sees herself to be in radical discontinuity with God, a sinner "before God," as Kierkegaard would say; but, again, it is precisely this conviction that enables her to accept the Eternal in time when it confronts her. Therefore, to talk

8. *The Sound and the Fury,* 295.   9. *Ibid.,* 297, 315.
10. Kierkegaard, *Fear and Trembling,* in *Fear and Trembling and The Sickness unto Death,* trans. with introduction and notes by Walter Lowrie (Princeton: Princeton University Press, 1954), 57.

about God in terms of "the blood of the Lamb" is to encompass both facets of her faith: the "scandal of particularity" (that God chooses blood, lambs, monkey-faced preachers to make himself known in time and place) and the "scandal of sin" (that she cannot "back into" the Eternal because she is absolutely incommensurate with the Holy God). The *only* answer, after the Incarnation, would have to be paradoxical. All other attempts at "rational" or "sensible" answers would fail.

Dilsey's brand of faith is implicit in all of her words and actions throughout the whole novel. On the day Benjy's name was changed, she had made the same kind of affirmation she would make after the sermon on Easter:

> *My name been Dilsey since fore I could remember and it be Dilsey when they's long forgot me.*
>
> *How will they know it's Dilsey, when it's long forgot, Dilsey, Caddy said.*
>
> *It'll be in the Book, honey, Dilsey said. Writ out.*
>
> *Can you read it, Caddy said.*
>
> *Wont have to, Dilsey said. They'll read it for me. All I got to do is say Ise here.*[11]

This is a faith rooted and grounded in eternity. Unlike Jason, who becomes so engrossed with the finite that he eventually forgets to choose himself or even to remember what his name is ("in the divine understanding of it"), she recalls her name and is able to choose herself because she has already been chosen.[12]

The most important clue to Dilsey's modality of existence involves her reaction to time. In contrast to Quentin and Mr. Compson, who succumb to the tyranny of time and who look on a timepiece as "the mausoleum of all hope and desire," Dilsey gets the best of time: "On the wall above a cupboard, invisible save at night, by a lamp light and even then evincing an enigmatic profundity because it had but one hand, a cabi-

11. *The Sound and the Fury*, 77.
12. *The Sickness unto Death*, 166–67.

net clock ticked, then with a preliminary sound as if it had cleared its throat, struck five times. 'Eight oclock,' Dilsey said." She knows the right time no matter what the old clock on the wall might say. Hyatt Waggoner perceptively writes:

> Knowing a "time not my time," she is able to *use* time practically and humanely, without haste and with the only constructive results achieved by anyone on the Compson place. She has time to take the unneeded hot water bottle slowly, painfully up the stairs and time to make a birthday cake for Benjy. She is the only major character not obsessed . . . by time. She acts as though she had "all the time in the world." And of course in a sense she has, if her religious beliefs are justified. She lives in two worlds, one in and one out of time. For her, Christ was crucified, not worn down by the minute clicking of little wheels. She has tried to celebrate His resurrection and to take Benjy with her. She does not need to hurry. She is not anxious.[13]

Dilsey's ability to make sense out of the clock (and hence time) arises out of her simple but profound faith that her validity as a self is "grounded transparently in the Power which posited it."[14] She does not have to resign herself to Fate (the aesthetical); she does not have to will despairingly to endure her lot (the ethical). She simply accepts herself because she knows herself to be already accepted ultimately and finally. This fundamental disposition of her existence thus determines the way in which she approaches time. Past, present, and future are all aspects of eternity, because all are held within the grasp of God. She is able to be *present* because she lives in absolute relationship to the Eternal. "Is we gwine to church," Luster asks. "I let you know bout dat when de time come," Dilsey replies.[15] It would all be taken care of in her own microcosmic vision of "the fullness of time."

There is no doubt but that Dilsey dwells within Kierke-

---

13. Hyatt Waggoner, *William Faulkner: From Jefferson to the World* (Lexington: University of Kentucky Press, 1959), 51.
14. *The Sickness unto Death*, 147.
15. *The Sound and the Fury*, 302.

gaard's religious category. Whereas the aesthetical person attempts to escape time and the ethical man attempts to conquer time (the Enemy), Dilsey can live simultaneously in time and in eternity. She makes what Kierkegaard calls "the double movement." That is, she long ago realized that God required of her but one thing—her self—which she offered up with utter confidence. The form of this sacrifice was service to the Compsons. As a poor, ignorant black woman in a demented white household, she could have rebelled and sought ways to escape her lot, but she did not. Indeed, she seems to have found herself in serving the various members of the Compson family. Not that she felt in any way forced into service or that she saw service as a way of gaining favor with the Eternal but that service was the place and destiny assigned her by Providence. Of course, to claim that God has put someone in such a lowly and demeaning position is repugnant to those of us who stand for social justice, but it was precisely in the midst of her day-to-day work among the Compsons that Dilsey made the double movements between time and eternity. She never knew anything other than that God was to be encountered in those (finite) surroundings. Kierkegaard would have said that she "resigned everything infinitely, and then . . . grasped everything again by virtue of the absurd." In short, she gave up her self but received it back again, infinitely blessed.[16]

"They endured," then, means that she triumphed, and "endure" is probably not a positive enough word. Faulkner must have realized this in his Stockholm speech, when he elaborated on the concept: "I believe that man will not merely endure: he will prevail . . . because he has a soul, a spirit capable of compassion and sacrifice and endurance."[17] He was doubtlessly speaking of the Dilseys of the world. She does not merely endure in the sense of passively accepting a menial place in the scheme of things; she prevails in that she can

16. *Fear and Trembling*, 49ff.
17. Faulkner, *Essays, Speeches, & Public Letters*, ed. James B. Meriwether (New York: Random House, Inc., 1965), 120.

choose her self as the self grounded transparently in the Power that originally posited it; she prevails because she sees that her life (her time) is summed up with the rest of her universe in the providential care of God. Certainly her life and action stand as a judgment on those around her. None of them seem to be able to accept life, much less to endure it. Everyone in his own way is in retreat, whereas Dilsey meets life head-on and embraces it.

Characters who occupy such crucial positions in Faulkner's work have more than thematic consequence. They usually play important roles structurally as well. As we have already seen, Lena Grove's appearances in the first and last chapters of *Light in August* serve as a frame for the others who are caught up in mad and irrational pursuit in the main body of the novel. She is the "bride of quietness," who quite unselfconsciously keeps in touch with the vital forces around her. It is, therefore, of more than passing significance that after Joanna Burden was murdered, and just at the moment when the Grand Jury is gathering to consider the case, Lena gives birth to a child. And that the lynching and castration of Joe Christmas, which may be considered the culmination of the novel, is the next event (chronologically) to occur. Thus, in the midst of sterility and death there occurs birth and life.

In the same way, Dilsey's section in *The Sound and the Fury* serves structurally to underline what Faulkner is trying to do in that novel. Perrin Lowrey makes a case for this and observes that the reader gains a correct perspective on the Compson household by viewing it through Dilsey's eyes. Furthermore, her sense of time serves as a corrective to the distortions of time suffered in the first three sections of the book. He writes:

> Her concept of time is put into direct contrast to both Jason's and Ben's . . . Ben's wailing, which 'might have been all time and injustice and sorrow become vocal for an instant by a conjunction of the planets,' is set against Dilsey's thoughts as she sits stroking Ben's head and says, 'Dis long time, O Jesus, dis long time.' And while Dilsey is thinking of

how Christ's birth and the present and eternity are all related in time, Jason, through his compulsion of haste, has
come to the end of his rope in Mottson, . . . It is with Dilsey's section that the keystone to the arch of the whole book
is dropped into place.[18]

In contrast to the other sections of the book, which persistently offer obstacles to the understanding, Dilsey's section illuminates the dark and murky impressions of the earlier
chapters and brings together into a meaningful whole all of
the loose ends. This is no mere happenstance but is part of
the art and scheme of the whole, for as the fourth section
becomes the unifying section, so Dilsey becomes the unifying
character of the work. By her actions *she* illuminates the
dark and murky actions of the other characters, and by sheer
force of her personality she gives what order and meaning
there is to a household that is disintegrating before her eyes.
At the last she utters, "I've seed de first en de last . . . I seed
de beginnin, en now I sees de endin." [19] Some critics say this
means that she has seen the rise and fall of the house of
Compson. Perhaps. An interpretation more consistent with
her own modality of existence is this: she is able to see all
of "the sound and the fury" of life within the larger context
of the Alpha and the Omega; what *seems* to be meaningless is
made meaningful within the larger wisdom of God. And because she is the only major character who consistently stays
in touch with God, she is the only one who can have such a
serenely detached attitude toward the chaos which threatens
to engulf everyone else in the book. Indeed, we can go further
than that. She's Faulkner's Abraham. No one else in the entire
Faulkner canon dwells within her modality; all others may be
seen in relation to hers. As Abraham is the Kierkegaardian
model for faithfulness, so Dilsey is Faulkner's paradigm of
religiousness, not only for *The Sound and the Fury*, but for

18. Perrin Lowrey, "Concepts of Time in *The Sound and the Fury*,"
English Institute Essays: 1952, ed. Alan S. Downer (New York: Co-
lumbia University Press, 1954), 81–82.
19. *The Sound and the Fury*, 313.

all the novels and short stories that together make up his richly populated fictional world.

But lest the reader think that Faulkner's conceptions of religiousness are, at all points, coterminous with Kierkegaard's, there is one important distinction yet to be made. Kierkegaard wrote, he would have said, as an "apostle"— one who self-consciously chose to write about Abraham, the classic exemplar of faith, from within an explicitly Christian framework and for one purpose only: to convert the reader. On the other hand, he would have called Faulkner an "aesthetic genius," in that his perception of true religiousness was achieved quite unself-consciously. Faulkner, of course, acknowledged that he was no theologian but that he did use, as needed, the scraps of Christianity that anyone could have picked up in the midst of Southern culture. Thus, his brilliant characterization of Dilsey as the heroine of faith was made, so to speak, in spite of himself, which is yet a greater testimony to his already towering achievement. In the figure of this humble black woman he enabled us to see true religiousness, refracted through the prism of his genius. He obviously magnified qualities available to any observer—the natural qualities of the immanent world—like her capacity to suffer, endure, and prevail. But his portrayal is so sensitive that the alert reader can catch a glimpse of Eternity in even her most mundane actions. All this, at a time when a number of people have given up on religion altogether.

Index

257

Index

—"Verse Old and Nascent: A Pilgrimage," 220
Faust, 24, 34, 57n, 76, 119
Ford, Ford Madox, 184–85
Frank, Erich, 214n
Frater Taciturnus, 79, 90, 93
Frony (Dilsey's daughter), 245–46

God: Compson's attitude about, 198; defiance toward, 168–73; invoked by Doc Hines, 49–50; Faulkner on, 7; indirectly present in modalities, 88; how known, 20, 89–90, 92–93; not subject to intellect, 71, 74–76; potentiates sin, 155–56, 236, 238; sums up time, 179; wrathful, 52–54
Goodwin, Lee, 120
Greek culture. *See* Christianity
Grimm, Percy, 217
Group, the, 17, 80
Grove, Lena, 58, 223, 253

Head, Herbert, 201
Hearing: the most spiritual sense, 119
Hegel, G. W. F.: and the System, 67–71 *passim;* the Idea, 92
Hero, tragic, 41, 54–55, 157–58
Hemingway, Ernest, 7
Hightower, Gail, 217, 219, 220, 223, 224
Hines, Eupheus (Doc), 48–50, 52, 54
—Milly, 48
—Mrs., 50, 219
Humor: as a modality, 85
Hunt, John W., 11, 186, 197

Idea, the, 92
Immediacy: 85, 111, 114
Incarnation: central to Kierkegaard's work, 24–30 *passim*, 32, 34
Indirect method, 11, 24, 37
Individual, the, 17, 80
Instant, the, 211. *See also* Moment
Inwardness, 18, 74–75, 240
Irony: as a modality, 85, 200; as a method, 95–96

Jiggs (of *Pylon*), 207
Johannes Climacus: on ethics, 153–54, 159–60; on nature, 240; on sin, 234–35; mentioned, 139, 155, 237, 239
Johannes *de Silentio:* exposes the

ethical, 231; on love, 106, 109–10; mentioned, 139, 156, 232, 233, 239
Jolivet, Regius, 104

Keats, John, 120–21, 220
Kierkegaard, Søren: attitude toward art, 98–99; authorial strategy, 8–10, 39, 77, 139; on God, 20; on the group, 17, 80; as empiricist, 68; personal irony, 95–96; indirect method, 11, 24, 37; on Old Testament, 16; as phenomenologist, 68–70, 76, 77–78; on privatism, 21n; relation to pseudonyms, 39–40; on the public, 20, 21, 211; on Shakespeare, 16; twentieth century influence, 11–12
—*The Concept of Dread*, 25, 43, 46, 50, 58, 72, 77, 177–83 *passim*, 190, 240
—*The Concluding Unscientific Postscript*, 39, 68n, 70–77 *passim*, 83–96 *passim*, 114, 148, 155, 156, 160, 215, 221n, 234–35, 239–42, 246
—*Crisis in the Life of an Actress*, 94n, 99
—*Either/Or*, 8, 16, 24, 29–35 *passim*, 38, 40–43, 47, 56, 59, 77, 85, 88, 103, 101–104, 111, 114, 117, 119, 135, 139, 142, 143–47, 195n, 224
—*Fear and Trembling*, 20, 77, 85, 156, 158–59, 232, 237–39, 252
—*Journals*, 12, 68, 70, 139, 239n
—*Point of View*, 8, 24
—*Prayers of Kierkegaard*, 80
—*The Present Age*, 15, 21, 23, 204, 210–11, 244
—*Repetition*, 181–82, 242–43
—*The Sickness unto Death*, 35, 36, 59, 63, 78, 111–12, 127, 131, 133, 137, 140, 148, 154, 155, 164, 168–69, 172, 194, 199, 204–205, 207, 209–210, 236–37, 250, 251
—*Stages on Life's Way*, 5n, 77, 79, 85, 105–110, 152, 153, 196, 202
Knight of faith, 20, 232–39. *See also* the Unrecognizable

Lamar, Ruby, 124, 226
Language: aesthetical, 91, 118–19; ethical, 238
Laverne (of *Pylon*), 208
Leap, the: transition between modalities, 87

259

Index

Levelling, 19–20, 22
Lorraine (Jason Compson's Memphis friend), 197, 201–202, 206
Lowrey, Perrin, 253–54
Lowrie, Walter, 5, 86
Love: an expression of the ethical, 161–73 *passim;* pagan, 29; perorations on, 105–109; sensuousness, 33–35
Luster (Dilsey's grandson), 244

Macbeth, 72
Magny, Claude-Edmonde, 225–26
Marriage: the ethical paradigm, 82, 148–52; rejected by Jason Compson, 196; rejected by Joe Christmas. *See also* William, Judge
Mass man, 19
Modality of existence: defined, 4–5; mentioned, 67, 86
McCord (of *The Wild Palms*), 165–66, 169–70
McEachern, Simon, 52–53, 61
Moment, the, 47, 111, 179–81. *See also* the Instant
Money: as an abstracting force, 164–66, 196–98, 201
Music: expresses sensuousness, 32, 47

Nature, 240
Niebuhr, H. Richard, 80–81
Novel, the: of ideas, 5–6

Objectivity: discussed, 32*n*, an expression of madness, 72; of Greek culture, 37–44 *passim*
Oedipus, 54–55
Olsen, Regine, 96
Old Testament, 16
Othello, 117

Pain: expressed in tragedy, 42–43
Paradox, the, 85, 158–59, 234–37
Pascal, Blaise, 141*n*
Passion: in the modern era, 15–17: in relation to God, 74–75
Philosophy: compared with sensualism, 104; discussed, 67–73
Plato, 26, 181
Poet-existence, 118
Popeye, 125–26, 223
Poteat, William H., 54–55

Pneuma, 26. *See also* Spirit, Universe
Primitives: Faulkner's, 213–15
Privatism: Kierkegaard on, 21*n*
Pseudonyms: Kierkegaard's relation to, 39–40
Psyche, 26, 27. *See also* Cosmos
Psychology, depth, 29
Public, the: Kierkegaard on, 20, 21, 211

Ratliff, V. K., 131, 191
Recollection, 147–48, 156, 181–82, 215, 235, 242
Reflection: and alienation, 15–16, 21; impossible for Greeks, 37; lacking in Joe Christmas, 61; mentioned, 93–94, 111–13
Religiousness *A*, 82–84, 92–93, 235
Religiousness *B* (Christian or paradoxical): in Abraham, 156–60, 233, 238–39; in Dilsey, 22–23; alternative to ethics, 153–55; and silence, 238–39; mentioned, 82–84, 85, 92–93, 96, 235
Repentance, 147
Repetition, 242–43
Resignation, 148–49, 231–33
Respectability: Faulkner on, 18, 206; Harry Wilbourne, 166; mentioned, 131
Rittenmeyer, Charlotte, 169*n*, 231
—Francis (Rat), 164, 167, 171
Reporter, the (in *Pylon*), 191, 223

St. Augustine, 29
St. Paul, 21*n*, 29
Sartoris, Bayard, 121, 215, 224
Sartre, Jean Paul, 7, 225
Satin, Joseph, 39
Schleiermacher, Friedrich, 69
Self, the: its formation, 142–43, 146–47
Sewanee, 124, 200
Sexuality: Narcissa Benbow's, 122; Joanna Burden's, 51, 57–59
Shegog, Brother, 245–46, 249
Shumann, Roger, 208–209, 211
Sickness: unto death, 114
Silence: and religiousness, 238–39
Sin: as contradiction, 40, 234; the ethicist's problem, 147, 154; as the existence medium, 234–35; as igno-